FREEDOM'S SEEKERS

Antislavery, Abolition, and the Atlantic World

R. J. M. Blackett and James Brewer Stewart, SERIES EDITORS

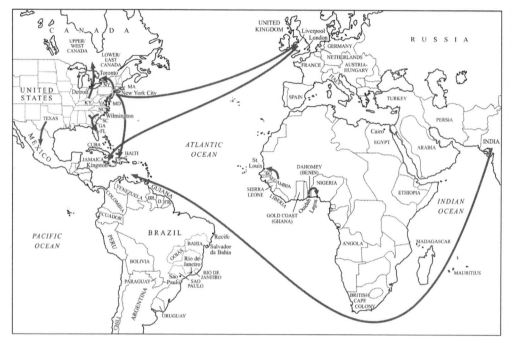

Global dimensions of freedom's seekers.

FREEDOM'S SEEKERS

Essays on Comparative Emancipation

JEFFREY R. KERR-RITCHIE

LOUISIANA STATE UNIVERSITY PRESS ✴ BATON ROUGE

Published with the assistance of the V. Ray Cardozier Fund

Published by Louisiana State University Press
Copyright © 2013 by Louisiana State University Press
All rights reserved
Manufactured in the United States of America
FIRST PRINTING

DESIGNER: *Mandy McDonald Scallan*
TYPEFACE: *Whitman*
PRINTER AND BINDER: *Maple Press, Inc.*

Maps created by Mary Lee Eggart

Library of Congress Cataloging-in-Publication Data
Kerr-Ritchie, Jeffrey R.
  Freedom's seekers : essays on comparative emancipation /
Jeffrey R. Kerr-Ritchie.
    p. cm. — (Antislavery, abolition, and the Atlantic world)
  Includes bibliographical references and index.
  ISBN 978-0-8071-5471-7 (cloth : alk. paper) — ISBN 978-0-
8071-5472-4 (pdf) — ISBN 978-0-8071-5473-1 (epub) — ISBN
978-0-8071-5474-8 (mobi) 1. Slaves—Emancipation—America—History. 2. Slaves—Emancipation—United States—History. 3. Antislavery movements—America—History. 4. Antislavery movements—United States—History. I. Title.
  HT1050.K47 2013
  306.3'62097—dc23

                                        2013028477

CONTENTS

PREFACE

Comparison can be used both to stress the uniqueness of the historical process, which appeals to the dyed-in-the wool historicist, and to find common traits in the unique historical events and sequences. Comparison in history actually covers a middle ground between overemphasis of uniqueness and sociological generalization which by necessity remains within the realm of forms: it can synthesize the substance of history.

　　—FRITZ REDLICH

We need to know much more about abolitionism, especially about the role and impact of diaspora Africans, not only in the United States and Brazil but for all former slave areas.

　　—JOSEPH E. HARRIS

The notable absence of any truly workable, comprehensive account of emancipation in formal comparative terms is perhaps indicative of the difficulties in this instance. It may well be that studies of the diaspora that was slavery have been enabled by the fact that despite its institutional diversity there is a recognizable, coherent set of parameters that give it shape.

　　—THOMAS C. HOLT

Free your mind, and the rest will follow.

　　—EN VOGUE

This book compares, contrasts, and connects the quest for emancipation by slaves, self-liberators, slave soldiers, black abolitionists, freedwomen, freed children, and freedom's first generations throughout the nineteenth-century African Diaspora.

Its origins are simple enough. In the fall semester of 1990, I taught a freshmen seminar titled "The Age of Emancipation" at the University of Pennsylvania. The 1980s had ushered in some exciting emancipation studies by Robin Blackburn, Eric Foner, Thomas Holt, Ira Berlin, Steven Hahn, Gavin Wright, Rebecca Scott, Seymour Drescher, Peter Kolchin, George Frederickson, and Stanley Engerman, among others. Students seemed familiar with the rudiments of slavery (mostly in the United States) but were less clear on what happened after emancipation (especially in the United States). The class was well received. I became interested in comparative history. Over the next two decades, I taught courses on comparative slavery and comparative emancipation at both the undergraduate and graduate levels at several U.S. universities. Students usually received these classes with a great deal of enthusiasm. Some history department colleagues were less impressed. How could students comprehend several national and colonial histories when they did not even know their own nation's history? Did not comparative work put method before empirical research? In which field did comparative studies fit?

I should mention that I had entered U.S. graduate school after escaping the stifling class and racial hierarchy of Margaret Thatcher's Tory Britain during the mid-1980s. Imagine my surprise encountering Ronald Reagan's United States, in which the civilized liberalism of Jimmy Carter was slowly being throttled by a ruthless ideological crusade against the poor and minorities domestically, as well as internationally against leftist regimes such as Maurice Bishop's Grenada, Daniel Ortega's Nicaragua, and Mikhail Gorbachev's Soviet Union. Even more disturbing was entering a U.S. academic world after gaining the history doctorate and encountering a sort of programmed conformity about ways to argue and present oneself as a historian, educator, and colleague. I still recall the so-called advice of an esteemed colleague at a small liberal arts college in New England who informed me that it would serve me better if I learned to disagree less passionately in order to fit in with the rest of the department! The problem, of course, is that, although English is the *lingua franca* of Anglo-American academe, it is argued through in very different ways, as British academics in U.S. universities and U.S. academics in British universities know all too well.

Somewhere along these paths, I decided to write a book on emancipation from a comparative perspective. Part of the inspiration also drew from my discomfort with notions of the United States' historical uniqueness—an ideology that resonated profoundly with those of us in U.S. academe once fed a regular diet of peculiar British liberties throughout our official education. (Hang on, this exceptional U.S. argument sounds familiar!) Part of the intellectual interest further derived from research for my first book, on the political economy of the post-emancipation tobacco South, in which it became increasingly clear that politicians, planters, freedpeople, journalists, abolitionists, and others in the U.S. South were very much aware of previous emancipations elsewhere in the nineteenth-century Americas and often sought to compare these—either favorably or critically—with emancipation in the postbellum South. Building upon this contemporary awareness, my second monograph examined the commemorative and ideological links of West Indies Emancipation across the English-speaking Atlantic world between the 1830s and 1860s. This book, however, was very specialized, and remained trapped within the very framework it sought to escape—namely the Anglo-centric model of Black Atlantic studies. The next work, I decided, must be much more inclusive of emancipation outside of the Anglophone world. Unfortunately, the resulting hemisphere-wide topic called *The Great Emancipators: How Slaves Destroyed Slavery in the Americas* met with a tepid response from some quarters of the U.S. historical establishment. Moreover, although bits and pieces were presented at conferences and published as articles, others were rejected after ridiculously long review processes. This negative outcome might have been due to the uninspiring nature of the topic, although I doubt it. It might have been because the role of slaves in ending slavery is now old hat to scholars and others (oh, how I wish this was so!). One anonymous reviewer of an abbreviated essay version of the project eventually rejected by *The Journal of American History* opined that the manuscript's distinctiveness "is more a matter of tone than of substance," and went on to dismiss the essay because of a "thesis that is not nearly so novel as its author claims."[1] My argument was, and remains, primarily concerned with the methodological potential of comparative emancipation. Another possibility, however, is that sweeping approaches to the past—for example, Fritz Redlich's sociological generalizations—are not popular with some dyed-in-the-wool empiricist members of our increasingly narrow and specialized academic discipline.

This was the context in which I decided to write *Freedom's Seekers*. There are no claims here for either a universal or a complete statement on how to compare emancipation. Instead, I offer a series of arguments stating what I consider to be some of the major tenets of comparative methodology for emancipation studies. More specifically, I demonstrate that there were historical experiences and people's lives that were inherently transnational and can best be understood through comparative approaches. This agenda shapes the structure of the book into two major sections: "Experiences" and "Lives," with each part containing three chapters.

The time period runs from the late eighteenth century and the age of revolutionary emancipation through the final abolition of slavery in Cuba and

Brazil during the late nineteenth century—what I call the century of emancipation. Sometimes, the lens is very wide and embraces several decades; at other times, it covers a three-decade period or generation; and, occasionally it focuses upon one or two key years. The epilogue extends the analysis into our contemporary era. The chronology should prove helpful.

The spatial dimensions embrace the Atlantic Americas, especially North America (the United States, Canada, Mexico), the French, Spanish, Danish, Dutch, and British Caribbean, Latin America, especially Brazil, and European empires. There are also comparative references to emancipation on the African continent. We also look at the Indian Ocean, especially colonized areas such as India and Mauritius. Africa and India offer parallel developments concerning slavery and emancipation, imperial conduits beyond the Atlantic Americas, as well as cross-imperial connections.[2]

There are four basic demographic points that should be borne in mind when comparing emancipation in the nineteenth-century African Diaspora. First, there were some 6.2 million enslaved Africans who were exported during the nineteenth century: around 4.0 million in the Atlantic slave trade; some 1.2 million in the trans-Saharan trade; about 492,000 forced across the Red Sea from Ethiopia; and, approximately 442,000 from East Africa dispersed throughout the Indian Ocean.[3] Most exported slaves during the nineteenth century went through the transatlantic slave trade and ended up in plantation production in Brazil and Cuba, not in the United States or the British and French Caribbean. Second, the total enslaved population in the 1860s Americas was around 6.0 million, of which 3.9 million (two-thirds) were in the United States, 1.7 million in Brazil, and over 370,000 in Cuba.[4] Emancipation wrought major social transformations in the slave societies of the United States, Brazil, and Cuba, compared to societies with slaves in the Atlantic Americas.[5] Third, the free black population in the French and English Caribbean, together with the United States, was usually 5 percent or less compared to around 20 to 30 percent in Brazil and Cuba.[6] This meant that the experience of freedom before official abolition was less prevalent in the former than the latter societies. Fourth, more women were freed before abolition elsewhere in the Americas than in the United States; and more women were freed after abolition in the United States compared to elsewhere in the Americas. This gender difference has important implications for comparing freedwomen across the nineteenth-century Americas.

During the 1970s and 1980s, there were numerous attempts to compare

U.S. emancipation with other post-abolition societies. The key objective was to transcend the problem of the American past as being exceptional by revealing some of the similarities as well as compelling differences concerning slavery and emancipation in the United States compared to other societies. One unintended consequence, however, was to reify the uniqueness of the U.S. experience. This was particularly the case with an older generation of historians whose comparative work on post-abolition political systems determined the prevalence of greater democratic freedoms in the post-emancipation United States compared to elsewhere in the Caribbean and Latin America. The argument was unpersuasive and U.S. centered. What rendered it especially problematic, however, was its dissemination by leading scholars in the profession— what we might refer to as the founding fathers of comparative emancipation. Their footprint remains visible in more recent emancipation studies. The introduction to *Freedom's Seekers* examines this historical mistreatment of comparative methodology, providing a critical and polemical examination of the limitations of a comparative analysis that ends up trumpeting national differences.

The book's subsequent chapters should be seen as a positive response to this critique by focusing on major ways in which to compare emancipation through similarities, differences, and connections that seek to avoid replicating the methodological problems of uniqueness and nation-state boundaries. These chapters are grouped into two parts. The first section examines the experiences of self-emancipators, slave soldiers, and slave rebels comparatively. The second part moves from the individual life of a prominent black abolitionist to the collective lives of freedwomen and children and freedom's first generation.

Over the past few decades, there has been a welcome rise in the historical literature dealing with fugitive slaves and their attempts to escape southern U.S. slavery. At the same time, there has been an explosion of public history associated with commemorating local sites on the Underground Railroad. There have been similar academic and public developments in Canada. What is striking, however, is the extent to which these academic and public activities are pursued as national projects independent of one another. Thus: fugitive slaves are studied and memorialized in Canada and the United States with much less attention to their cross-national activities. This is no doubt because governments, universities, and research institutes seek to fund historical projects that contribute toward the making of multiculturalism.

Yet, self-liberators often crossed national borders in the ultimate quest to achieve and protect their liberty. Their actions sometimes shaped international relations between nation-states. Their relocation also helped create new abolitionist organizations. They also established the first free black communities on the edge of slave societies. In other words, these self-emancipators were transnational figures whose lives and actions fit awkwardly within nationalist narratives. We must always embrace studies of the subaltern and the voiceless over the endless tomes on history's personages. On the other hand, both national funding agencies and local historical initiatives tend to render invisible the international dimensions of these freedom seekers. Their continental stories, and the important implications of their actions, are the subject of chapter 1.

During the nineteenth century, slaves who opposed slavery were frequently reported as murderers, savages, rebels, discontents, troublemakers, outsiders, and so forth. Less frequently, they were depicted as warriors, heroes, freedom fighters, and soldiers. The last two decades have witnessed the emergence of a stimulating scholarly literature on the role of slaves as soldiers who fought during wars of national independence and against human bondage throughout the nineteenth-century Americas. Much of this impressive literature, however, continues to operate within established national frameworks. Thus, we read about black patriots or loyalists during the American War of Independence and U.S. Colored Troops as Unionists during the American Civil War. Slaves who fought during the Haitian Revolution and Cuba's First War for Independence are usually heralded for their contributions to the making of new Caribbean nations. Such research on slave soldiers will continue, presumably at smaller levels such as regimental histories, dramatic episodes, and chronological turning points. In contrast, chapter 2 provides a broader framework for comparing the extent, experience, and participation of slave soldiers on the battlefield. It is only through a comparative analysis that we can appreciate the historical significance of slave soldiers in wars of national independence, the abolition of slavery, and developments in the nineteenth-century African Diaspora. Although some attention is directed toward connections and compelling differences, this chapter's major emphasis is on the general similarities of slave soldiers as freedom's seekers, the implications of their quest, and the limitations of patriotic narratives.

This idea of similarities is what most people think of when one mentions the comparative method. The word "compare" derives from the Latin *compar*, meaning like or equal. In my comparative history courses, most students begin with the assumption that comparing slaves and ex-slaves entails searching for what is similar. Less familiar is the idea of examining compelling differences—also an important part of comparative methodology. But there is another aspect to the comparative method that is best described as transnational or cross-national. Slaves were never citizens, while blacks who were legally free had to constantly struggle for civic inclusion in slave societies, societies with slaves, free societies, colonial societies, independent republics, and constitutional monarchies. Sometimes they met with success, other times less so. This lack of equal citizenship created a void often filled by extra-national identities, including Christian abolitionists who promoted the idea of brotherhood (and sisterhood) as well as slaves and free blacks' construction of common causes and homelands. Chapter 3 examines examples of slave revolt, legal abolition, and post-emancipation developments throughout the nineteenth-century Americas. Its specific concern is with the transmission and nature of slave revolt and abolition in one area inspiring slave self-emancipation in other places, and its ramifications. It pursues connections among slaves seeking freedom in colonial states as well as the first black republic's responses to these actions. It explains the intersection between slaves' original desires for freedom and the impact of external factors. Slave revolt is broadly defined as both collective rebellion as well as smaller acts of self-emancipation, while borders are delineated as national boundaries on land and at sea as well as between states in federal territories. It has three objectives. It seeks to expand the spatial and temporal dimensions of the "common-wind" approach to slave revolt studies beyond Haiti as well as the Age of Revolution. It aims to reveal connections between the Caribbean, Central America, North America, and South America overlooked by national and regional historiographies independent of each other. The third goal is to contribute to the conceptualization of African Diaspora scholarship. In sum, this first section employs a comparative methodology to reveal the cross-national dimensions of emancipation experiences usually overlooked in local, regional, and national studies.

The second section of *Freedom's Seekers* examines emancipated lives at the individual and collective levels. Many self-emancipators were remarkable figures. One such was Samuel Ringgold Ward. Slave-born in Maryland, Ward became a Presbyterian preacher in upstate New York before becoming a leading antislavery campaigner in Canada and the United Kingdom during the 1850s. He spent the last decade of his life propagating the faith in Jamaica. Despite this transnational traveling life, and constant border crossings, however, scholars usually define Ward in national terms as an American ex-slave, an African American, or a refugee from his homeland. In contrast, I think his life and labors provide a fascinating example of the freedom seeker crossing borders—in this particular case those of the British Empire in the decades after it abolished colonial slavery. At the same time that the United States was building a slave empire in the continental Southwest, Great Britain was transforming its colonial slave system. Where these bordered, so fugitive slaves were attracted. I must confess that the idea of an ex-slave finding sanctuary in the British Empire is a little inconvenient for someone with a lifelong commitment to anti-colonialism. (Some readers will no doubt read this fourth chapter and still conclude that it represents a celebration of British imperialism!) But it did not bother thousands of self-liberators and those like Ward who sought human relief and greater freedoms under the Lion's paw. Much like later generations of Afro-Caribbean peoples who lived and labored in post–World War II Britain, Ward sought to put some black in the Union Jack in the post-abolition empire.[7]

The application of gender analysis to slave studies has been recently replicated in emancipation studies. Scholars who have drawn upon gender theory, as well as pursued the implications of slave women studies, have now given us a much richer picture of not only how freedom was different for freedwomen compared to freedmen, but also the centrality of gender in the emancipation experience. At the same time, comparisons of this different experience remain at their infancy for two obvious reasons: much of the research remains to be done; and, that already done remains within local, regional, or national parameters. In chapter 5, we pursue an explicit comparative analysis of ex-slave women and children in the nineteenth-century Caribbean, United States, and Latin America. There are two central arguments. First, a comparative treatment reveals compelling contrasts based on demographic and legal developments that often get overlooked. These differences are pursued through women's manumission during slavery as well as the reconstruction of ex-slaves' household economies. Second, women and children were historical agents who helped shape the emancipation narrative. These similarities are explored through women and children as self-emancipators during social crises as well as ex-slave women functioning as political agents before and after emancipation. Our major objective is to steer between the rock of U.S. uniqueness and the rapids of universal gender categories.

Chapter 6 further broadens this collective perspective by providing a comparative examination of the first generation of ex-slaves in post-abolition societies. Since the spatial, temporal, and demographic dimensions are a little large—three continents, a century plus, and several million people—the analysis is not comprehensive. Rather, it compares reduced cash crop production, the ubiquitous quest for land by ex-slaves, and relations between emancipation and forms of dependency as three specific ways to argue for similarities, differences, and connections respectively in the lives of generations of ex-slaves after abolition in the Caribbean, the United States, and Brazil. In contrast to a proliferation of studies on freedpeople and the meaning of freedom, this chapter offers a comparative approach as a way of thinking cross-nationally about emancipation's founding generations and their struggles during the first thirty years after abolition.

The epilogue concludes with a succinct statement concerning the value and necessity of comparative emancipation methodology. Moreover, it examines several issues pertaining to emancipation today such as cross-border workers and refugees, the imposition of new national boundaries, and the rise of neo-slavery globally. Rather than trying to survey the contemporary globe's political travails, the epilogue seeks to expand the previous comparative analysis by providing an additional temporal dimension linking past and present.

Freedom's Seekers has several major objectives. The first is to reach a broad audience of students and general readers interested in studying emancipation beyond national frameworks. Another aim is to encourage scholars, disciplines, and institutions to examine emancipation outside conventional spatial, temporal, and conceptual categories. A third and related goal is to encourage Anglophone scholars—especially those examining U.S. and British colonial emancipation—to pursue and embed questions and interpretations drawn from non-Anglophone studies of emancipation within their own work. A fourth concern is to use comparative methodology to challenge the claims of several exceptional historiographies: unique U.S. democracy in post-abolition societies, the Haitian Revolution as the only successful slave revolt, pioneering British liberties ahead of all other colonial abolitions, and so forth. A fifth task is to replace national and imperial boundaries with multiple imperial overlaps for a broader comparative approach.

In addition, this book contributes to the theory of the African Diaspora. The historical examination of slavery, homelands, and modern social/cultural movements dominates university courses and academic publications on the African Diaspora. In contrast, there has been much less work on abolitionism and emancipation two decades after Joseph Harris's call.[8] This book goes some way to addressing this oversight through specific investigations into the role and impact of Diaspora Africans in former slave societies. But it also makes a methodological contribution. The comparative methodology of similarities, differences, and connections in abolition societies will hopefully encourage scholars of the African Diaspora to adopt this analytical approach for studies of slavery, homeland, social/cultural movements, and so forth. These two important aspects of the African Diaspora—abolition and comparisons—are pursued throughout this book in three specific ways: the *centering* of people of African descent; an emphasis on *movement*, both coerced and free; and, the making of imagined racial *communities* beyond the local, ethnic, and national. The book's key agenda is a re-conceptualization of the field of emancipation studies through comparative methodology.

It is of course up to the reader to decide whether these aims are achieved. What should be recognized at the outset are two problems inherent with comparative methodology. First, the search for similarities can squash differences. Thus, the similarities of slave soldiers' or ex-slaves' quest for land might only be superficial and undermined by more local and applied documentary research. The alternative, however, is empirical studies revealing more and more unique historical events and sequences that move us further and further away from useful sociological generalizations. Second, how to write transnational history without making points and arguments, or marshalling evidence, that is not nation-based? It is not only easier to cast paragraphs this way, but most of the historical literature on emancipation—or whatever other subject one cares to compare—has been (and is) written in national terms. One of the lessons I have learned from reading, organizing, and writing this book is that there is a good reason why comparative studies do not proliferate, and it has little to with the efficacy of the method and all to do with the challenges of its implementation!

The bibliography lists most of the works used in this collection. It is important to note that it contains only those works that I have found most useful for comparing emancipation rather than all of the studies that have informed my thinking and teaching on slavery and emancipation over the past two decades.

There might be times in what follows (especially the introduction) when it seems I am presenting myself as the sole authority on comparative emancipation. Let me conclude this preface with the acknowledgment that I build on the shoulders of many others who have labored in the vineyard of emancipation studies. More specifically, I have incurred numerous debts in putting together this volume. I would like to thank Howard University for a New Faculty Research Grant between 2007 and 2009 that helped kick-start this project. Thanks to my graduate assistants John Tilghman and Neil Vaz in the History Department at Howard University for tracking down sources at the Library of Congress. I especially want to give a shout-out to Mr. Vaz for his timely assistance with the chronology, map, and proofing of the manuscript, and to Kate McMahon for indexing and page proof corrections. The Library of Congress holds a remarkable collection of sources from which I have benefited immeasurably. Their helpful staff deserves special praise for not only bringing published sources to my desk number 342 every Wednesday for several years, but doing so at a time when under-appreciated federal employees face unjustifiable job and benefits cuts from a stingy federal legislature. *Merci beaucoup* to Ashraf H. A. Rushdy for improving the book's organization, Ana Araujo for saving me from making some facile generalizations about abolition in Brazil, and to both for warning me about my colorful language!

Most of the chapters have benefitted from the intellectual work, critical feedback, and general support of Ana Araujo, Richard Blackett, Bob Engs, Robert Gregg, Edna Medford, Ashraf H. A. Rushdy, Daryl Scott, and Robert Waters. An outline of the introduction was first delivered at the National Humanities Center, Durham, North Carolina, in April 2004. Thanks to Kent Mulliken for the invitation to speak and to the participants. A revised version was presented at Clare College, Cambridge University, in May 2010. Thanks to Brian Ward for the invitation and the participants. I would also like to thank Brian Ward, David Brown, and Bill Link for editorial improvements to the written version. An earlier draft of chapter 1 was presented at the Newberry Library, Chicago, in September 2008, and published as "Fugitive Slaves across North America," in *Workers Across the Americas: The Transnational Turn in Labor History,* edited by Leon Fink (New York: Oxford University Press, 2011), 363–83. Chapter 2 was outlined at the forty-second annual meeting of the Association of Caribbean Historians in Christ Church, Barbados, in May 2010. Thanks to the selection committee and the conference participants. Chapter 3 was outlined at Virginia Commonwealth University, Richmond, in April 2010. Thanks to Bernard Moitt for the invitation and to the participants for their questions. Parts were also delivered at the nineteenth annual meeting of the British American Nineteenth Century Historians, Northumbria University, Newcastle, England, in October 2012. Cheers to David Brown and

David Gleeson for their support. I would also like to thank two anonymous readers for *Atlantic Studies* for their critical comments on an earlier draft subsequently published as "Slave Revolt Across Borders" in the *Journal of African Diaspora Archaeology and Heritage* 2, no. 1 (May 2013): 65–92. Chapter 4 was presented at the University of Liverpool, United Kingdom, in April 2009. My thanks to Fionnghuala Sweeney for editorial improvements on the written version subsequently published as "Samuel Ward and the Making of an Imperial Subject" in *Slavery & Abolition: A Journal of Slave and Post-Slave Studies* 33, no. 2 (June 2012): 205–19. *Shukran* to Ashraf Rushdy and *obrigado* to Ana Araujo, who helped me rethink chapter 5 in important ways. I would also like to thank Jennifer Cubic, Marian Horan, and Jennifer Erdman for interesting papers on gender and emancipation that made me rethink some of my original ideas. The title and approach pursued in chapter 6 draw from the inspirational scholarship of my friend and former doctoral advisor Bob Engs.

Finally, I express my warmest appreciation to Elizabeth R. Lindquist, who is my greatest advocate and favorite critic. This volume is triply dedicated: to Bob Engs, who passed away unexpectedly in early 2013; to all of my students who have taken classes comparing slavery and emancipation since 1990; and, to Alexander R. Kerr-Ritchie, who saw first light on the River Cam, Cambridge, and taught me *ab initio* to greet the rising sun in Durham, North Carolina.

JKR
March 2013

NOTE ON LANGUAGE

Freedom's Seekers offers alternative meanings and broader definitions of terms in the spirit of comparative methodology. It employs the terms "self-emancipators" and "self-liberators" rather than "fugitives," "runaways," and "escapees" used by contemporaries and scholars. The former provide a more accurate reflection of what slaves wanted rather than the latter which reflect the language of the propertied class. Besides, the former viewed themselves as fugitives from moral injustice rather than legal justice. I like to use the phrase *barefoot plebiscite* to describe slaves' voting on the system of slavery with their feet. I have used it in the past to describe self-emancipators in the antebellum United States. Here is it employed more broadly across regions, time, and genders. I prefer the term *ante-emancipation* to *ante-bellum* because the latter has a specific U.S. connotation in contrast to the former, which offers a broader comparative meaning. Besides, it compliments *post-emancipation* which is the preferred term in this book to *post-bellum*. I have adapted the phrase *freedom's first generation* from the U.S. context to provide a broader comparative framework for understanding the generational experiences of ex-slaves throughout the hemisphere. I have not used the phrase *race relations* because the book's emphasis is on the experiences and lives of those who sought freedom in comparative perspective.

CHRONOLOGY

1763	British annex Florida.
1763–1841	Canada divided into Upper (Ontario) and Lower (Quebec).
1772	*Knowles v. Somersett* decision against slaveholding in England.
1775	Lord Dunmore offers freedom to loyalist slaves in Virginia.
1776–83	War of Independence between United States and Britain.
1777	Vermont abolishes slavery.
1780	Pennsylvania abolishes slavery.
1783	Florida returned to Spain.
1789	*The Interesting Narrative of the Life of Olaudah Equiano.*
1789–99	French Revolution.
1791	Slave revolt in St. Domingue.
1793	Fugitive Slave Law in United States.
	Imperial Act prohibits slave importation to Upper Canada.
	British invade St. Domingue.
1794	France abolishes colonial slavery.
1795	Slave revolts in Curaçao, Grenada, and Louisiana.
1795–1808	British West India regiments of ex-slaves.
1798	British withdraw from St. Domingue.
1802	France reinstitutes colonial slavery.
1803	Louisiana Territory purchased by United States from France.
1804	Haitian independence and abolition of slavery.
1805	Slave conspiracy in Trinidad.
1806–18	Civil War in Haiti.
1807	Britain legislates abolition of its transatlantic slave trade.
1808	United States abolishes transatlantic slave trade.
	Britain implements abolition of its transatlantic slave trade.
1808–26	Spanish American Wars of Independence.
1811	Slave revolt in Louisiana.
	Free Womb Law in Chile.
1812	José Aponte's revolt in Cuba.
	Slave conspiracy in Peru.
1812–14	War between the United States and Britain.
1813	Free Womb Law in Argentina.

1816	Slave revolt in Barbados.
	New Constitution in Haiti.
	Simón Bolívar visits Haiti.
1817	Samuel Ward born in Maryland.
	Deep Nine goes to Haiti.
1817–18	First Seminole War in Florida.
1819	Adams-Onis Treaty between United States and Spain.
1821	Mexican independence.
	Free Womb Law in Columbia and Peru.
1822	Haiti invades Santo Domingo and abolishes slavery.
	Denmark Vesey's conspiracy in South Carolina.
1823	Chile abolishes slavery.
1825	France recognizes Haiti for 150m franc indemnity.
	Free Womb Law in Uruguay.
1826	Slave revolt aboard the *Decatur*.
1827	New York abolishes slavery.
	Mary Prince goes to London and becomes free.
1829	Mexico abolishes slavery.
	David Walker's *Appeal to the Colored Citizens of the World*.
	Slave revolt aboard the *Lafayette*.
1830	Wilberforce Settlement in Upper Canada.
1831	Nat Turner's revolt in Virginia.
	Mary Prince's *The History of Mary Prince*.
1831–32	Slave revolt in Jamaica.
1833	British Emancipation Act legislates colonial abolition.
1834	Great Britain implements colonial abolition.
1835	Slave revolt in Salvador da Bahia, Brazil.
1835–42	Second Seminole War in Florida.
1837	William Lyon McKenzie's rebellion in Upper Canada.
1837–1917	Asian indentured workers transported to British Caribbean.
1839	Slave revolt aboard the *Amistad*.
1841	Slave revolt aboard the *Creole*.
	Slave conspiracy in lower Mississippi Valley.
1841–67	Canada divided into West (Ontario) and East (Quebec).
1841–68	Dawn Settlement in Canada West.
1842	Webster-Ashburton Treaty between United States and United Kingdom.
	James Silk Buckingham's *The Slave States of America*.
	British East India Company abolishes slavery in India.
1845	Florida becomes twenty-seventh state.
	Texas becomes twenty-eighth state.

1845–49	Great Potato Famine in Ireland.
1846–48	War between the United States and Mexico.
1847	Liberia declares independence.
1848	France abolishes colonial slavery.
	Denmark abolishes colonial slavery.
	Treaty of Guadalupe Hidalgo between United States and Mexico.
1849	Henry Bibb's *Narrative of the Life and Adventures of Henry Bibb*.
1850	Fugitive Slave Law in United States.
	Elgin Settlement in Canada West.
	Brazil abolishes transatlantic slave trade.
1851	Anti-Slavery Society of Canada.
	Voice of the Fugitive in Canada West.
1852–55	Civil War in Peru.
1853	Henry Bleby's *The Death Struggles of Slavery*.
	Argentina abolishes slavery.
1854	*Provincial Freeman* in Canada West.
	Peru abolishes slavery.
	Venezuela abolishes slavery.
1855	Samuel Ringgold Ward's *Autobiography of a Fugitive Negro*.
1856	Rebellion in British Guyana.
1857	Eureka settlement in Mexico.
	Dred Scott v. Sandford in United States.
1859	John Brown's raid in Virginia.
1861	Dominican Republic reverts to Spanish control.
1861–65	U.S. Civil War.
1862–65	Cotton cultivation in India, Egypt, and Brazil.
1863	Netherlands abolishes colonial slavery.
	Emancipation Proclamation in United States.
1864	Massacre of black soldiers at Fort Pillow, Tennessee.
1865	United States abolishes slavery.
	Revolt at Morant Bay, Jamaica.
	Dominican Republic declares independence.
1865–70	War of Triple Alliance.
1866	Samuel Ward dies in Jamaica.
	Jamaica reverts to Crown Colony status.
	Spain abolishes transatlantic slave trade.
1867	Canada adopts Dominion status in British Empire.
1867–77	U.S. Congressional Reconstruction.
1868–78	First War of Independence in Cuba.
1870	Free Womb Law in Spanish Antilles.

1871	Free Womb Law in Brazil.
1873	Spain abolishes colonial slavery in Puerto Rico.
1876	Centennial of U.S. independence.
1878	Pact of Zanjon ends First War of Cuban Independence.
1879–80	*Guerra Chiquita* in Cuba.
1882	British colonize Egypt.
1884	Berlin conference carves up Africa for European powers.
1885	Sexagenarian Law frees sixty-year-plus slaves in Brazil.
1886	Spain abolishes colonial slavery in Cuba.
1888	Brazil abolishes slavery.
1889	Brazil becomes republic.
1896	*Plessey v. Ferguson* "separate but equal" ruling in United States.
1912	Onslaught against the *Partido Independiente de Color* in Cuba.
1928	Britain abolishes slavery in protectorate of Sierra Leone.
1957–62	Zenith of de-colonization in Africa and Caribbean.
1958	Chinua Achebe's *Things Fall Apart*.
1989	Edward Zwick's *Glory*.
1998	Schenger Agreement in Europe.
2005	Revolt in France.
2011	Revolt in London.
2010	Earthquake in Haiti.
2011	Arab Revolution.

Was U.S. Emancipation Exceptional?

Yet we also need to be mindful of the capacity of the United States to construct a triumphalist narrative of its own history and absorb the world's history into that narrative. To phrase the problem more bluntly, [comparative] approaches might constitute simply another form of U.S. intellectual hegemony.
—JULIE GREENE

The most severe limitation of comparative literature has been its national and nationalist bent. . . . As such, there is a tendency among comparativists to compare large social structures, ideologies, or organizations to explain the nature of the American variant. The desire is to use some other nation's history to help explain 'American slavery,' 'American race relations,' 'American working-class formation or class consciousness,' and so on. That there might be connections between these two American forms and those others being compared is either ignored or not taken sufficiently into account; nor is the fact that there might be differences within the United States that defy the label 'American' and lead one to reconsider its usage.
—ROBERT GREGG

Comparisons, no matter how well conceived, can hide connections.
—MATTHEW PRATT GUTERL

I. FOUNDING FATHERS

On July 4, 1876, hundreds of thousands of Americans gathered throughout thirty-nine states to commemorate the centennial of the founding of the U.S. republic. They listened to orations, speeches, songs, and poems. These public presentations covered numerous themes: the current economic crisis facing the nation, America's providential roots, the inevitability of national progress, and the importance of reunion after a fractious civil war. The recent abolition of slavery in 1865 was also mentioned and widely praised. In Philadelphia, prominent New York state lawyer William M. Evarts proclaimed the centennial "crowns with new glory the immortal truths of the Declaration of Independence by the emancipation of a race." "Thanks be to God, who overrules everything for good," former Massachusetts Senator Robert C. Winthrop told a large gathering in Boston, "that great event, the greatest of our American age . . . has been accomplished; and by his blessing, we present our country to the world this day without a slave, white or black, upon its soil." According to the Baptist Reverend Thomas Armitage, abolition was not only the greatest American event, but it was also unique compared to the practices of other nations. Unlike the abolition of slavery by Great Britain, explained the Reverend, emancipation in the United States had been a principled act: "She [Britain] adopted it merely as a policy and paid for it as a bargain, failing largely to bring down the doctrine of freedom to the question of man's rights as the root of his humanity." In case his audience in New York City missed the point, he reminded them "the American Republic has done more for liberty and against bondage than all other people have done before."[1]

These ideas of God's republic, national progress, and exceptional emancipation—together with an evocation of the unique frontier spirit of the American people—meshed during the era of the professionalization of U.S. history in the late nineteenth century. The subsequent emergence of a historiography of American uniqueness has been well explained and critiqued by Ian Tyrell, Robert Gregg, and others and requires little elaboration here.[2] What is important to note is that it was in response to the chauvinistic, parochial, and unique aspects of this historiography there emerged the first generation of comparative U.S. emancipation scholars. Comer Vann Woodward, one of the pioneers of modern southern historical studies teaching at Yale University, sought to compare the role of the American Civil War in ending slavery with other abolition processes in the nineteenth-century Americas.[3] Eric Foner, one of the major historians of nineteenth-century American political history at Columbia University, compared the extension of political rights to former slaves in the United States with ex-slaves in other post-emancipation societies.[4] George Frederickson, an influential scholar of comparative history at Stanford University, compared race relations in the postbellum American South, post-abolition Jamaica, and fin de siècle South Africa.[5] As we shall see, although their comparative approaches have broadened our understanding of nineteenth-century U.S. history, they have also resulted not only in privileging U.S. emancipation, but further buttressing the argument for the uniqueness of America's past compared to other national experiences. A geo-spatial framework, expanded to situate the U.S. South in the Atlantic world, ended up generating its own kind of exceptionalist narrative.

There were several specific reasons why these scholars thought it important to pursue comparative work. There was a belief that such work would prove as efficacious as the comparative study of slave systems. The publication of Frank Tannebaum's *Slave and Citizen: The Negro in the Americas* in 1946 had heralded a generation of rich historical scholarship comparing slave systems both in the New as well as the Old World.[6] Woodward explained that one reason for his comparative study was that, since there were as many abolitions as slave systems, "it might be presumed that as much light could be shed upon the American experience by the comparative study of the one as the comparative study of the other."[7] Moreover, this comparative work set out to slay the behemoth of America's exceptional past epitomized by the remarks of Winthrop and Armitage at the 1876 centennial commemoration. Woodward's description of the problem of the triumphant narrative of historical progress in U.S. history remains compelling: "One habit of mind that has complicated American ways of dealing with the problem of failure," he argued, "has been the isolation of American experience from comparative reference."[8] Foner points out that "comparative analysis permits us to move beyond 'American exceptionalism' to develop a more sophisticated understanding of the problem of emancipation and its aftermath."[9] It should be added that Foner's *Nothing But Freedom* was published while he was preparing his massive synthesis, *Reconstruction: America's Unfinished Revolution,* with both works insisting on major historical change in the postbellum United States in opposition to numerous studies that focused on its continuity.[10] According to Frederickson, a comparative approach toward racial attitudes after the abolition of slavery might further our knowledge of post-emancipation race relations as well as enlarge our geographical knowledge. New cases for comparison, he adds, "might significantly aid our understanding of the processes involved in racial classification."[11] In other words, comparison with racial attitudes in other carefully selected environments might help us learn more about the nature of American racial attitudes.

These prominent historians at major research universities have shaped the ways in which generations of scholars, students, and general readers comprehend nineteenth-century U.S. history both at home and abroad. They have been particularly successful in situating U.S. emancipation within the broader contours of hemispheric and Atlantic history. Collectively, three comparative arguments stand out. First, the American Civil War represented a unique abolition process in the Americas. Woodward argued that its "unique magnitude,"

together with its "association with a terrible war," made it a historical experience unlike any other.[12] Second, the postbellum United States represented an
exceptional moment in the expansion of national democracy, especially during Reconstruction. Woodward writes: "For nowhere in Plantation-America
during the nineteenth century did the white man share with black freedmen
the range of political power and office that the Southern whites were forced
to share for a brief time with their freedmen."[13] Frederickson agrees: "Such
an extension of full citizenship to a mass of propertyless and largely illiterate
former slaves was, by nineteenth-century standards, an extraordinarily bold
and radical innovation."[14] The most insistent statement on this remarkable
expansion of democracy was provided by Foner, for whom "Reconstruction,
in a comparative context, stands as a unique and dramatic experiment in interracial democracy in the aftermath of slavery."[15] Black workers' struggles in
the rice fields of post-abolition South Carolina, he tells us, "reveal how the
existence of sympathetic local and state governments during Reconstruction
afforded American freedmen a form of political and economic leverage un-
matched by their counterparts in other societies."[16] Indeed, this insistence on
the remarkable enfranchisement of former slaves into the American polity
compared to other post-emancipation societies would not have sounded alien
to the 1876 celebrants.

The third argument claims there was a post-Reconstruction nadir in race
relations unique to the American South compared to other post-emancipation
societies. Frederickson's comparison of local white responses to the freeing
of slaves and the abolition of legal and political distinctions based on race or
color in three areas—the southern United States, the Cape Colony of South
Africa, and Jamaica—concludes that the "reaction of southern whites to the
new racial order seems on the whole to have been less affected by purely
economic concerns [i.e., labor relations] than that of the white Jamaicans
or the majority of the Cape colonists. Emancipation presented itself to most
southern whites pre-eminently as a racial or social challenge—a threat to
the elaborate structure of caste privilege that had developed before the Civil
War."[17] Although both Woodward and Foner eschewed comparing race relations in post-abolition societies, their findings imply that they would not have
disagreed with Frederickson's argument.[18]

In sum, then, what did these early comparative U.S. emancipation studies
add up to? The abolition of slavery in the United States was unique because
of its magnitude and origins in a bloody and terrible war. The postbellum po-

litical terrain was transformed primarily because former slaves gained unique access to political power. It was because of all these factors—bloody war, slave abolition, and Congressional Reconstruction—that race relations were to become so bad in the post-Reconstruction South.

II. THE NEW EXCEPTION

Let us proceed with a critical examination of these comparative arguments. First, was the American Civil War of greater magnitude in ending U.S. slavery compared to the abolition of slavery elsewhere? This argument is unpersuasive given the central role that military conflict played in bringing about immediate abolition in St. Domingue during the 1790s, Peru in the 1850s, and Spanish Cuba in the 1870s–80s, as well as gradual abolition in Spanish America between the 1820s and 1850s. Recent scholarship suggests that revolution, colonial invasions, and national independence struggles played an indispensable role in slave abolition struggles throughout the nineteenth-century Americas.[19] To be precise, the role of military conflict in the abolition of slavery was part of a familiar pattern in the nineteenth-century Americas instead of being unique to the United States. Rather than being the exception to all other emancipation experiences, as implied by Woodward and others, revolutionary emancipation in Haiti should be seen as entailing similar carnage to the American Civil War and Cuban national independence, albeit the most bloody variant. Indeed, if there was a major exception to this linkage between war and emancipation, it occurred in Brazil, in which the abolition of slavery in 1888 was preceded by several years of social unrest rather than military conflict.[20]

Moreover, if the loss of human life serves as the measuring stick of abolition, then the American Civil War was not of the greatest magnitude. Around 620,000 Americans died fighting during the Civil War, including 36,000 soldiers of African descent. This amounted to about one-sixtieth of the white population and one-thirteenth of the black population. Most white Americans fought either to preserve the Union or for southern independence, with more dead southerners than northerners. Most black Americans fought for their own freedom, the destruction of U.S. slavery, and preservation of the Union. Compare this loss of life over abolition during the American Civil War with the devastating decline of Cuba's population from 1.4 million to 1.2 million between 1862 and 1877. This drop in Cuba's population was largely due to the First War of Cuban Independence that hastened Cuban abolition in 1886.[21]

Haitian emancipation was even bloodier with between 100,000 to 200,000 people of African descent forfeiting their lives between 1791 and 1804.[22] The loss of between 20 to 40 percent of Haiti's population resembles a demographic disaster on par with France's loss of 1.6 million soldiers, or almost 20 percent of military-aged men, in the First World War between 1914 and 1918.[23] Thus, the American Civil War exemplified rather than deviated from the link between war and emancipation, while the price of liberty was of enormous magnitude across the nineteenth-century Americas, especially for those who fought for their own liberty.[24]

An additional interpretive challenge with this comparison concerns how to reconcile the view of the American Civil War with its terrible loss of life as a national tragedy with the final overthrow of a system of brutal slavery stretching back to the seventeenth-century Chesapeake region. Woodward never fully extricated himself from the belief that the Civil War was a national tragedy. This point remains deeply embedded within the American psyche as continually demonstrated at contemporary history conferences as well as in battlefield reenactments and on personal websites. But many abolitionists viewed the war and its outcome as a necessary path toward liberty and national redemption. And black soldiers who fought for the Union in an epic battle to destroy U.S. slavery did not see the Civil War as an unfolding tragedy. Black veterans of these wars of liberation remained proud of their military contribution. (For them, the tragedy was postwar America's refusal of racial equality to those who had risked their lives on behalf of the Union.) Edward Longacre's recent history of the Fourth U.S. Colored Infantry persuasively concludes that "the regiment's war record was a never-ceasing source of pride to its veterans."[25] Triumph trumped tragedy in the recollections of other veterans of wars of emancipation. After the legal abolition of slavery in 1886, former slave soldiers in Spanish Cuba claimed they won their freedom through fighting for it rather than receiving it as a governmental boon.[26] There is little doubt that Haitian veterans who battled and defeated British, Spanish, and French troops for individual liberty and national independence during the Haitian Revolution felt the same way. In short, who could disagree with Woodward's evocation of Robert E. Lee's famous quip that war is a terrible thing, except for former slaves across the nineteenth-century Americas for whom the horrors of war were usually the only realistic way to destroy the terrors of slavery?

Second, was U.S. Reconstruction exceptional? Foner successfully inverts an older racist historiography depicting the "Africanization" of the postwar

South with Reconstruction representing an important moment not only for the "Americanization" of former slaves, but also for the realization of the American ideal of freedom first passionately expressed by W. E. B. Du Bois in his monumental *Black Reconstruction*, published in 1935.[27] It is important, however, not to forget the structural restraints on ex-slaves' political power during U.S. Reconstruction. Republican Reconstruction of the southern states always depended upon the approval of the federal Congress that provided for revised state constitutions and voter registration buttressed by the presence of the Union Army. Furthermore, Reconstruction legislatures between 1867 and 1877 consisted of coalitions between northern republicans, southern unionists, and African Americans (former slaves and formerly free blacks), with the latter often serving in a minor role. About one thousand delegates participated in the rewriting of southern state constitutions, of which around one-fourth were African Americans.[28] Black American delegates were a demographic majority in Louisiana and South Carolina, about 40 percent in Florida, 20 percent in Alabama, Georgia, Mississippi, Virginia, and around 10 percent in Arkansas, North Carolina, and Texas.[29] It is useful to recall an important generalization made by Kenneth Stampp in his revisionist study of U.S. Reconstruction published the same year as the passage of the U.S. Voting Rights Act in 1965: blacks "did not control any of them [state legislatures]" during Reconstruction.[30] The irony of over-emphasizing freedmen's politics during U.S. Reconstruction is that it echoes a traditional white South's view of dominant black political power facilitated by federal intrusion into the region.

Moreover, while ex-slaves in the U.S. South enjoyed more political power than ex-slaves in Jamaica, Cuba, and Brazil, they did not do so compared to Haiti. In 1804, a black elite comprising former slaves and *ancien libres* (long-term free blacks) controlled the government after overthrowing the French colonial state and its administrative apparatus. It is true that Haitians did not exercise the constitutional right to vote, but this was primarily due to the revolutionary nature of the transition to power. In the same way, there was not an expansion of democratic rights in post-revolutionary England (1650s), France (1790s), Russia (1920s), China (1950s), and Iran (1980s). This contrasts with the American Civil War in which one political party (the Republicans) sought to consolidate its wartime advantage by extending the suffrage to former slave men in the virtually solid South (Democrats). The key point is to heap qualification upon qualification to the statement that emancipated southern blacks enjoyed more political power than other newly freed peoples. They were enfranchised for the purpose of political expediency. They rarely enjoyed local political domination. They lost influence in federal politics by 1877, and eventually at the state level in North Carolina by 1898 and Virginia by 1902. Most important, their brief political power pales in comparison to that of black elites in post-abolition Haiti. In short, an argument for the uniqueness of American Reconstruction says more about historians' unshakeable belief in national democratic ideals than it does about ex-slaves' political power in comparative perspective.

Moreover, this argument for unique U.S. democracy has been indirectly challenged by the recent claims of some scholars for the Haitian Revolution's global political significance. Laurent Dubois claims the revolution "forever transformed the world" whose destruction of slavery in the Americas was "a crucial moment in the history of democracy, one that laid the foundation for the continuing struggles for human rights everywhere."[31] Robin Blackburn has recently echoed his call that the Haitian Revolution was historically significant for ushering in a global agenda of human rights.[32] This revolutionary optimism has recently been challenged by Philippe Girard, who claims the revolution was led by a greedy rather than ideological black elite.[33] My argument for an alternative interpretation of Haiti as a racially imagined community is pursued in chapter 3. The salient point, however, is that an older view of U.S. unique-ness is being replaced by a new argument for Haiti's uniqueness.

One final point about the uniqueness of U.S. Reconstruction concerns the skewing of its inspirational source. Du Bois's *Black Reconstruction* sought to challenge existing racist depictions of the postwar South by stressing the na-tion's democratic moment. Foner and others have subsequently pushed this argument further to make a claim for American democracy's exceptionalism compared to other post-emancipation societies. But this has served to down-play an important argument made by Du Bois concerning certain common-alities among the wretched of the earth during the 1930s. After an eloquent indictment of racist historians of U.S. Reconstruction, Du Bois writes: "Im-mediately in Africa, a black back runs red with the blood of the lash; In India, a brown girl is raped; in China, a coolie starves; in Alabama, seven darkies are more than lynched; while in London, the white limbs of a prostitute are hung with jewels and silk. Flames of jealous murder sweep the earth, while brains of little children smear the hills."[34] This poetic passage connotes the similarities of oppression rather than unique democratic differentiation. It also recalls other worlds beyond the U.S. South and the Atlantic.

The argument that the extension of political rights made the post-abolition U.S. South unique among post-emancipation societies has been most strongly contested by *The Political Languages of Emancipation in the British Caribbean and the U.S. South,* published in 2002.[35] Its author, Demetrius L. Eudell, completed his dissertation under Frederickson at Stanford University. Drawing upon J. G. A. Pocock's dialectical concept of political languages, Eudell examines competing paradigms and ideologies of planters, government officials, and racial scientists to argue for the similarity of racial debasement in post-abolition Jamaica and South Carolina. "In both postslavery situations," argues Eudell, "the dominant society found a way to disempower (Jamaica) or disfranchise (South Carolina) its respective Black majorities and still continue to see itself as being a nation that embodied free and democratic principles."[36] In contrast, former slaves in Jamaica and South Carolina "appropriated and expropriated the dominant languages of liberty and freedom" to provide alternative understandings of what they thought freedom entailed.[37]

Eudell's *Political Languages of Emancipation* is in serious disagreement with the notion of exceptional U.S. emancipation. At the end of his chapter comparing the "civilizing" policies of Freedmen's Bureau officials and special magistrates representing the British Colonial Office, Eudell explains that such an understanding "can provide the basis for an analysis of the postslavery Anglo-America from a new angle," namely the work of Reconstruction.[38] More generally, Eudell offers a more static interpretation of the post-abolition past compared to Foner, for whom U.S. emancipation represented a radical break, and Frederickson (as well as Woodward) for whom without this radical rupture, there is no satisfactory explanation for the breakout of vehement racism in the late-nineteenth-century American South. Most reviewers of Eudell's book managed to ignore his key comparative points, with the unfortunate consequence that the author's challenge to earlier views of exceptional U.S. emancipation went unrecorded.[39]

These contributions by Eudell are both informative and positive, but the question is what exactly are we learning anew about the limits of freedom and post-abolition societies more generally through the comparison? So much work has already been done on post-abolition Jamaica and South Carolina (as implied by the ten pages of secondary sources listed in the book's bibliography) that his comparison often reads thinly. Furthermore, the choice of a colony (Jamaica) and a state (South Carolina) for regions (British Caribbean, American South) as being representative is debatable. These places are chosen, we are told, because they were "significant" places in slave and post-slavery politics, they contained black numerical majorities, and limited access to land became a major political bone of contention in both areas.[40] Although most southern states did not have black majorities (except Mississippi and South Carolina), this was not the case for the British colonies, all of which had large black majorities, and it is hard to separate any of these three factors (politics, demography, land) from the post-abolition experience of British colonies and Southern states. In addition, when Eudell informs us that the southern Black Codes and British colonial acts had "local variations" but "contained some unifying elements," we are left wondering why the analysis of Jamaica and South Carolina is *necessarily* more useful than between any other post-abolition British colony and southern state.[41] After all, both Foner's optimism about striking black rice workers and Eudell's pessimism concerning former slaves' limited democracy are simply reverse sides of the same post-abolition South Carolina coinage. This recalls one of the problems of the first generation of comparative emancipation scholars, for whom a place often took the proxy of a nation. Indeed, although Eudell's argument for a similar racial subjugation clearly differs from his former doctoral advisor Frederickson's view that the post-emancipation South was far worse than anywhere else, including Jamaica, both draw upon questionable representative units. Finally, it is unclear how this comparison advances our understanding of post-emancipation developments. Because both emancipation experiences are conflated, there is a stress on similarities rather than differences. Consequently, we are treated to a fairly familiar account of two emancipation experiences whose comparison (re: similarities) reveals little that is actually innovative.

The uniqueness of post-abolition U.S. democracy has been powerfully restated by Steven Hahn. Currently a professor of history at the University of Pennsylvania, and former member of the Freedmen and Southern Society Project, Hahn completed his doctorate under Woodard at Yale University on the political and social transformation of life among yeoman farmers in postbellum upcountry Georgia. A comparative dimension to this work was its conceptual affinity with the famous transition debate from feudalism to capitalism that hallmarked European historiography for a generation.[42] In a 1990 journal article, Hahn provided a comparative treatment of the links between abolition and nation-building among the *fazendeiros* (planters) of Brazil, the Prussian Junker landlords, and planters in the American South, concluding that "what stands out in the course of emancipation and unification is the swift and dramatic decline in the fortunes of the Southern planter class."[43] This was an argument—minus the comparison with Brazil and Prussia—many southern opponents of federal Reconstruction made at the time; it was also eloquently expressed in Woodward's magnum opus, *The Origins of the New South*.[44] It might have been because of Hahn's lack of attention to the subject of "race" in the nineteenth-century South that persuaded him to turn to rural black southerners and their political mobilization after the abolition of slavery. The result is a deep documentary excavation revealing kinship, work, communication, and mobilization among generations of black southerners, culminating in a social politics of rural working peoples' struggles.[45] At the same time, the author situated these social politics within a comparative post-emancipation framework. The participation of blacks in the local politics of southern courthouse towns was of a "magnitude unprecedented in the region, nation, or hemisphere." "In the history of slavery and freedom in the Atlantic world," Hahn concludes, "there never has been nor ever would be anything quite like it."[46]

Hahn's *A Nation under Our Feet* has been rightly praised as a major work in U.S. historiography. Most of the reviews, however, ignored the book's comparative statements. Furthermore, it seems a little odd that a book concerned with revealing the rural southern roots of black nationalist ideology should fail to draw upon a vibrant black nationalist historiography articulated long ago by Herbert Aptheker, Sterling Stuckey, Lerone Bennett, John Blassingame, Vincent Harding, and Mary Berry, among others. The comparative argument for a unique democratic experiment is highly debatable: limited ex-slave political power in the postbellum South; ex-slaves' winning of state power in Haiti, and so forth. Indeed, Hahn's arguments for *both* ex-slaveholders' decline *and* ex-slaves' political rise are part of the same argument for the exceptional expansion of democracy in the postbellum South. But this argument for the uniqueness of U.S. Reconstruction simply reminds us that an explicit argument is already implicit because of its existing assumption of the revolutionary (and unique) dimensions of the American Civil War.

The third rebuttal of unique U.S. emancipation concerns the argument for the nadir of race relations in the postbellum South. First, there were obvious regional differences that were more important than national differences. The activities of Ku Klux Klan chapters as well as spectacle lynching appear to have been more marked in states in the Lower South compared to those in the Upper South.[47] White supremacist attitudes might well have been more akin between extremists in South Carolina and the Boer Republic and between moderates in Virginia and the Cape Province rather than for the entire post-emancipation South compared with *fin de siècle* South Africa.

Moreover, if the nadir refers to racial violence during the post-abolition decades, then we have to look beyond the post-abolition American South for its most extreme expression. In the aftermath of colonial abolition in the British West Indies, there were riots and rebellions in 1856 British Guiana (now Guyana), 1876 Barbados, and 1884 Trinidad, resulting in considerable death and destruction. The Morant Bay revolt in Jamaica in 1865 claimed the lives of 20 whites and more than 430 blacks.[48] In 1912, the Afro-Cuban political organization *Partido Independiente de Color* pursued armed struggle for the "relegalization of their party" twenty-six years after the abolition of Cuban slavery. The Cuban state's response was a race war against the militants, resulting in the deaths of between 2,000 and 6,000 rebels. One contemporary reported that "the roads are strewn with dead bodies."[49] It was Haiti, however, that witnessed some of the worst racial violence. The members of the First Civil Commission to St. Domingue estimated that 400 whites had been killed in the four months after the uprising began in August 1791.[50] During the war of national liberation in 1802–3, the French military invading forces under General Leclerc followed by General Rochambeau tried to reassert colonial control through a systematic campaign of terror and torture to intimidate the local black populace. General Jean Jacques Dessalines responded by massacring white men, women, and children, leaving "stacks of corpses rotting in the sun to strike terror into the French detachments."[51] In April 1804, president Dessalines ordered the systematic extermination of all remaining French citizens in the new nation-state. This act was designed to both mobilize national sentiment as well as warn French citizens to stay away from Haiti.[52] In other words, struggles over power between freedom's new generations and older custodians of colonial control and white domination were an inimitable part of post-abolition racial disorder. From this comparative perspective, the emergence of white supremacy in the U.S. South was not unique but part of a broader racist reaction to post-emancipation developments throughout the nineteenth-century Atlantic world.

In short, there are two major problems with the argument for exceptional U.S. emancipation. First, it seems that an explicit argument is already implicit because of the assumption that the American Civil War constituted a social revolution. This notion of sweeping revolutionary change is shared by all of these comparative emancipation scholars. In which case, we are reading either a more sophisticated version of an existing argument, or we are reading about American history in more cosmopolitan ways. These are welcome challenges to the parochialism of U.S. history, but what exactly are we learning that is new through the comparison? Second, the nation-based approach toward comparative analysis ends up supporting rather than challenging American difference. The result is that studies motivated by a genuine desire to demonstrate the difference of the American experience through comparison with other national case studies end up providing a more sophisticated version of America's unique historical trajectory.

III. BEYOND THE ATLANTIC

One possible objection to these challenges to comparative U.S. emancipation studies is that they rely on research and perspectives unavailable to earlier scholars. This criticism, however, is unpersuasive for two reasons. First, it ignores the tremendous influence that this first generation of scholars has had on reshaping our understanding of post-abolition societies despite the emergence of new scholarship. Second, it overlooks the easy assimilation of the original approach and findings into more recent studies. Woodward's view of the revolutionary nature of the American Civil War remains uncontested in Hahn's comparison of U.S. emancipation. The limitations of representative units for comparative analysis remain unchallenged in the work of Frederickson's former student Eudell. The Anglo-Atlantic world serves as the epicenter of emancipation, with other movements in West and Central West Africa, Central and South America either peripheral or absent altogether.[53]

Influential economic historian Stanley L. Engerman, a teacher at the University of Rochester since 1963, has spent a long career examining the economics of U.S. slavery and emancipation, especially family structure, demographic patterns, and the treatment of slaves. He has also published extensively on various aspects of slavery and emancipation in the British Caribbean including black fertility, contract labor, land and labor ratios, and regional demographics. It was this expertise that helps explain his selection to deliver the prestigious Walter L. Fleming Lectures at Louisiana State University on April 13–14, 2005.[54] These were subsequently revised and published in 2007 as *Slavery, Emancipation, and Freedom: Comparative Perspectives.*[55]

It provides a comparative examination of slavery, emancipation, and freedom within a largely Anglo-Atlantic framework. The first chapter concludes that, "by world standards, slavery in the American South was not an unusual institution."[56] What was unusual about American slavery was its demographic difference from other slave societies, in particular its higher fertility rates, more equal sex ratios, and more stable family units. This was to be explained by "some combination of better nutrition, lesser work demands, and a more favorable disease environment," with consequences for understanding "differences in slave culture, the nature of slave revolts and resistance, and the question of African survivals."[57] The book's second chapter turns to emancipation and focuses on certain commonalities. Thus, most slave emancipation was accomplished with some form of compensation for former slaveholders, while the abolition of slavery, with its "combination of increased leisure time, a lessened intensity of labor, and lowered labor force participation rates," had similar positive effects for ex-slaves.[58] The heart of the chapter, however, compares U.S. emancipation and argues for its exceptional nature in two familiar ways. Former slaves' enfranchisement "compared favorably" with that of other ex-slaves as well as citizenship struggles of European immigrants.[59] And the "level of violence" in the postbellum South compared to other post-emancipation societies was unprecedented.[60] Engerman's postscript expands the temporal lens by comparing past slavery with contemporary forms of unfree labor, concluding that many existing evils have little in common with the "permanent purchase and sale of individuals for lifetime labor and with inherited status."[61]

This book's publication met with fulsome praise, as suggested by glowing endorsements on the dust jacket by fellow scholars of slavery and abolition studies, including David Brion Davis, Seymour Drescher, and Hebert Klein. But its contribution to comparative U.S. emancipation studies seems less evident for several reasons. First, the unique reproductive rate of slaves in the antebellum South is a very familiar argument in comparative slave studies. Second, the comparative generalization that abolition was often accompanied by compensation is misleading. Slaveholders were compensated in the British West Indies, the Dutch West Indies, and Spanish Puerto Rico, while Haiti was forced to indemnify France twenty-one years after independence in exchange for diplomatic recognition. But abolition was not accompanied by compensation in Mexico, the French West Indies, and the Danish West Indies. Most important, emancipation was not followed by compensation in the major slave societies of Brazil, Cuba, and the United States. The distinction is an important one because emancipation was rarely an orderly legal process as implied by Engerman's comparative compensation approach. Third, the comparative framework is outdated. In 1959, Stanley Elkins's *Slavery* argued that slaves in the American South had been infantilized by unimpeded capitalism compared to slaves elsewhere in the hemisphere. Students of slavery (and abolition) all owe an inestimable debt to Professor Elkins for provoking many scholars to prove him wrong, resulting in slave studies periodically becoming one of the most vibrant fields in U.S. historiography. Yet Engerman's preface to his 2007 book can still refer to "two critical questions" about slavery's legacy and master/slave psychology first raised by Elkins in 1959![62] Fourth, much of the exciting historical literature exploring the local, regional, national, and comparative dimensions of slave and emancipation studies is absent. Many pre-2007 publications listed in the endnotes, below, do not show up in Engerman's bibliography. Furthermore, the author fails to engage exciting new historical literature on topics like the imperialist and gendered dimensions of Asian indentured servitude since the 1990s by Verene Shepherd, Bridget Brereton, Barbara Bailey, Madhavi Kale, Rosemarijn Hoefte, Patricia Moham-med, and Andrew Wilson.[63] As one reviewer reminds us, what is missing "is a full explication of race and the issues of cultural survival and regeneration," issues germane to most current studies of slavery and emancipation.[64]

Most important for our purposes, Engerman fails to move the comparison of U.S. emancipation beyond its original moorings. In other words, U.S. aboli-tion was exceptional in its enfranchising of ex-slaves, while racial violence in the post-emancipation American South was unprecedented in its ferocity. Moreover, the author's insistence on the demographic uniqueness of U.S. slav-ery is not pursued into the post-emancipation era. Engerman's reiteration of the familiar argument of higher fertility rates, a more balanced gender ratio, and greater familial stability among southern U.S. slaves compared to slaves elsewhere should have made American post-emancipation developments ex-ceptional compared to other post-abolition societies with less fertility, more males than females, and less stable family units. Instead, Engerman concludes that ex-slaves' desires to "become family farmers on small units" in the Ameri-can South was also common in the post-abolition British Caribbean. How, we might reasonably inquire, could such profoundly different social conditions of slavery result in strikingly similar post-emancipation outcomes?[65] The au-thor's conclusion begs questions concerning the significance of slave/ex-slave demographic differences in the British Caribbean and the American South as well as their intra-regional comparison.

This introduction is less concerned with providing a comprehensive overview of U.S. emancipation studies and other comparative treatments of abolition than in seeking to show the significance of the choice and interpretation of comparisons and their legacy.[66] One of the major problems of comparative U.S. emancipation scholarship is its national and nationalist focus. The consequence is that studies motivated by a genuine desire to demonstrate the difference of the U.S. experience through comparison with other national case studies end up providing a more sophisticated version of America's unique historical trajectory. Thus, U.S. comparative emancipation has become a new secular version of an older narrative of God's republic. Moreover, this comparative approach transcends its particular historical moment of the 1970s and 1980s stretching back into the past (1870s) as well as into subsequent comparative studies (post-1990s). In short, although U.S. emancipation was far from exceptional, the view that it was unique and special continues to exert a major influence in the field of emancipation studies.

In addition, there are several drawbacks with existing geo-spatial frameworks for comparing U.S. emancipation. First, the expansion of the spatial framework makes little difference if there is a nationalist bent to comparative emancipation studies. When the framework is expanded to situate the American South in the Atlantic world, it remains exceptional. Race relations in the post-abolition American South were unique in their violent breakdown compared to Jamaica and South Africa. The extension of political rights to former slaves in the American South was unique compared to other post-emancipation societies in the Atlantic world. Second, the claim for exceptional U.S. emancipation downplays the significance of emancipation in other regions of the hemisphere. For instance, the argument for the revolutionary nature of slave abolition in the United States implies a greater degree of continuity elsewhere in post-abolition societies. Yet some slave societies experienced total revolutions (Haiti), others went through political transformations associated with the establishment of national independence (Cuba), and others were transformed from monarchies into republics (Brazil). Third, comparative U.S. studies ignore *connections* between the United States and emancipation elsewhere in the Americas. The overthrow of slavery in Haiti had a major impact on slaveholders, abolitionists, free blacks, and slaves especially in the United States and Cuba throughout the nineteenth century.[67] The passage of British colonial abolition during the 1830s was to play a significant role in the mobilization of antislavery protest movements throughout the English-speaking Atlantic world.[68] The legal abolition of slavery in the United States in 1865 contributed toward the ending of the Cuban slave trade in 1867. It also left Cuba, Puerto Rico, and Brazil as the sole surviving slave regimes in the Americas, a disjuncture yet to be fully explored by historians.[69]

Finally, if the subjects concern slavery and emancipation, then the nineteenth-century Atlantic and the Western Hemisphere must be privileged geospatial frameworks over the Pacific Rim and continental territories because this was the time and place for slavery and emancipation. There are limitations to a comparative method with expanded spatial dimensions, however, especially if the premise is the national unit of organization or if the expanded framework serves to confirm a pre-existing argument of magnitude.

Let us return to 1876. It is evident that, even though too many comparative U.S. emancipation studies smack of a new version of uniqueness, these are beyond the sort of celebratory nationalist rhetoric of the first centennial. It would be foolish and disingenuous to reduce the critical deliberations of well-meaning liberal and committed leftist scholars to the ebullient shouts of nationalist cheerleaders. At the same time, one is struck by the compatibility of U.S. history in comparative perspective. We live in a particular historical conjuncture during which time the United States has been busy spreading "liberty" globally over the past two decades. This is exemplified in rhetorical triumphs like western celebrations over the fall of the Berlin Wall and modest proclamations that the end of history culminates in democratic free-market systems like the United States. It is also buttressed by U.S. military enforcement in Kuwait and the Balkans during the 1990s and imperial wars in Afghanistan and Iraq during the early twenty-first century. Only future historians will be able to reveal the contours of this historical moment as well as its impact on comparative U.S. scholarship. What is disturbing is the lack of discontinuity between existing U.S. policies of spreading freedom globally, arguments for exceptional U.S. emancipation compared to other abolitions, and the boisterous claim by British-born Thomas Armitage at the 1876 centennial that America has done more for liberty and against bondage than all other people.

PART ONE
EXPERIENCES

CHAPTER 1

Self-Emancipators across North America

Although a slave without men's right am I, My will of steel can reach the starry high.

—ANTARAH

[To organize in America] would greatly endanger the liberty of thousands of self-emancipated persons.

—HENRY BIBB

Sam Castle (son): What are Borders? Maurice Castle (father): It's where one country ends and another begins.

—GRAHAM GREENE

Most fugitive slaves in nineteenth-century continental North America did not leave the colonial or independent polity. Slave escapees in British Canada, Spanish Florida and Mexico, and independent Mexico stayed within national/colonial boundaries. Most scholars agree that fugitive slaves escaped southern U.S. slavery for local, regional, or northern destinations during the antebellum era.[1] Whether they traveled near or far, slave runaways carved out niches of freedom within the territorial confines of the colonial society or nation-state. Their search for the starry high was confined to national parameters, albeit ones in which borders between bondage and freedom were constantly shifting.

At the same time, however, a significant number of self-emancipators crossed national borders in search of permanent freedom. Some crossed international borders in continental North America.[2] We begin with examples of self-liberators crossing borders in search of individual liberation. During the nineteenth century, territorial conflict abounded between the British, Spanish, Americans, and Mexicans. This conflict provided a gateway to freedom for thousands of self-emancipators who gravitated toward free areas beyond the borders of the U.S. republic, including Spanish Florida, independent Mexico, and British Canada. This demographic undercurrent deserves greater attention than it has received thus far. The second section of this chapter examines the consequences of these activities in the diplomatic arena, especially attempts to agree on international treaties to extradite and prevent fugitive flight. The role of self-liberators in provoking these agreements has not been sufficiently understood, and the conventional treatment of these treaties within national frameworks ignores their transcontinental context. The third part analyzes the contributions of self-emancipators to antislavery mobilization across borders. These organizing efforts in different nations, colonies, and territories took place because such efforts were either illegal or difficult to accomplish within the existing confines of the nation-state. The concluding section examines the creation of free settlements across borders, especially in Florida, Canada West, and Mexico. These black communities served as beacons of freedom and were among the first post-emancipation settlements on the North American continent.[3] This chapter's major objective is a cross-national examination of movement, law, activism, and community-formation in support of the practice of transnational history.

I. SOUTH AND NORTH OF THE BORDER

During the seventeenth and eighteenth centuries, imperial tensions between the British and the Spanish facilitated self-emancipation from the British mainland colonies of South Carolina and Georgia to Spanish Florida. In 1688 and 1689, for instance, colonial officials noted that fugitive slaves had sought refuge in the Spanish colony.[4] In 1728, English planter Thomas Elliott and others requested government assistance because they had "fourteen Slaves Runaway to St. Augustine." That same year, the colonial governor of South Carolina complained to the London colonial office that the Spanish were "receivieing [sic] and harbouring all our Runaway Negroes."[5] The extent of this flight, together with the usefulness of fugitives as laborers, translators, and settlers, encouraged the Spanish to establish a fugitive slave settlement near Saint Augustine called Gracia Real de Santa Teresa de Mose in 1739. Although the English established the colony of Georgia as a buffer during the early 1730s, this simply transferred the fugitive "problem" to the southern border of the new colony. The fugitive "problem" disappeared with the British annexation of Florida in 1763, when fugitive slaves were no longer able to seek Spanish asylum, until Florida was returned to Spain at the end of the American Revolutionary War in 1783.[6]

The establishment of a slaveholding U.S. republic did not reduce national rivalries and guaranteed the continuation of self-liberation. During the War

of 1812, international conflict between the United States and Great Britain facilitated the southward escape of slaves to Spanish Florida. Self-emancipators
continued to flee the plantations and farms of the southeastern seaboard,
with mixed results. Some obtained and retained their freedom by mixing with
the Seminole Indians and fought in two major wars (the First and Second
Seminole Wars) to protect their way of life. Others were either returned to
American slavery or re-enslaved by American Indians. The area was annexed
by the United States in 1819 and eventually made safe for emigrant slaveholders with the establishment of Florida as the twenty-seventh state in the Union
in 1845.[7]

Two years after the annexation of Florida, the Spanish Empire was further
weakened by the loss of one of its oldest and most valuable colonies. During
the sixteenth and seventeenth centuries, enslaved Africans worked the cities, mines, plantations, households, and stores of New Spain.[8] The expense of
slave labor, together with the difficulties of supply and high mortality rates,
resulted in the gradual demise of slavery by the early nineteenth century. Between 1810 and 1821, Mexico fought and won its independence from Madrid.
The same year as independence was declared, a commission estimated fewer
than three thousand slaves in the new nation, mostly located in the coastal
areas of Veracruz, Acapulco, and elsewhere. On October 13, 1824, the federal
government abolished the slave trade. Between 1825 and 1827, several states
outlawed slavery. On September 15, 1829, President Vincente Guerrero issued
a decree abolishing slavery throughout the Mexican republic. The decree was
passed to commemorate national independence, enhance "public tranquility,"
and restore natural rights to all.[9]

It is clear that this sequence of events encouraged slaves to invest the
United States–Mexico border with, as one scholar puts it, "liberationist significance."[10] The U.S. continental slave trade from the 1810s onwards brought
hundreds of thousands of new slaves into the expanding southwest regions of
the national republic.[11] After the winning of Mexico's independence in 1821,
slaves crossed the Rio Grande. Benjamin Milam, an early frontier settler,
complained to Joel Robert Poinsett, the first U.S. minister to Mexico: "I have
been in the frontiers of Texas for some time and have observed that the stait
of Louisiana [since 1812] have lost a grait maney slaives that have taken refuge
in this Republick of Mexico."[12] Free soil south of the Rio Grande continued to
attract freedom's seekers after abolition in 1829.

During the mid-1830s, slaves were reported to have headed west across the

Sabine River in search of free soil, much to the chagrin of Texan slaveholders.[13] War on the borderlands often proved conducive to slaves' self-emancipation. In April 1836, Mexican General José Urrea recorded in his diary: "Fourteen Negro slaves with their families came to me on this day and I sent them free to Victoria."[14] In December 1844, twenty-five mounted and armed slaves departed from Bastrop for Mexico. Around seventeen had been caught by early January, but seven to eight made a successful escape.[15] Union officers marching to the Rio Grande in 1845 recorded "three slaves of officers have run away."[16]

It is hard to estimate exactly how many slaves crossed into Mexico after the abolition of slavery. Colonel John S. Ford, Texas Ranger, journalist, and politician, estimated that the 3,000 fugitive slaves from Texas who were living in Mexico in 1851 had increased to 4,000 by 1855.[17] One former slave from Virginia informed journalist, abolitionist, and future public-park designer Frederick Law Olmsted of some 40 escapees during a three-month period in 1854.[18] Rosalie Schwartz suggests "several thousand" ex-slaves inhabited Mexico by the 1850s.[19] What is certain is that slave self-emancipation to Mexico was not popular with Texan slaveholders. In May 1855, the San Antonio *Herald* lamented: "Something should be done to put a stop to the escape of Negroes in Mexico." Four years later, the same newspaper declared: "We have often wondered why some bold and enterprising men in our state do not club together and go into Mexico and bring away the large number of fine likely runaways known to be not far over the line, forming a pretty respectable African colony."[20]

Slaves continued to self-liberate across the borderlands during the American Civil War. The Treaty of Guadalupe Hidalgo in 1848 had ended the U.S. war with Mexico, setting the international boundary along the southern edge of Texas on the Rio Grande. After the Confederate states' creation in 1861, this border served as the new southern nation's sole land frontier with a neutral nation.[21] Cotton, weapons, and supplies crossed the new border; so did self-liberated slaves. Jacob Branch, a former slave in Texas, witnessed these crossings: "After [the] war starts lots of slaves runned off to git to de Yankees. All dem in dis part heads for de Rio Grande river. De Mexicans rig up flat-boats out in de middle river, tied to stakes with rope. When de culled people gits to de rope dey can pull deyself 'cross de rest de way on dem boats. De white folks rid[e] de Mexican side dat river all de time, but plenty slaves git through, anyway."[22]

Branch's recollection is striking for several reasons. Many scholars have noted fugitive flight to Union lines during the American Civil War, but less so border-crossings to Mexico. Furthermore, Branch depicts Mexicans helping slaves escape from Texas, although without any explanation as to why they would do so. The reasons included the belief that a weakened slave institution in Texas would limit American territorial expansion and the establishment of military colonies of ex-slaves and Indians would serve as a useful protective buffer.[23] In addition, this account suggests that slaves were not deterred from self-liberation despite regular patrol efforts to prevent escapes. Finally, Branch's account is vivid: slaves pulling themselves across the river in the hot sun while patrols ride up and down the other side chasing down and shooting fugitives. No wonder he recalled it in such detail more than eight decades later.

Mexican freedoms long continued to resonate in the memories of African Americans. Former slave Felix Haywood of San Antonio, Texas, told an interviewer: "In Mexico you could be free. They didn't care what color you was, black, white, yellow, or blue. Hundreds of slaves did get to Mexico and got on all right. We would hear about 'em and how they was goin' to be Mexicans."[24] Sallie Wroe recalled her father escaped by paddling a bale of cotton across the Rio Grande.[25] There is something rather poetic about a slave crop serving as a vehicle of liberation. In the modern era, Mexico still held promise for gifted artists like African American Elizabeth Catlett, who relocated to Mexico in the late 1940s after which she became a prominent and successful sculptor and print-maker until her death in 2012.[26]

Mexico's free soil before American slaves had several consequences. First, slaveholders in the United States repeatedly sought extradition treaties with Mexico to include the return of fugitive slaves from the 1820s through the 1850s and repeatedly failed. There is little doubt that this failure fueled slaves' cross-border self-emancipation efforts. Second, the passage of the Fugitive Slave Act in 1850 transformed the continental United States into an empire of slaveholder's property rights. This made it harder for self-liberators to elude southern slaveholders because of the federal government's complicity in supporting the latter's pursuit of human chattel. Those who crossed either the southern border into Mexico or the northern border into Canada were guaranteed greater security. Third, it was these slaves' self-emancipation actions that transformed Mexico into a powerful symbol of freedom and antislavery. The fact that some were captured, others died in the attempt, and still others ended up eking out miserable lives in their new domicile should not detract from the importance of the original motivation. After all, there are not many reports of fugitive slaves in Mexico volunteering to return to U.S. slavery. As the Greek slave Aesop is reputed to have quipped: better beans in freedom than bread in slavery.

Former slaves and free blacks in the United States also crossed northern borders into the British colony of Canada. This became particularly pronounced in the years following the passage of British colonial abolition during the 1830s. Robin Winks estimates some 12,000 fugitive slaves living in British Canada by 1840.[27] But the real exodus occurred during the 1850s. As a result of the passage of the Fugitive Slave Act in 1850 in the United States, many fugitive slaves and free blacks left the northern states for the comparative safety of Canada. It has been estimated that about 3,000 fugitives relocated in the months immediately following ratification of the law. Self-liberators Anthony Hollingsworth, Daniel Lockhart, Fred Wilkins, and Jerry McHenry— all rescued from American slave catchers—relocated to Canada. Those who aided and abetted their escape, like Samuel Ringgold Ward and John Lisle, also crossed over to Canada to avoid federal prosecution. In his *Autobiography of a Fugitive Negro*, Ward explained that he and his family decided to move to Canada because of the lack of prospects in the United States and the possibility of incarceration for assisting in the escape of fugitive Jerry McHenry from Syracuse, New York, in contravention of the 1850 Fugitive Slave Act: "I had already become hopeless of doing more in my native country; I had already determined to go to Canada. Now, however, matters became urgent."[28] Furthermore, numerous self-liberators worked their way via the Underground Railroad through the midwestern states of Ohio, Illinois, and Michigan into the southern reaches of Canada West. This region bordering the Detroit River and Lake St. Clair contained the counties of Essex and Kent. Many towns in the area—Windsor, Sandwich, and Amherstburg—saw a large increase in their black populace. Scholars estimate between 40,000 and 60,000 persons of African descent were living in Canada by 1860, with some historians claiming a populace of more than 100,000. Most of these resided in Canada West, and most arrived during the 1850s.[29]

The actions of these self-liberators on the North American continent were paralleled on the African continent. In West Africa, slaves often gravitated toward free colonial zones. During a resurgence of the Cuban slave trade in the late 1850s, numerous domestic slaves from Ouidah, Dahomey, and other neighboring towns in coastal West Africa escaped to the British-controlled port of Lagos where slavery had been abolished. They "all state as the cause of their desertion," it was reported, "the dread of being sold to the Spanish slave-dealers and carried away from their country."[30] After the French abolition of colonial slavery in 1848, slaves (*Jaam* in Wolof) in Senegambia fled to the coastal port of St. Louis because the city offered a haven of freedom from domestic slavery.[31] According to Paul Lovejoy, those slaves who fled to free zones on the African continent during the late nineteenth century contributed to an abolitionist impulse leading to the eventual demise of a very old institution.[32]

In short, an impressive number of slave self-emancipators crossed international borders in pursuit of their own liberty. They did this at various times and in a variety of ways. Territorial conflict between rival powers and states provided a gateway to freedom for slaves, and they did not balk at the chance to repeatedly exploit these tensions. This self-emancipation occurred within the context of expanding U.S. slavery, the emergence of British colonial abolition in Canada, and imperial rivalries between the Americans, British, Spanish, and Mexicans. The primary inducement was less official state policies than the prospect of permanent freedom during a time of shifting national and free/unfree borders. The transformative role of self-liberators, and how this took on continental significance, goes unappreciated if the focus remains confined to individual escapees and their movements within national boundaries.

II. CAUSE CÉLÈBRE

As a result of fugitive flight across the North American continent, treaties were drawn up between nation-states and colonial powers to return fugitive slaves as well as to prevent future escapes. These treaties between the United States, Mexico, and British Canada during the 1820s through 1840s met with limited success. (At the same time, new fugitive laws within the United States pointed to shifting borders between slave and free territories that became increasingly important.) As a consequence of these diplomatic failures, territories adjacent to slaveholding lands were annexed to secure borders. Although these territorial grabs proved successful, and new lands were added to the slaveholding American South, the borders continued to prove porous as self-emancipators simply crossed them.

In the aftermath of the establishment of the independent republic of Mexico in 1821, many new emigrants settled in the state of Coahuila y Texas. These included slaveholders and their slaves. One consequence was self-emancipation to Mexico. Benjamin Milam, an early frontier settler, complained to Joel Robert Poinsett, the first U.S. minister to Mexico: "I have been in the frontiers of Texas for some time and have observed that the Stait of Louisiana have lost a grait maney slaives [sic] that have taken refuge in this Republick of Mexico."[33] Between 1825 and 1832, a series of diplomatic initiatives between the two republics began. The major purpose was to establish relations of amity, commerce, and navigation between the two nations; but no less important for the Americans was the need to arrange for the return of former slaves from Mexico to U.S. territory. Despite vigorous treaty negotiations, strong consideration of two separate articles concerning fugitive slave return, and powerful U.S. pressure to get the treaty and these articles ratified, the Mexican Chamber of Deputies repeatedly rejected the addition of a fugitive slave clause. Their opposition was motivated by several factors: natural rights law; the utility of free labor in an underpopulated area, and potential security for the border region. Both nations ratified the treaty on April 5, 1832, but without the fugitive slave clause.[34]

As we have seen, British colonial abolition was followed by slave self-emancipators gravitating toward Canada West. Their status prompted U.S. slaveholders' requests for extradition. Recognizing the irrelevance of American fugitive law in Canada, U.S. slaveholders tried to use an 1833 British-Canadian extradition act for returning escaped criminals as a means of repatriating fugitive slaves. Anglo-American relations were tested by three cases involving escapees from Kentucky to Canada and U.S. requests for their extradition between 1833 and 1837. Thorton Blackburn and Lucie Blackburn were arrested in Detroit, Michigan, under the 1793 U.S. Fugitive Slave Act but were rescued by their supporters and crossed into British Canada, where they settled in eastern Toronto. Solomon Mosely stole himself and his master's horse and was arrested and ordered returned, but a group of antislavery supporters helped him to escape to Canada West. Jesse Happy also stole himself and a horse to aid his escape. These fugitives' thefts were considered instrumental to personal escape by the colonial authorities. As Sir Francis Bond Head, lieutenant governor of Upper Canada, put it in a letter to Lord Glenelg, the British colonial secretary in London: "It may be argued that a slave escaping from bondage on his master's horse is a vicious struggle between two parties of which the slave owner is not only the aggressor, but the blackest criminal of the two—it is the case of the dealer in human flesh versus the stealer of horse flesh."

This pattern of fugitive escapes, extradition requests, and colonial denials continued until the Nelson Hackett case in 1842. Hackett, a self-emancipated slave from Arkansas, stole a horse, coat, saddle, and gold watch, as well as himself. Since some of these items were not considered indispensable to his escape, the governor-general of Canada West ordered Hackett's return for criminal intent, according to the 1833 extradition treaty with the United States. This was the first time a fugitive slave had been returned from Canada. The combination of abolitionist furor and the legal ambiguities of the Hackett case resulted in the passage of the Webster-Ashburton Treaty in 1842. The new law eased border disputes between the United States and British Canada, and, although some abolitionists feared it would create new slave catchers, it appears that no fugitive slave was extradited from Canada under the 1842 treaty.[35]

These fugitive cases between 1833 and 1842 highlight three important points concerning the relationship between British imperial abolition and U.S. slavery. First, self-emancipators from the United States deemed British soil safer after the legal abolition of colonial slavery during the 1830s. Although they were to subsequently encounter racism and exclusion in British Canada, self-liberators were originally motivated by their belief in greater liberties under the British flag. As William and Jane Pease neatly summarized: "If the tales of a Canadian paradise were in part misleading, perhaps it was just as well, for they guided the Negro to a land where the law both promised and gave what in the United States was denied him."[36] Second, British denials of U.S. extradition can best be understood within the broader context of an unfolding imperial commitment toward abolition and paternal governance. The position of fugitive slaves in British Canada had already been determined by a series of important legal decisions: Chief Justice Mansfield's decision against slaveholding in England (not the colonies) in 1772, Lieutenant Governor Simcoe's ruling against slave importation to Upper Canada in 1793, the legal abolition of the British transoceanic slave trade in 1807, and the complete cessation of British colonial slavery in 1838. By the late 1830s, slavery had become illegal throughout the British Empire, any former slave was instantly free on British soil, and the empire was *de facto* a paternal entity.[37] Third, black and white mobs of antislavery activists often proved more important in freeing fugitives than either British legal decisions fueled by colonial paternalism or Anglo-American diplomacy. Both the Blackburn family and Solomon Mosely gained their freedom through armed struggle. This collective stance represented a continental means of self-defense and liberation, a cross-national form of resistance otherwise lost in local, regional, and national narratives.[38]

In the aftermath of the victorious American war on Mexico during the late 1840s, southern slaveholders demanded federal support for locating and returning runaway slaves. The continental expansion of the American Empire brought with it the spread of slavery and demands for federal protection of personal property, especially fugitive slaves. Authored by Virginia senator and slaveholder James M. Mason, the Fugitive Slave Act was debated, passed, and finally signed by President Millard Fillmore on September 18, 1850. It empowered federal marshals to support southern slaveholders' efforts to—in the language of the act—"pursue and reclaim" fugitive slaves "from service and labor" through either a warrant or legal seizure "without due process." It essentially beefed up the pursuit, capture, and return of fugitive slaves by buttressing state rights with federal legislation. It further betokened a legal assault on the pursuit of freedom by slaves, posed a massive new threat to self-liberators living in free states, and opened up the potential for kidnapping people of African descent who had been born free.[39]

The same year the Fugitive Slave Act was passed, the Texas legislature approached the U.S. Congress requesting an agreement with Mexico that "all criminals, robbers, persons held in bondage, or fugitives from justice" should be returned. This legal language says a great deal about the way these politicians understood justice and property rights; it stands in marked contrast to the perspective of self-liberators, whose search for freedom was against injustice and what they would have considered criminal acts of enslavement. (In this sense, they paralleled the landless and destitute of seventeenth-century England who desired liberty not from but *against* the law.)[40] Texas's politicians failed, and Mexico continued to refuse to return fugitive slaves from its territory. Similar efforts at extradition in 1857 also proved fruitless.[41]

Much of the historiography on fugitive slaves focuses upon *cause célèbres* like Anthony Burns, Frederick Wilkins, and the Christiana rescue. But there were also important examples of self-emancipators who crossed borders with major diplomatic ramifications. Individual acts by self-liberators forced governments into diplomatic negotiations. People with no citizenship status forged their liberation out of that cauldron, while also testing the national borders that rendered them enslaved in one spot, free in another.[42] Along with failed extradition treaties, and the loss of valuable personal property, a further fear of slaveholders and their political representatives was the potential of free soil for organizing against U.S. slavery.

III. ANTISLAVERY MOBILIZATION

Much like fugitive slave escapes, abolitionist and antislavery activities usually occurred within the parameters of the nation-state.[43] Historians have devoted a great deal of attention to these activities, including the Underground Railroad, the antislavery movement, and the politicization of opposition toward the southern slave power. One striking example was the passage of personal liberty laws by northern and western states as a means of challenging federal support for returning fugitive slaves during the 1840s and 1850s. At the same time, we cannot ignore the unprecedented power of the federal government in clamping down on these activities. Fugitive Anthony Burns and thousands of his abolitionist supporters could not prevent the combined might of U.S. military personnel, the Massachusetts militia, and the Boston police from returning Burns to slavery in Virginia in June 1854.[44] Famous altercations like these proved that antislavery activities were difficult in northern states, and becoming harder after 1850. One lesson was they were more likely to be successful beyond U.S. borders.

One of the most important consequences of the fugitive exodus to Canada West was the continental expansion of antislavery mobilization. Six months after the passage of the U.S. Fugitive Slave Act, the Anti-Slavery Society of Canada was formed at City Hall, Toronto, Canada West, the first major antislavery organization in the colony. Its auxiliary, the Toronto Ladies' Association for the Relief of Destitute Colored Fugitives, was formed in April 1851. Over the next two years, the Anti-Slavery Society of Canada established regional branches in Kingston, Hamilton, London, and St. Catherines. Its successful expansion was partly due to the uncompromising organizing efforts of Maryland fugitive Samuel Ringgold Ward, who had relocated to Canada. Moreover, this period saw the pioneering establishment of an antislavery press in Canada West. The *Toronto Globe*, established in 1844, increasingly attacked U.S. slavery under the editorial direction of Scottish emigrant George Brown. In March 1854, the *Provincial Freeman* began regular publication under the nominal editorship of Ward. This soon passed to Mary Ann Shadd, free-born in Wilmington, Delaware, who moved to Windsor, Canada West, in 1851, where she opened a school for black children. It was through the pages of these newspapers that readers first learned about West Indian Emancipation Day celebrations, annual meetings every first day in August drawing large numbers of people of African descent and their white supporters with the dual aims of commemorating British colonial abolition in the past and mobilizing for the future abolition of U.S. slavery.[45]

This mobilization was also very pronounced in the region of southwest borderlands of Canada West, where many self-liberators ended up relocating. Between January 1851 and February 1852, these freedom seekers played a central role in the establishment of an antislavery newspaper, a major black convention, and a new organization. One of the key individuals involved in these developments was Henry Bibb. Bibb was born in Shelby County, Kentucky, in May 1815, to enslaved mother Mildred Jackson and slaveholder James Bibb. As a youth, he was separated from his mother and endured several harsh periods as a hired slave. Of this period, he later wrote: "I was a wretched slave, compelled to work under the lash without wages and often without clothes enough to hide my nakedness." In 1834, he married Malinda, an enslaved woman, and they had one child, Mary Francis. After several unsuccessful escape attempts and forced returns to Kentucky between 1837 and 1841, Bibb made his final successful bid for freedom and settled in Detroit, Michigan. He searched for his family for the next three years, but ceased after finding out they had been sold and that Malinda had become the mistress of her new owner. Bibb threw himself into antislavery work and became quite successful. In 1848, he married Mary Miles, a free black woman and teacher working in the Boston abolitionist movement. The following year, he published *Narrative of the Life and Adventures of Henry Bibb, an American Slave*. After the passage of the 1850 Fugitive Slave Act, Henry and Mary crossed the border and settled in Sandwich.[46]

It was from this small town that they started the *Voice of the Fugitive* on January 1, 1851. This bimonthly newspaper called for abolition in the United States along with temperance, educational reform, agricultural development, and emigration to Canada West. It published numerous articles on fugitive slave cases, abolitionist meetings in the United States and Canada West, and post-emancipation conditions in the Caribbean. It also advertised and reported annual commemorations of British colonial abolition, along with articles on temperance and moral reform, together with advertisements for small black businesses, including confectioners, boarding houses, clothiers, and barbers. Within one year, the *Voice of the Fugitive* claimed more than one thousand paid subscribers. Many readers in the British colony first learned about major fugitive slave cases, like the Shadrach rescue in Boston and the rescue at Christiana, Pennsylvania, from the pages of this newspaper. The same journal played an important role in informing readers in the United States about the formation of antislavery organizations, the establishment and welfare of black communal settlements, and Anglo-Canadian politics. Moreover, the *Voice of the Fugitive* listed selling agents throughout Canada West, as well as in Michigan, Massachusetts, New Jersey, New York, New Hampshire, Ohio, and Pennsylvania. Martin Delany was the Pittsburgh correspondent, and

James T. Holly was the agent for Burlington, Vermont. Its reach even extended to the United Kingdom: African American visitors Henry Highland Garnet and James W. C. Pennington corresponded from London.[47]

The *Voice of the Fugitive* was also the organ used by Henry Bibb to call for a North America Convention of Colored People to convene in Toronto during the second week of September 1851. To hold such a meeting in the United States, he observed, "would greatly endanger the liberty of thousands of self-emancipated persons." In contrast, Canada West "bids defiance to all fugitive slave laws," and Toronto was a great commercial metropolis and central meeting place. Although the major objects would be brought before the convention, several correspondents informed Bibb what these might be, and he subsequently published them:

1. The immediate and everlasting emancipation of our race from slavery, and a manifestation of gratitude to the government of Great Britain, which has so nobly protected us in the enjoyment of liberty, whenever and wherever, we have stepped on her soil.
2. To abandon menial employments, as far as it may be practicable, and become owners and tillers of the soil.
3. To consider the vast interests of moral, mental and physical improvement.
4. To inculcate the idea of every man becoming the owner of his homestead.
5. The vital importance of our people becoming agriculturalists as a means of making themselves independent.
6. To recommend the emigration of free people of color, from the United States, for the settlement of Canada land.
7. To take proper steps for sustaining such presses only as will faithfully vindicate the rights of our people.
8. To bear testimony against the American colonization to Africa, as being prejudicial against color and proslavery.
9. To pledge ourselves to the defence of that government only that protects us in the enjoyment of liberty.[48]

This agenda deserves quotation in full because its emphasis on liberation, the benefits of free soil, independence through land and home ownership, racial improvement, emigration to Canada, honest newspaper reportage, anti-colonization, and self-defense of liberty constitute the self-liberators' manifesto in an era replete with capitalist, communist, and reactionary manifestos.[49]

Over three days at the NACCP the delegates discussed numerous resolutions in "spirited debate," including the unchristian nature of American slavery; the moral improvement of temperance, education, and wealth accumulation; and the cultivation of free soil. Earlier calls for immigration to Canada West were repeated. It was resolved "that the convention recommend to the colored people of the U.S. of America, to emigrate to the Canadas instead of going to Africa or the West India Islands, that they, by so doing, may be better able to assist their brethren who are daily flying from American slavery."[50]

In the aftermath of the meeting of the NACCP, three of the delegates—Henry Bibb, John Fisher, and James Tinsley—issued "An Address to the Colored Inhabitants of North America," which was published in the October 21, 1851, edition of the *Voice of the Fugitive*. As one might expect from a representative address, many of the convention's themes and resolutions were repeated, including outrage at the Fugitive Slave Act, calls for moral improvement, and emigration to Canada West. But there was also a more militant tone to this address, anchored in the politics of self-emancipation. After outlining the unique oppression of "colored inhabitants," the hypocrisy of U.S. republican slavery, and the nominal freedom of free coloreds in the United States, the address turned to its main theme of stressing that abolition was in the hands of the people of color in North America. While grateful to "the truehearted abolitionists, who have stood by us in the darkest hours of adversity," the manifesto stressed that it is we who should be "standing in the front ranks of the battle, until our kinsmen, according to the flesh are disenthralled." The history of the oppressed demonstrates that they have succeeded in liberating themselves only through their own exertions. To follow the English poet George Byron: "Hereditary bondsmen! know ye not, Who would be free, themselves must strike the first blow?" The best way to accomplish this was through slave rebellion: "Three millions and a half of men, armed with the righteous cause of freedom, and the God of Justice on their side, against two hundred and fifty thousand tyrants [southern slaveholders], could sweep them like chaff before the wind." Moreover, fugitive slaves would undermine the system of U.S. slavery. "We believe it to be an indispensable duty," read the address, "that every 'hereditary bondsman' owes to himself, first to run away from slavery, and to carry off with him whatever may be necessary to effect his escape." This last sentence drew from a long tradition of self-emancipation, stretching from the seventeenth century Chesapeake to the Kentucky cases in the late 1830s, through to two of the address writers—Bibb and Tinsley—who had escaped from U.S. slavery.[51]

IV. BLACK BEACONS

Along with antislavery organization and mobilization, self-liberators also crossed borders to create new free settlements in Spanish Florida, British Florida, British Canada, the Republic of Mexico, and elsewhere. These settlements met with mixed success. Furthermore, they often served as footballs in an ideological game between defenders of slavery, who argued that such poor settlements proved that emancipation did not work, and abolitionists, who disseminated an opposing view that they demonstrated the unequivocal success of ex-slaves' freedom.[52] Amid the polemics, however, let us not forget why self-emancipators crossed borders, what they hoped to accomplish, and the role such settlements played in provoking territorial expansion.

The creation of the United States did not prevent slaves from continuing to escape. This led to the creation of new settlements in Spanish Florida. By 1812, black settlements among the Seminole Indians consisting of "several hundred fug[i]tive slaves from the Carolinas & Georgia" were reported by irate southern slaveholders. A U.S. surveyor described separate villages with well-constructed houses and carefully cultivated fields and large herds of livestock.[53] In late 1814, British troops built a fort called British Post at Prospect Bluff, near Pensacola, which included some 100 self-liberators who had enlisted in the army in exchange for guaranteed freedom. In the following year, an estimated 1,000 former slaves settled in the fort's environs, protected by a garrison of about 300 self-liberators and some Choctaw and Seminole warriors led by a black leader called Garcon. This black fort was to become a "beacon light" for slaves, who flocked to its promise of freedom and guaranteed protection.[54]

It also served as a constant threat to the security of southern slave owners along the borders. The U.S. authorities were eventually persuaded to attack and destroy the fort, blowing up 270 of its inhabitants and capturing 64 prisoners. As a consequence, the survivors fled eastward, where they built villages down the seacoast to Tampa Bay. Here, they lived and drilled in preparation for the impending invasion by the Americans. When it came, a thousand Seminole Indian and ex-slave soldiers proved no match for General Andrew Jackson's 3,300 professional troops, including American Indians opposed to the Seminoles. By the summer of 1818, the black and Indian settlements had been destroyed, their former residents killed, captured, or exiled. In February 1819, the Adams-Onis Treaty was signed between the United States and Spain. It ceded all of Florida for $5 million, dropped the U.S. claim to territory north of the Forty-second Parallel in the Pacific Northwest, and ceded the U.S. claim to Texas. The treaty established the border between the United States and Spanish territories across the continent to the Pacific Ocean. More important, a territory that had provided a refuge for fugitive slaves, virtually without interruption since the late seventeenth century, was now made safe for the expansion and protection of U.S. slaveholding interests. Kenneth Porter makes the key point: "The original impulse behind these invasions was general American expansionism, inspired by the same frontier land-hunger as was also directed in the same general period against Canada; but another objective, which became increasingly important and eventually developed into a primary purpose, was to safeguard the slave system in adjacent states by breaking up the runaway Negro settlements in Florida."[55] He could have added Mexico to the equation.

Self-liberators from the United States also settled north of the border in Canada West. In 1830 and 1842, fugitives settled at Wilberforce and Dawn. Although these new settlements were plagued by poor land, lack of alternative employment opportunities, and leadership problems, they did at least provide the basis for the creation of free black institutions—families, churches, schools—as well as asylum and relief from U.S. slavery, with its slaveholders, slave catchers, federal officials, and system of slave laws.[56]

Probably the most renowned settlement was Elgin. Named after British Canada's governor, it was incorporated on August 10, 1850, as the "King's Settlement" at Buxton, Ontario. Benjamin Drew's 1856 collection of fugitive slave narratives in Canada, A Northside View of Slavery, estimates its population numbered nearly eight hundred adults, many of them fugitive slaves who had originally resided in the northern United States before relocating to Canada. According to the director's fourth annual report of 1853:

> 130 families have settled on the lands of the association, and improved farms in the neighborhood: these families contain 520 persons in all. 500 acres are cleared and under fence; 135 cut down and partially cleared. Of the cleared land, 236 acres are in corn; 60 acres in wheat; 29 in oats, and 90 in other crops: making in all 415 acres under cultivation. The number of cattle in the settlement is 128. There are 15 horses,

30 sheep, and 250 hogs. The temperance principle is strictly acted on through the whole settlement,—no intoxicating drinks being either manufactured or sold. The Sabbath is generally observed; and most of the settlers attend some place of worship. The number of children at the day school is 112; at the Sabbath school, 80. They were all improving, both in secular and scriptural knowledge: a number of the more advanced pupils were studying Latin, with a view to future usefulness.

Isaac Riley's personal story humanizes this Gradgrind-like statistical report. Although he recalled a benevolent form of slavery in Missouri, he still decided to escape "with my wife and child to Canada." "Among the French near Windsor [Canada]," he continued, "I got small wages—2s. or 1s. 6d. a day, [at] York: and morning and night up to my knees in water,—still I preferred this to abundance in slavery. I crossed over and got work and better pay in Michigan. They would have liked to have me remain, and offered to build a house for me. But I did not feel free in Michigan, and did not remain. I went to St. Catharines, and got fifty cents a day. By and by, I heard of Mr. King's settlement,—I came here, and have got along well. My children can get good learning here." Dr. Samuel R. Howe, who represented the Freedmen's Inquiry Commission, agreed that this "settlement is a perfect success."[57]

Another settlement was the Refugee's Home Society. This organization was rooted in changes along the Detroit-Windsor frontier. The rapid influx of fugitive slaves had resulted in the meeting of a local black convention at Sandwich, Canada West, in 1846. Its major objective was to form a new black settlement to aid escaped slaves through the provision of land, homes, and education. Over the next few years, the Sandwich Mission obtained about 1,200 acres, which were to be divided into 10-acre lots and resold to black settlers, with 25 acres reserved for a school and a church. Although little came of this plan, the Sandwich group became the basis for the Fugitives Union Society, a black moral improvement association located in Windsor, Canada West. In May 1851, a new group of white abolitionists in Detroit was moved to form an organization whose primary object was to "extend to them [fugitives] the helping hand in their struggle to establish homes among strangers, whose laws protect them from the grasp of the American slave hunters." The resulting body merged with the Sandwich group to form the RHS in January 1852. Its leaders included white abolitionists E. P. Benham and Horace Halleck in Detroit, American Missionary Association worker David Hotchkiss in Amherstburg, ex-slave and settlement leader Josiah Henson, and Henry and Mary Bibb in Windsor. The RHS plan was to buy "50,000 acres of farming land, in Canada, on which to settle refugees from slavery." By 1855, it had purchased 2,000 acres and provided homes for 150 fugitive slaves. Three years later, the RHS acquired another 290 acres along the Puce River east of Windsor, thus expanding the existing black community.[58]

There were also settlements of people of African descent south of the Rio Grande. On October 13, 1857, U.S. Consul Franklin Chase, based in Tampico, Mexico, wrote to U.S. Assistant Secretary of State John Appleton in Washington, D.C., about one of these settlements: "A decree was issued at the city of Mexico on the July 2, 1857, granting the formation of a new colony in the state of Vera Cruz and District of Tampico called 'Eureka.' This concession is made to a person by the name of Luis N. Fouche, a colored native of the State of Florida, who has obligated himself to furnish his colony with one hundred families of the same race. They are to be considered as Citizens of the Mexican Republic but exempted from the payment of all taxes other than municipal, and also from the performance of military service, except in the case of foreign invasion, when they are to come under all obligations of other Mexican Citizens."

It is unclear why this decree was issued, beyond the Mexican government's desire to populate regions with productive emigrants, as well as potential fighters against U.S. incursions. (One can imagine these recent newcomers to Mexico would have been as eager to repulse U.S. slaveholder incursions as their northern cousins in Canada West.) Consul Chase continued: "Several families have already arrived here, and preliminary preparations are in progress for the final establishment of the new Colony, but from the information I have obtained from them, I feel convinced that their new enterprise will not be attended with success."[59] The emigrant poverty described earlier by Frederick Olmsted supports Consul Chase's feeling, although it does not appear to have stopped cross-border emigration. In 1857, forty people of African descent left New Orleans for Vera Cruz and formed another settlement at Tlacotalpan. Other black settlements were reported at Nacimiento, Coahuila, and elsewhere in Mexico. Although conditions were often hard, wages low, and the language and culture initially alien, many self-emancipators embraced their new lives of freedom. Much like their cousins in British Canada, these emigrants were attracted by an alternative set of freedoms, as well as official protection offered by cross-border movement and settlements that were guaranteed by the existing government.[60]

It should be evident that national borders played an important role in self-emancipation, as well as the establishment of free settlements. Crossing borders was more likely to result in permanent freedom, as well as the opportunity to begin a new life away from the travail of slavery. At the same time, there were borders within national borders that facilitated such movement. We have already seen this with the shifting of borders between slave and free states in the ante-emancipation United States. The Great Dismal Swamp, situated along the North Carolina–Virginia border, is 1.3 million acres of quagmire, bog, and inhospitable terrain. It was once peopled by a motley crew of poor whites from the two states, American Indians especially of the Tuscarora nation, and self-liberators. According to one recent researcher, this massive swampland consisted of concentric rings of external and internal residents, many of whom spent their entire lives within its confines. There were also maroon communities deep in the interior regions, which, according to Edmund Jackson of *The Liberty Bell* in 1852, constituted a "singular community of blacks, who have won their freedom and established themselves securely in the midst of the largest slaveholding State of the South . . . [and] from this extensive swamp, they are seldom, if now at all, reclaimed."[61] Refuges like the Great Dismal Swamp suggest that long-term self-emancipation was even possible within national borders.

This cross-border treatment of self-emancipators, laws, mobilization, and settlements is noteworthy for several reasons. First, those self-liberators who crossed borders were much more likely to remain permanently free because the long arm of the slaveholding state could not reach them. This was not always the case. A citizen from Washington County, Texas, reportedly crossed into Mexico with a posse and captured and returned a fugitive.[62] On the other hand, the lesson of the failure to extradite fugitives from Canada West and the Mexican Republic to the United States during the 1830s and 1840s sent a clear message to slaves; it was also no doubt the reason for so many crossings after the passage of the 1850 law, as well as during the American Civil War. Second, self-liberators abroad were a major loss of capital investment for slaveholders because it was so difficult to obtain their return. Seven fugitives who sought to escape to the North via ship from Pensacola, Florida, in June 1844 were estimated to have been worth about $600 each, or $4,200 in total.[63] Samuel Ward estimated that each fugitive from the American South in the mid-1850s "carried off in his own person from 400 to 2,000 dollars."[64] If 1,000 fugitives left annually, Ward's estimates suggest that slaveholders would have lost between

$400,000 and $2 million each year. This explains the wide array of political activities by southern slaveholders and their supporters—extradition treaties, national slave laws, territorial annexation—to try to protect and retrieve their lost property. Third, some domestic laws had an important cross-national impact. The emigration of free blacks and self-emancipators from the northern United States across the border to British Canada as a consequence of the 1850 U.S. law is one clear example. Another is the 1829 abolition of slavery in Mexico, after which slaves in the southwest United States headed for the Rio Grande. Their actions get overlooked if such laws are examined solely in national terms.

Moreover, annexation was driven by the need to stamp out potential refuges for fugitive slaves. This simple point, made nearly seventy years ago by Kenneth Porter in the pages of the *Journal of Negro History,* was probably also true regarding carving the state of Texas out of northern Mexico. If we are familiar with the notion of the southwest territories being made available for U.S. slaveholders, we should also become more acquainted with the notion that these new territories provided beacons of liberty to enslaved people. In addition, free settlements not only inspired numerous enslaved people but also—as the first post-emancipation communities in North America—challenged the disingenuous argument of proslavery ideologues that African slaves could not exist without U.S. slavery and would perish if left to their own devices. The continental struggles of self-liberators suggests otherwise. Most important, self-emancipators who crossed borders *knew* that the nation-state, with its laws, boundaries, and territorial integrity, could be indispensable to the successful realization of long-term freedoms. They were aware of the significance of national borders, even if some contemporary scholars dismiss the relevance of the nineteenth-century nation-state in the lives of ordinary men and women. Finally, these cross-national movements constitute a long tradition of continental pathways to freedom beyond our conventional understanding of national struggles for rights and freedoms.

CHAPTER 2

Slave Soldiers

Mourn lions who in fields of honor fell, Mourn who, in fray, acquits himself
so well.

—ANTARAH

The black soldiers fighting in the French revolutionary war were of a similar
type to the black soldiers fighting in the Civil War.

—C. L. R. JAMES

But there is one thought which every white man thinks when he sees a black
army marching past. "How much longer can we go on kidding these people?
How long before they turn their guns in the other direction."

—GEORGE ORWELL

Older historical narratives of wars of national independence and abolition
struggles in the nineteenth-century Americas that ignored the roles of people
of African descent are increasingly being replaced by a vital historical literature acknowledging slaves and free blacks as military participants. Much of
this important scholarship, however, is produced within national frameworks
as historians seek to show the contributions of black soldiers toward the creation and consolidation of nation-states.[1] Rarely is this historical work comparative, and when it is, the primary concern is with political elites and why
they armed bondsmen during social upheavals.[2]

   In contrast, this chapter provides a comparative approach centered on
slave soldiers. Specifically, it examines the decisions, actions, experiences,
and consequences of slaves taking up arms in the wars of American and Spanish American Independence, the Haitian Revolution, the American Civil
War, and the First War for Cuban Independence. There is no attempt to be
encyclopedic. Rather, it makes three comparative points. First, slaves fought
during wars, revolutions, and social crises across the Americas to a remarkable
extent. Second, slaves armed with guns usually transformed existing conditions. Third, slave soldiers' military contributions were significant, including

the destruction of slave systems. These three points, especially the latter, can best be appreciated through a comparative framework. Although we explore differences and connections, the major comparative focus is on similarities. The central aim is to challenge a scholarly approach toward slave soldiers that is too often reduced to a simplistic and unsatisfying patriotism.

I. EXTENT

Slave soldiers participated in wars of national liberation throughout the nineteenth-century Americas. During the American War of Independence, around 5,000 black soldiers fought on the patriot side in state militias and the Continental Army. Many were free blacks; others were former slaves. In response to British occupation, the new state of Rhode Island offered slaves liberty in exchange for military service while their owners were compensated 120 pounds sterling. Cuff Greene, Dick Champlin, and Jack Champlin were among the first recruits. Eventually, one in four able-bodied male slaves in Rhode Island served in what became known as the Black Regiment.[3] Opposing these black patriots were around 15,000 black loyalists who supported the British Crown. Most of them were former slaves who labored and fought in exchange for their personal liberty. The vast majority of the Ethiopian Regiment organized by Governor John Earl of Dunmore of Virginia, for example, consisted of self-emancipated slaves from Virginia and Maryland who saw the British as their best hope for freedom.[4] A generation later, history was to repeat itself. During the War of 1812, several thousand free blacks labored and fought for the United States while several hundred former slaves served as laborers, spies, messengers, and soldiers for the British.[5] During the mass upheaval against French colonial slavery and the struggle for independence in St. Domingue, the insurgent army grew from 10,000 strong in late August 1791 to between 23,000 to 30,000 regular troops with local militias of 10,000 by early 1802. Although these included white soldiers, *gens de coleur* (free people of color) and *ancien libres* (long-term free blacks like Toussaint Louverture), the majority of insurgent military forces were former slaves.[6]

Soldiers of African descent had been active in Spanish America since the sixteenth century, but the extent of their activities increased markedly with national independence struggles during the early nineteenth century.[7] In 1812, slaves fought in the guerilla army under the leadership of Francisco Gomez, Juan Bautista, Mariano Mota, and José Maria Alegria in the sugar plantation region of coastal Veracruz during the war for Mexican independence.[8] In Argentina, between 4,000 to 5,000 slaves enlisted with patriot armies between 1813 and 1818. *Libertos* (freed slaves) made up half of General José de San Martín's invading army into Chile in 1817 and one-third of General Simón Bolívar's army in Ecuador.[9] In 1821, royalists conscripted 1,500 slaves to defend Lima, Peru, in exchange for liberty after six years of service. By January 1822, the rebel army under General San Martin consisted of between 4,000 to 5,000 slave soldiers.[10] It has been estimated that literally "thousands" of slaves joined rebel armies in Cuba's First War for Independence between 1868 and 1878.[11] In short, scores of thousands of slave soldiers participated in wars of national independence in the British, French, and Spanish Americas from the 1770s through the 1870s. And they fought on *both* sides for liberty.

Moreover, slaves frequently pursued individual liberation during opportune moments such as fractious civil wars within newly independent nations. Thirty years after gaining independence from the Spanish Crown, Peru became embroiled in a vicious civil conflict with slaves fighting on either side to gain their freedom. On November 18, 1854, President José Rufino Echenique issued a decree that "every domestic or hacienda slave who enlists in the army will receive his freedom." He later claimed that 350 slaves responded. Rebel leader Ramon Castilla also issued a decree on December 3, 1854. One report estimated between 2,000 to 3,000 slaves enlisted in the rebel army as a consequence.[12] Nearly eight decades after winning independence from the British, the United States split apart because of political disagreement over slavery. By the end of the American Civil War, about 179,000 black men had fought for the Union Army, and roughly 18,000 black men served in the Union Navy.[13] Twelve fugitive slaves joined the crew of the Union steamer Minnesota at Fortress Monroe, Virginia. Apparently, they were "the only men who could be trusted to go ashore without an officer and still return on time and sober."[14] The vast majority of black Union troops (between 150,000 to 165,000) were former slaves who fought for their liberty and not free black volunteers as depicted in Edward Zwick's 1989 *Glory* about the 54th Massachusetts Infantry Regiment.[15] If scores of thousands of slaves participated militarily in wars of national liberation, hundreds of thousands fought for their liberty during civil wars.

Slave soldiers also participated in more general forms of warfare and military conflict. The French revolutionary and Napoleonic wars were not restricted to the European mainland but were also fought out in New World colonies between the 1790s and the second decade of the nineteenth century.

One response by the British government was to offer bounties to free blacks and freedom to slaves if they would fight on behalf of the Crown. Between 5,000 to 6,000 slaves fought for the British during their occupation of St. Domingue between 1793 and 1798. Armed with a musket and machete, wearing a red jacket, coarse pants, and round hat, these black troops received British pay and rations.[16] Roger Buckley estimates that 6,858 slaves were recruited at a cost of 484,080 pounds sterling between 1798 and 1807 to fight for the British Empire mainly in the Caribbean. These recruits were organized into twelve regiments consisting of both Caribbean and African-born slaves, amounting to about 10,000 troops by the latter date.[17] On May 1, 1865, Brazil allied with Argentina and Uruguay against Paraguay in a fractious territorial dispute that was to last for five years until March 1, 1870. Some 6,905 Brazilian slaves were bought from their owners and offered their liberty in exchange for serving as soldiers and sailors on behalf of the Brazilian empire.[18] Of these slave soldiers, around 1,518 had been formerly enslaved in Bahia.[19] It is obvious that political elites turned to the arming of slaves during desperate situations. There is little reason to doubt, however, that many of these slave soldiers—whether in the British or Brazilian empires—cared primarily about freedom-seeking opportunities and only secondarily about the specific complexities of these political crises. In sum, there were few military conflagrations in nineteenth-century slave societies and societies with slaves that did not involve the active participation of slave soldiers.

II. EXPERIENCES

It is, of course, very difficult to capture the range of military and social experiences of slave soldiers in the field across a hemisphere and spanning a century. Apart from the gargantuan dimensions of such a project, other challenges include the paucity of documents produced by slave soldiers as well as the nascent state of the historiography on slaves in the military.[20] Our focus will be on three key aspects of slaves' military participation: reasons to serve, battlefield activities, and the price of liberty. These are pursued in comparative terms with the aim of shifting scholarly attention toward slaves fighting rather than political elites' decision-making to arm slaves.

The principal reason slaves fought in armies was to win individual liberty. An unnamed slave in Buenos Aires, Argentina, fought for the *patria* to win the "most sacred right of freedom."[21] Francisco Estrada explained his reasons to a Buenos Aires court in 1813: "We chose the generous system of the *Patria* [homeland], we sang the hymns of Freedom, and we linked our desires, our hearts, to the holy principles of the just system of Freedom. Together we renounced forever and with indignation that cruel, unhappy, and disorganized government that degrades men and refuses to permit those who are called slaves to reclaim, if they so wish, the rights of humanity."[22]

One private from the Fourth United States Colored Troops "had left his home a slave, but he returned in the garb of a union soldier, free, a man."[23] In 1864, company D of the Fifty-fifth Massachusetts Infantry matched private Estrada's rhetoric: "we came to fight For Liberty justice & Equality. These are gifts we Prise more Highly than Gold For these We Left our Homes our Families Friends & Relatives most Dear to take as it ware our Lives in our Hands To Do Battle for God & Liberty."[24] Although written by a company of black men in a northern regiment made up of free blacks rather than former slaves, this petition reflected the views of many other black troops. It is likely that the enlistment of nearly seven thousand former slaves to fight for the Brazilian Empire during the War of the Triple Alliance was based more on the prospect of gaining liberty than on helping to resolve an international dispute in Latin America.[25] Cuban slave Pedro de la Torre self-liberated to a rebel camp near Holguin during the opening months of the First War for Cuban Independence in 1868 because of a "desire to sustain the Holy Cause."[26] In short, "military service meant freedom," as David Geggus put it describing slave soldiers fighting for the British in St. Domingue.[27]

Another reason why slave soldiers engaged in military activities was the prospect of compensation. Scholars have demonstrated that some slaves were paid for their services as hired factory workers, merchant seamen, market sellers, and so forth. Most slaves, though, were not financially compensated in plantation economies in the nineteenth-century Americas.[28] Wartime service brought financial rewards. In Venezuela, ex-slave Pedro Camejo explained that a slave who went to war left without a shirt and peseta and returned with a uniform "and with money in his pocket."[29] The common soldiers' monthly wage of six pesos was standard throughout Spanish America.[30] The slave soldier in the British West India Regiments earned the same pay, allowances, and privileges, as white soldiers.[31] During the American Civil War, black soldiers were compensated for their services in the U.S. Army although the pay scale oscillated. They began receiving $13.00 plus a clothing allowance of $3.50 per month, the same as white soldiers. This was reduced to $10.00 per month with a $3.00 deduction for clothing. The original figure was eventually reintroduced after black regiments protested and refused to accept the unequal pay scale.[32] Although more detailed research needs to be done on the extent, range, and consequences of compensation for slave soldiers on the front during the nineteenth century, the important point is that military service brought financial compensation, and this proved an attractive proposition to many of those who previously had toiled without pay.

A second comparative theme in the slave soldiers' experience concerns their activities on the battlefield. In comparing this aspect of slave soldiers' experiences, we should distinguish between those engaged in actual combat and those who served in an auxiliary capacity. During the French revolutionary and Napoleonic wars, about one-third of the soldiers in the British West India Regiments fought on the battlefield while about two-thirds served in a secondary role.[33] In wars of independence in Spanish America, some slaves fought on the battlefield. Cuban slave rebel Eduardo was caught "with weapons in his hands" during the First War for Independence.[34] Many slaves, however, served as artisans, wranglers, and laborers to marching armies.[35] The military activities of slave soldiers during the American Civil War also combined fighting and support work. Many of them served in support units as scouts, road and rail builders, teamsters, cooks, spies, and so forth. In North Carolina, the Fourteenth U.S. Colored Heavy Artillery served as a regular labor force and never fought on the battlefield; unlike the Thirty-fifth, Thirty-sixth, and Thirty-seventh U.S. Colored Troops who skirmished and battled throughout South Carolina and Florida.[36] Slave soldiers both labored and fought for individual liberty and national independence against French, British, and Spanish troops during the Haitian Revolution.

Slave soldiers' wartime activities, however, did not come without a heavy price in human life. We lack even an approximate tally of the number of slave soldiers who died in these military conflicts, but it must have run into many scores of thousands. Better armed and trained patriot militias decimated Lord Dunmore's regiment of black soldiers at the battle of Great Bridge on December 9, 1775, during the American War of Independence.[37] Thousands of slave soldiers died in St. Domingue resisting Spanish and British colonial invasions as well as French colonial slavery.[38] Countless numbers of slave soldiers lost their lives during wars of independence in Spanish South America. English observer Samuel Haigh described the price of freedom at Maipu, the second great battle for Chilean independence near Santiago in April 1818: "The carnage was very great, and I was told by some officers who had served in Europe that they never witnessed anything more bloody than occurred in this part of the field."[39] The American Civil War also proved very costly for slave soldiers. Colonel James S. Brisbin provided his federal superiors with a sobering casualties report after the Fifth U.S. Colored Cavalry's operations in West Virginia in October 1864: "Out of four hundred engaged, one hundred and fourteen men and four officers fell killed or wounded."[40] During four years of war, some 36,000 black soldiers are estimated to have died serving the Union.[41] In short, one in six black soldiers who fought in the U.S. military during the American Civil War gave their lives.

Why was the mortality rate so high for slave soldiers in all of these wars? The view that slaves made poor soldiers because they were unprepared is unpersuasive for two reasons. First, the Atlantic slave trade frequently landed African veterans in the Americas. Tim Hashaw's recent study of the first generation of Africans in the seventeenth-century colonial Chesapeake points out that "most of them would have been experienced Ndongo soldiers who had been captured in Angola while fighting the Imbangala and Portuguese in 1619, or Kongolese Jaga militants who had been taken prisoner in the Nsundi rebellion against the Manikongo at the same time and loaded onto the Bautista with the Ndongo."[42]

In 1696, the governor of the Dutch Caribbean colony of Curaçao was advised to arm imported slaves because "we have been told that the Negroes shipped there, and in particular the Angolans, are men who have served in wars in their country, and know how to handle a gun."[43] In the opening chapter of his autobiography, published in 1789, Olaudah Equiano describes combat readiness in his African homeland: "All are taught the use of these weapons; even our women are warriors, and march boldly out to fight along with the men. Our whole district is a kind of militia: on a certain signal given, such as the firing of a gun at night, they all rise in arms and rush upon their enemy. It is perhaps something remarkable that when our people march to the field a red flag or banner is borne before them."[44]

John Thornton and Matt Childs have shown that African veterans played decisive roles in the 1739 slave revolt in Stono, South Carolina, and José Aponte's 1812 rebellion in Cuba.[45] The participation of African veterans in the Haitian Revolution is described in several documents. After the 1791 uprising began, black leaders warned white colonists of "a multitude of negroes from the Coast [of Africa] who barely know two words of French but who, however, in their country were accustomed to making war."[46] Captain Colville from Britain described the military tactics of a corps of slaves in action during early 1793: "[They have] a bush fighting warfare peculiar to themselves. . . . Their appearance was . . . very grotesque—instead of the drum and fife they used the Banger and Coromantee flute, the musical instruments of their native country. Some had firearms; others, bill hooks fastened to long poles and plantation watchmen's hangers, and were in general wretchedly attired in their osnaburgh frocks."[47]

Léger-Félicité Sonthonax, member of the Second National Commission to St. Domingue, wrote his superiors in Paris claiming the insurgents' "method is to harass our camps with night attacks; they charge vigorously, rarely try to hold a position after a first round of firing and, when they are pursued, they usually retreat into the mountains or the woods where it is almost impossible to follow them."[48] African-born Minas, Mozambiquans, Mocos, and Congolese were among the thousands of slaves who fought for the British against the French in St. Domingue between 1793 and 1798.[49] Between 1798 and 1807, 710 out of a total of 812 recruits for the Fifth British West India Regiment were African born.[50] The leading authority of the largest urban slave revolt in the Americas points out that "Nagos [Brazilian term for ethnic Yoruba] brought with them either the Oyo militaristic tradition or their experience resisting that tradition." João José Reiss goes on to explain that the rebels in Salvador da Bahia in January 1835 "were stirred not solely by religious fervor but also by men with experience in intra- and interethnic warfare, that is, in civil and national wars."[51]

This argument linking African veterans with slave soldiers in the Americas should not be overstated. The ending of transoceanic slave trades in the nineteenth-century Atlantic world would have cut off the supply of many of these veterans to slave societies, especially to the British Caribbean and the United States after 1808. Slave soldiers during the American Civil War were largely trained by the federal military. But, a long history of slave revolts before the enlistment of slave soldiers suggests that combat was not a totally new experience.[52] Moreover, illegal slave trading continued for decades after official abolition. According to David Eltis and David Richardson, some 1,189,500 slaves embarked illegally for the Americas between 1837 and 1867.[53] This number is probably underestimated because of the clandestine nature of such trading. In other words, African veterans did not cease entering the Americas on slave ships. Moreover, the abolition of the Atlantic slave trade does not negate the major point: many slave men were experienced fighters in their African homelands; they put their military knowledge to good use at opportune times in the slave Americas; they were fighting to regain their recently lost freedom; and this was a continuous transoceanic exchange over three to four centuries.

The second reason to reject the view that slaves died in massive numbers because they made poor soldiers was unequivocal evidence of their fighting prowess. In 1837, Scottish-born American and Canadian journalist and politician William Lyon McKenzie led a national independence struggle to free Canada from British colonial rule. Sir Francis Bond Head, lieutenant governor of Upper Canada, wrote to his colonial superior in London: "They [black men] hastened as volunteers in wagon-loads to the Niagara frontier to beg from me permission that in the intended attack upon Navy Island they might be permitted to form the forlorn hope." Black men in Chatham, Canada West (now Ontario), formed their own militia company from 1837 through 1843.[54] The 1850 U.S. Fugitive Slave Act betokened the prospect of U.S. annexation of the Canadian provinces in order to pursue, capture, and return fugitive slaves. Former slave and recent arrival Samuel Ringgold Ward was in no doubt as to the reaction: "We blacks, having tasted of the genial sweets of true British freedom, would no more comment or submit to be made bondmen again, than we would deliberately jump into perdition. We would see every slaveholder in the bottomless pit, before we could, or would submit to such a thing. Some of us fought in the wars of our native country: others fought in defence of our adopted government, fourteen years ago [1837 Rebellion]; all of us would fight till our last blood was spilt, before we should be subjected again to the tender mercies of American barbarism."[55]

Frederick Douglass, former slave and prominent abolitionist in the United States, is often credited with urging the enrollment of black troops during the American Civil War. "Let the slaves and the free colored people be called into service," he proclaimed, "and formed into a liberating army, to march into the South and raise the banner of emancipation among the slaves."[56] But this much quoted statement ignores a long tradition of self-emancipators and free blacks' preparedness to fight against slavery and its national expansion. In the antebellum northern American states, black men consistently protested their exclusion from state militias; self-liberators often armed themselves to prevent being recaptured by slaveholders; and northern vigilance committees sought to protect those who had escaped the slave south. From the late 1840s onwards, young black men began to organize dozens of independent armed militias that would publicly parade through town and city streets during annual commemorative events such as British West Indies Emancipation every first day of August. Indeed, Douglass recorded his surprise at a public parade during an 1855 West Indies Day commemoration of "two colored military companies, the 'NATIONAL GUARDS,' of Providence [Rhode Island], and the 'UNION CADETS' of New Bedford [Massachusetts]." "I never saw," wrote Douglass, "colored soldier[s] before, and before I saw them I had serious doubts of the wisdom of their coming out on that day."[57] According to one recent researcher of black involvement in John Brown's raid on Harper's Ferry in October 1859, three hundred armed black men arrived late because the raid was moved forward one week.[58]

Once the American Civil War began, black men began drilling unofficially in Rhode Island.[59] Former slaves willingly served in several unofficial regiments—three in New Orleans, one in South Carolina, and one in Kansas—with little federal support until the creation of the U.S. Colored Troops in the spring of 1863.[60] This was months before Douglass's famous call to arms.[61] The important point is that black men did not wait to be encouraged by abolitionist leaders to fight for the Union in 1861 or to be invited by the federal government to join the Union Army in 1863 in order to quash southern rebellion. They were either combat ready or fighting against slavery *before* political elites decided to arm them during political crises.

A more plausible explanation for high casualty rates among slave soldiers was the prevalence of filthy and disease-ridden conditions in which they fought and eventually died. The ranks of soldiers in Spanish America were decimated by yellow fever, malaria, typhoid, typhus, measles, and various parasites.[62] According to one scholar of slave soldiers in Argentina: "During the winter of 1824, slave troops fought in subfreezing temperatures without shoes or adequate rations. They returned to the capital crippled by frostbite and gangrene, many of them having lost toes, fingers, or parts of limbs. Well into the 1840s and 1850s, crippled black veterans begging in the streets were a common sight in Buenos Aires—as in Lima, Caracas, Cali, and other cities."[63] During the American Civil War campaigns of 1864, the Thirty-fifth U.S. Colored Troops marched and fought in South Carolina and Florida, losing 153 enlisted men. Of these, more than 50 had been killed in action, died of wounds, or were missing in action, and 43 died from smallpox and fever.[64] According to one reliable estimate for black soldiers' deaths during the American Civil War, disease claimed the lives of 11 men for each 1 killed on the battlefield.[65]

But perhaps the most compelling reason why slave soldiers died in such numbers was simply because they had the most to gain and the most to lose fighting in these wars. Contemporaries frequently commented on those who acquitted themselves so well on the battlefield. Speaking of the Haitian Revolution, Lemmonier-Delafosse wrote: "But what men these blacks are! How they fight and how they die!"[66] Argentine general Jose de San Martin claimed that the "best infantry soldier we have is the Negro and the mulatto."[67] A Black Seminole descendant recalled a family oral tradition about resistance to U.S. military aggression in Florida from her grandmother about "how the Old ones used to talk 'bout the look on them white soldiers faces when they see Black fighters looking like they grow outta swamp grass and the hammocks, coming at them with gun and cutlass."[68] According to one account, the United States spent $20 million and lost 1,500 soldiers winning the Second Seminole War.[69] On July 16, 1863, the Fifty-fourth Massachusetts Regiment attacked Fort Wagner, which guarded the port to Charleston, South Carolina. Of the 600 soldiers who participated, about half were killed, captured, or later died of their wounds.[70] "Of this fight I can only say men could not have behaved more bravely," declared Colonel Brisbin of his cavalry regiment in a campaign in Western Virginia. He continued: "I have seen white troops fight in twenty-seven battles and I never saw any fight better."[71] "Marvels of courage" was one speaker's succinct account at a recruitment rally at Camp William Penn, Pennsylvania, held on August 1, 1863.[72]

Such glowing reports could be attributed to stereotypes of black physicality, the special bravery of black men, or abolitionist propaganda designed to challenge the view that blacks would not fight for their own freedom. It is more probable that fighting for freedom turned slaves into formidable adversaries. The re-establishment of French colonial slavery in 1802 left the black occupants of Guadeloupe, Martinique, and St. Domingue with the option of either fighting to the death or being re-enslaved.[73] "Their Best Soldiers Are Black" is the title of the opening chapter of Kenneth Porter's *Black Seminoles*. It argues that the failure to repel U.S. annexation attempts of Florida would end established communal independence and introduce plantation slavery into the region.[74] Slave soldiers who served in rebel armies and were caught by royalists during wars of independence in early and late nineteenth-century Spanish America risked re-enslavement.[75] Black soldiers fought for the British Crown in 1837 because they feared an independent Canada might result in their being extradited to slavery in the U.S. South through slaveholder's influence.[76] Such fears remained palpable until the final destruction of U.S. slavery a generation later. Former slave Samuel Cabble, who joined the Fifty-fifth Massachusetts Infantry during the American Civil War, informed his wife: "great is the outpouring of the colered [sic] people that is now rallying with the hearts of lions against the very curse that has separated you and me."[77] On April 12, 1864, Confederate General Nathan Bedford Forrest's capture of the federal garrison on the Mississippi River at Fort Pillow, Tennessee, was followed by the indiscriminate slaughter of anywhere between several dozen to over two hundred mostly black Union troops who had already surrendered. General Forrest's tactic of killing black soldiers in order to deter future recruits backfired since black soldiers fought even harder after Fort Pillow, knowing that surrender would bring death anyway. Indeed, black Union soldiers were often reported going into battle after the spring 1864 yelling "Remember Fort Pillow."[78] The defense of newly acquired freedoms, together with the prospect of these being taken away and lost, explains why slave soldiers fought like lions and fell so frequently on the battlefields of the Americas.[79]

It is clear that the vast majority of these slave soldiers were male. The author of a report on the 1791 slave revolt in northern St. Domingue estimated that two-thirds of the 68,664 slaves in the region were women, children, and the infirm unable to take up arms.[80] This reflected the fact that the battlefield was a place where men fought. On the other hand, wars in which slavery was to become a crucial issue changed this landscape in several ways. Women were reported to have militarily participated in a number of conflicts. One scholar claims that over 14,000 maroon women were involved in the vital battle for Le Cap during the early stages of the Haitian Revolution in 1793.[81] Toussaint Louverture's military forces were said to contain some black women.[82] Women were also reported to have fought in the Spanish American wars of liberation. Simón Bolívar made the following observation about one conflict: "They [loyalists] have directed their deadly arms against the fair and tender breasts of our lovely women, spilling their blood and killing not a few[,] . . . and our women are fighting against oppressors and competing with us to overcome them."[83] This evidence is a little unclear: it feels like a call to arms for men to protect women, while it is not certain whether female fighting was literal or figurative.

Less ambivalent was female slave Josefa Tenorio, who claimed to have fought with patriot guerillas in Peru. She later explained: "Having heard the rumor that the enemy was trying to reenslave the *patria* once again, I dressed myself as a man and ran at once to the barracks to receive my orders and take up my musket. General [Juan Gregorio de] Las Hasas entrusted me with a flag to carry and to defend with honor. . . . Assigned to the forces of the commander general of guerrillas, Toribio Davalos, I suffered the rigors of the campaign. My gender has not impeded me from being useful to my *patria*."[84] During the American Civil War, at least several dozen black women served in the Union Navy. Their sex only became known once they were either injured or killed.[85] Women participated on other nineteenth-century battlefields. During the Taiping revolt in China, new regiments of Hakka women fought heroically in an unsuccessful attempt to occupy the Guangxi capital of Guilin in the spring of 1852.[86]

Women also proved useful on the battlefront serving as spies, nurses, cooks, servants, camp followers, and laborers. Harriet Tubman's claim for a pension in 1898 included an account of her services rendered for the federal government during the American Civil War: "My claim against the U.S. is for three years service as a nurse and cook in hospitals, and as commander of several men (eight or nine) as scouts during the late War of the Rebellion, under direction and orders of Edwin M. Stanton, Secretary of War, and of several Generals."[87] Tubman was one of scores of thousands of ex-slave women who ended up in Union Army camps working as nurses, cooks, servants, and laborers for the federal cause.[88] Peter Blanchard has outlined some of the major ways in which ex-slave women participated as spies, informers, and laborers in wars of independence in Spanish South America.[89] Ada Ferrer's study of wars of national independence in Cuba during the late nineteenth century shows how slave insurgents often included women who followed their husbands, brothers, and sons to the battlefront.[90] Although males constituted the demographic majority of ex-slave insurgents during the Haitian Revolution, it is not unreasonable to assume that ex-slave women played similar roles as spies and laborers who either followed loved ones to the front or got on with the business of familial obligations under difficult wartime conditions.[91] Much research remains to be done on ex-slave women and military conflicts in the nineteenth-century Americas. More work also needs doing on social constructions of masculinity and slave soldiers. One of the striking differences regarding black soldiers during the American Civil War compared to slave soldiers elsewhere in the wartime Americas was linking fighting with manhood, a discourse prevalent in the United States but seemingly absent in the rest of the Americas.

III. CONSEQUENCES

The military participation of slave soldiers in wars of independence and struggles over slavery in the nineteenth-century Americas had several important consequences. First and foremost, despite the real risks of death, disease, maltreatment, and re-enslavement, many slave soldiers achieved personal freedom. Those slaves who fought for the patriots during the American War of Independence during the 1770s as well as the much larger number who fought for the Union in the 1860s gained their liberty as soon as they were enlisted. This was also true for slaves who fought against colonial slavery and for national independence in St. Domingue between 1791 and 1804. The Pact of Zanjon, signed on February 10, 1878, freed an estimated 16,000 slaves in Cuba, including those who had served as loyalists to Spain as well as those who had served with the nationalist rebels. This sweeping abolition was a pragmatic measure because the colonial authorities in Madrid recognized that armed slave rebels would not put down their arms.[92] In other words, these slave soldiers fought for and won their liberation, despite the failure of Cuban independence. These thousands of small emancipations across the nineteenth-century Americas meant a great deal to freedom's seekers.

Moreover, slave soldiers contributed to the outcomes of numerous national liberation struggles in the nineteenth-century Americas. They helped prevent the success of William McKenzie's national independence movement in Canada West during the late 1830s. Black Union troops, most of whom were former slaves, contributed decisively to the military defeat of the Confederate States of America. As Joseph Reidy put it: "They helped alleviate a shortage of manpower at precisely the time that white northerners began seriously questioning the level of sacrifice that the federal government asked of its citizens."[93] The alternative would have been the establishment and consolidation of the most powerful slaveholding republic in the Western Hemisphere.[94] Although slave soldiers failed to help the British retain colonial control of their mainland colonies, other slave soldiers helped to win national liberation for the American colonies during the 1770s and to protect the United States from re-colonization by the British in the War of 1812. Slave soldiers also played an important supporting role in the establishment of independent republics in Spanish America during the first two decades of the nineteenth century. Their role in winning national liberation from French colonial rule to establish the independent republic of Haiti in 1804 was indispensable.

It is obvious that war was not the mother of all abolitions in the nineteenth-century Americas. Different circumstances account for the abolition of slavery elsewhere: in the British West Indies during the 1830s, in the French and Danish West Indies in 1848, in the Spanish Americas during the 1850s, in the Dutch West Indies in 1863, and Brazil in 1888.[95] In addition, slave soldiers also protected slave systems. According to the official record, British West India regiments proved "efficient" in "identifying Maroon habitats, locating the carefully camouflaged entrance points and the vulnerable nodes in Maroon defense and attacking their adversaries fiercely."[96] Slave soldiers also were reported to have played an important role in suppressing slave revolts in the British Caribbean.[97] On the other hand, slave soldiers did play a vital role in the destruction of some of the major systems of slavery in the region. In the Spanish American states, it was through the passage of free-womb laws. These laws required that the children of slave mothers were born free and that older slaves would be manumitted. These laws were passed either at the beginning of wars to gain slave support for independence (Chile in 1811, Argentina in 1813) or later to reward slave military service (Columbia and Peru in 1821, Uruguay in 1825).[98] In contrast to this gradual process of abolition in Spanish America, slavery was directly ended by the military participation of slave soldiers in Saint-Domingue/Haiti during the 1790s, 1850s Peru, and the United States during the 1860s. Indeed, it is hard to envision how slavery would have ended in these societies without the leading participation of slaves who were fighting for their freedom. Slaveholders wanted to retain their valuable property, while abolition was never a strategic objective of political elites *at the beginning* of these social upheavals. One of the least persuasive arguments for political elites arming slaves is the suggestion that slaves were "gifted" freedom from above. In actuality, they fought and died in large numbers for their own liberation and in the process helped to destroy the institution of racial chattel slavery in the Americas.[99]

The historical significance of slave soldiers in wars of national independence and the abolition of slavery cannot be fully appreciated without adopting a cross-national framework. Local, regional, and national approaches overlook the revolutionary role of slave soldiers in wars of independence and emancipation with international implications. Thus, Haiti's ex-slave army halted French imperial ambitions in North America. African American troops who fought for the Union military helped prevent the creation of what would have been the most powerful slaveholding republic in the Americas. Slave soldiers hastened the dissolution of the Spanish-controlled Americas on the mainland and in the Caribbean during the early as well as the late nineteenth century. Collectively, slaves helped to destroy systems of slavery either immediately or gradually across the hemisphere. These significant historical developments become apparent only through a cross-national examination rather than nationalist narratives of slave soldiers fighting for citizenship.

IV. CITIZENS?

According to a recent comparative study of gender and emancipation in the Atlantic world, emancipation benefited men more than women primarily because slave men fought against slavery, thus earning the right of citizenship. Mimi Sheller argues that "highly exclusive discourses of nationalized masculinity were deployed in the construction of republican citizenship and civic militarism" in nineteenth-century Haiti.[100] Post-emancipation societies, concludes Sue Peabody in her essay on two centuries of abolition in the French Caribbean, "created more opportunities for advancement and exercise of political agency by newly freed men than women, thus minimizing many of the advantages that universal freedom should have brought to women."[101] In the volume's introductory essay, the editors identify "a central theme of this book: that emancipation tended to benefit men more than women, particularly in the political sphere."[102]

This comparative claim that emancipation benefited men more than women is debatable for several reasons. Most obviously, it ignores the high death rate of slave soldiers as well as the benefits that emancipation wrought freedwomen concerning control over their own bodies.[103] But the more particular claim for soldiers earning citizenship is also questionable. Veterans of the Haitian Revolution in the north of the nation became subjects not citizens of King Henri's post-abolition realm. In the British Caribbean, ex-slaves could not claim equal civil and political rights alongside those who were formerly free before abolition, including white colonists. Mimi Scheller's interesting analysis of black masculine discourse in post-emancipation Jamaica cannot escape the fact that Jamaican freedmen did not have equal political rights.[104] This exploded into view during the Morant Bay uprising in 1865.

Moreover, it is hard to view veterans of the U.S. Colored Troops as equal citizens given their hard fight for equal pay during wartime, the need for federal protection of new civil and political rights during the 1860s and 1870s, and the withering away of legal rights during the immediate post-Reconstruction decades. Indeed, one of the commonalities of many memoirs written by white officers of black Union troops published during the 1890s was the importance of black soldiery to the Union war effort and by implication the injustice of political disfranchisement and Jim Crow inequality during the same decade.[105] We have already seen what happened to Afro-Cubans in the early post-abolition decades when they tried to assert their political independence. In addition, although many scholars would agree that former slaves won their legal freedom in late-1880s Brazil, few would argue that this entailed legal and civic equality that bestowed a greater advantage on freedmen compared to freedwomen.

One clear indication of slave soldiers' contribution was personal pride in their former military activities. It is unlikely that veterans from Haiti's wars against colonial slavery and for national independence soon forgot their triumph over slaveholders as well as powerful French and English armies. Although Spanish colonial officials constructed "racialized representations" of wars of independence in Cuba during the 1870s in negative ways, it is obvious that black veterans had a very different view of the conflicts in which they had participated and that had resulted in their gaining emancipation at the Pact of Zanjon in 1878.[106] In general, black veterans of the U.S. federal military after 1865 "could take pride in knowing that they had helped destroy slavery, save the Union, and establish republican liberty and the rule of law throughout the land."[107] More specifically, the 4,100 veterans from four black regiments in North Carolina that served the Union would not dispute their contribution toward ending American slavery.[108]

Moreover, black veterans were often promised rewards for past military service by grateful governments but with mixed results. During the epoch of revolutions in the late eighteenth century, the idea of payment to veterans was initiated. In 1775, the Continental Congress of the fledgling United States voted to provide a pension to those soldiers and sailors who would fight for national independence. This promise was only partially fulfilled after victory had been achieved.[109] In his farewell address to Rhode Island's Black Regiment, commanding officer Lieutenant Colonel Olney praised the soldier's "unexampled fortitude and patience," but also regretted "that such faithful service has heretofore been so illy [sic] rewarded, and painful indeed is it to him to see the officers and men retire from the field without receiving any pay, or even their accounts settled and the balances due ascertained."[110] Some veterans of the British West Indies regiments were provided with a temporary pension of "a bitt a day," but many were left to their own meager resources.[111] The same was true of others who had served in Her Majesty's forces. Around 976 former slaves who had served militarily with the British in St. Domingue were evacuated in 1798 and reduced to "unmerited and unspeakable distress."[112] The editor of the Toronto-based *Provincial Freeman* reported frequently encountering poor "colored men who are pensioners" throughout the Niagara region in 1850s Canada after military service with the British Crown.[113] In the United States, former servicemen received limited veteran pensions ranging from a few dollars a month to around twelve dollars a month to those elderly surviving ex-slaves. Although these were not great sums of money, they did provide ex-soldiers with a degree of financial independence.[114]

On the other hand, many black veterans of the American Civil War had sought land in exchange for their military service.[115] After the initial redistribution of land to black veterans and families by the Union military, the federal government reneged because it upset the free market ideology of northern business interests and Republican politicians.[116] This failure to redistribute land to black veterans was in marked contrast to the activities of political elites elsewhere in the post-emancipation Americas. In the war-torn areas of eastern Cuba, especially near El Congo, small land plots were granted between 1879 and 1885 to veterans of the Spanish armies, including former slaves.[117] In 1809 and 1814, land reform in southern and western Haiti resulted in the estimated redistribution of some 76,000 *carreaux* of land among 2,322 civil and military officers. In 1819, grants of land were distributed from 1 to 20 *carreaux* to veterans in northern Haiti.[118] In exchange for their service in the unsuccessful British war to retake the former American colonies in 1812, black veterans were transported to Trinidad in the southeast Caribbean and settled in company villages New Grant/Mount Elvin, Indian Walk, Mount Pleasant, Hard Bargain, Montserrat/Sherring Ville, and Matilda Bounty. Their descendants are still there.[119]

Along with pride in their work and compensation for military service, black veterans became politically engaged. Their mobilization took several forms. One was the unfinished business of emancipation. In the aftermath of the unsuccessful First War for Cuban Independence against Spain during the 1870s, slaves and former slaves continued to battle for their liberties. The principal leaders of this new insurrection known as the *Guerra Chiquita* were veterans of color including Jose Maceo and Guillermo Moncada.[120] Another aspect of this political work was the role of veterans after civil wars. Two years after gaining national independence in 1804, Haiti became involved in a fractious civil war between the republican South under President Pétion and the monarchical North under Christophe that lasted until 1818. Veterans from

Haiti fought on both sides. Indeed, part of the *raison d'être* for land reform by both leaders was to anchor veterans on their respective sides in the civil conflict.[121] The political mobilization of veterans took other forms in the post-emancipation U.S. South. Demobilized soldiers from the federal army went back to their communities and formed independent black militias. Around 10,000 black Marylanders, most of who fought for the Fourth, Seventh, and Thirty-ninth Regiments of the U.S. Colored Troops, were mustered out by 1866. By the following summer of 1867, they had formed independent black regiments including the Lincoln Zouaves, the Oakland Invincible Guards, the Hugh Lennox Bond Militia, the Henry Winter Davis Guards, and the Butler Guards.[122] Black veterans also formed independent militias in Wilmington, North Carolina, as well as throughout Georgia and South Carolina during the 1870s.[123] These black veterans played a prominent role in protecting voter registration and participation, as well as resisting racist attacks by white paramilitary organizations. On Saturday morning, July 24, 1875, for example, several hundred black soldiers paraded into Sandersville, Georgia, for a political rally, led by "the war-like sound of many drums."[124] These veterans also ran for local public office.[125] What this political mobilization of black veterans suggests is that, although the monster of slavery had been slain, the battles of freedom's first generations were by no means over.

Nation-centered frameworks have limitations. Nationalist historiographies draw upon the role of minorities as soldiers fighting for the country, yet what we have seen is that slaves fought on *both* sides in wars, revolutions, and social crises in the nineteenth-century Americas. Abolitionists during the American Civil War trumpeted the role of black soldiers as Union propaganda to silence those critics who doubted their capacity to fight; but a hemispheric perspective shifts the emphasis onto the actions and experiences of slaves on multiple battlefields. Political elites often depicted abolition as their gift, a view reinforced by scholars' focus on why slaves were armed, but it was slave soldiers who decided to fight and fought hard because of what was at stake. The social consequences of the actions of slave soldiers are best realized through cross-national perspectives on national liberation struggles, imperial and national wars, and the military destruction of slavery.

CHAPTER 3

Slave Revolt across Borders

Each country has its own laws, as you must know, sir, and fortunately for the cause of humanity, Hayti is not the only one where slavery is abolished.
—ALEXANDER PÉTION

[Madison Washington,] that bright star of freedom [who] took his station in the constellation of freedom.
—JAMES AND LOIS HORTON

In discussing the origin of Pan-Africanism, what one should look for is the period when the sentiments or concepts underlying it first attracted attention.
—P. O. ESEDEBE

In the second volume of *The Slave States of America* published in 1842, James Silk Buckingham penned the following: "The example of Hayti, with a free government of blacks, is before them; —the emancipation of all slaves in Mexico, is known to them;—the example of England in the West India Islands, is fresh and recent; and the exertions making for their abolition in their own Northern States, are, of course, familiar to them all. It is impossible but that all this must every year increase the general *desire* to be free."[1] Buckingham, an English traveler and writer sympathetic to the peaceful abolition of slavery in the United States, highlighted prominent examples of emancipation in the Western Hemisphere during the first four decades of the nineteenth century. In 1804, the new republic of Haiti had outlawed slavery. In 1829, Mexico had terminated slavery eight years after gaining national independence from Spain. The abolition of British colonial slavery—largely directed at its West Indies colonies—had been legislated in 1833, implemented in 1834, and concluded by 1838. Between 1777 (Vermont) and 1827 (New York), slavery was legally abolished in all northern states in the U.S. republic. Buckingham drew attention to these Caribbean, Central American, and North American examples of slave emancipation because he wanted to "avert the calamity" of slave insurrection in the United States.[2]

Building upon Buckingham's cross-national approach, together with

The Greater Caribbean region showing the proximity of slave and free borders.

an emerging historical literature on the transnational connections among slaves—what one scholar dubs "common winds"[3]—this chapter examines examples of slave revolt, legal abolition, and post-emancipation developments in the nineteenth-century Americas. Its specific concern is with the transmission and nature of slave revolt and abolition in one area inspiring slave self-emancipation in other places and its ramifications. Moreover, it pursues connections among slaves seeking freedom in colonial states as well as the first black republic's responses to these expectations. Most important, this chapter explains the intersection between slaves' original desires for freedom and the impact of external factors. Slave revolt is broadly defined as both collective rebellion as well as smaller acts of self-emancipation, while borders are delineated as national boundaries on land and at sea as well as between states within federal territories. Although organized around Buckingham's major abolition moments and their international impact on slaves, free blacks, and abolitionists, it also expands his framework to make a bolder argument for the historical significance of slave revolt across borders.[4]

The chapter has three key aims. It seeks to transcend the spatial and temporal dimensions of the "common-wind" approach beyond Haiti as well as the Age of Revolution. Most scholarly attention focuses on the generational period around the late eighteenth through early nineteenth century, but it is clear that, not only did the Haitian Revolution continue its impact throughout the nineteenth century, but it was accompanied by other influential slave revolts and abolitions in Mexico, the English Caribbean, the northern United States, and so forth. The second objective is to reveal connections between the Caribbean, Central America, North America, and South America usually overlooked because of national and regional historiographies independent of each other. This is obviously the consequence of the development of celebratory historiographies in the aftermath of national independence together with the gradual professionalization of history by the late nineteenth century and onwards. The earlier era, however, points to less concrete nation-centered experiences as well as more protean forms of communal identity (Buckingham was an international rather than English abolitionist). The third objective is to contribute to the conceptualization of emancipation in African Diaspora studies. Slaves moved across borders. Slaves sought free lives. Slaves suffered and protested, sharing a common skin color. These three components of the Diaspora theory—movement, homelands, and racial solidarity—require greater emphasis in global emancipation studies.

I. EXAMPLE OF HAYTI

The Haitian Revolution clearly inspired slaves across the Americas. During the 1790s, news of slave rebellion blew throughout the circum-Caribbean carried by soldiers, sailors, slaves, and others traversing borders stretching from French Louisiana to Spanish Venezuela.[5] In the summer of 1793, U.S. slaveholder John Randolph overheard slaves' conversation outside the windows of his home in Richmond, Virginia, in which one conversant reminded the other of "how the blacks *has* kill'd the whites in the French Island . . . a little while ago."[6] In April 1795, a number of slaves were arrested in Pointe Coupee, French Louisiana, for conspiring to kill slaveholders and destroy slavery. The trial summary determined that the conspiracy was inspired by the most radical phase of the French Revolution as well as the Haitian Revolution.[7] Four months later, in August 1795, Haitian revolutionary André Rigaud visited the Knip plantation on the Dutch colony of Curaçao. A few weeks later, Tula led some two thousand fellow slaves in an armed revolt for the abolition of slavery that was eventually crushed by several hundred soldiers, militia units, and some free blacks.[8]

The Haitian Revolution's cross-national impact was reported in several areas in 1805, the year following the founding of the new black state. An investigation into a slave conspiracy in the Cuban province of Puerto Principe revealed the influence of the Haitian Revolution.[9] Brazilian historian Luis Mott has documented slaves in Rio de Janeiro, Brazil, wearing necklaces stamped with the image of Haiti's first president, Jean Jacques Dessalines.[10] Hundreds of francophone slaves were discovered plotting a revolt at Christmas in northern Trinidad. After the discovery of the plot, several witnesses recalled a ceremony of oaths and song, including the following stanza:

Pain nous ka mange (The bread which we have eaten)
C'est viande beke (Is white man's flesh)
Di in nous ka boue (The wine we have drunk)
C'est sang beke. (Is white man's blood)
He! St. Domingo, song St. Domingo! (Hey! St. Domingo, recall St. Domingo!)[11]

In early January 1811, Creole-born driver Charles Deslondes led an army of some five hundred slaves from plantations along coastal Louisiana to seize New Orleans. Although historians differ on Deslondes's connections with Haiti,[12] the two regions—separated by approximately twelve hundred miles—were linked for more than a century by French colonial slavery and since the 1790s by numerous French planters fleeing the revolution, taking their slaves with them. While it is hard to document whether any of these incoming slaves participated in what some have called (incorrectly I think) America's largest slave revolt,[13] it is hard to think why they would not have shared news about this massive rebellion with other slaves. In 1816, planters and merchants in Sao Francisco, Bahia, Brazil, worried that "[t]he spirit of insurrection is seen among all types of slaves, and is fomented principally by the slaves of the city [Salvador], where the ideas of liberty have been communicated by black sailors coming from Saint Domingue."[14] During the Easter weekend of 1816, Barbados experienced its largest slave revolt since the late seventeenth century. The revolt—began because of rumors that emancipation was imminent but being impeded by planters—was influenced by the Haitian Revolution. After its brutal suppression, Robert, a slave on the Simmons plantation, told a Select Committee of the House of Assembly:

That Nanny Grig (a negro woman at *Simmons'* who said she could read) was the first person who told the negroes [*sic*] at *Simmons'* so; and she said she had read it in the Newspapers, [slaves to be freed on New

Year's Day] and that her Master was very uneasy at it: that she was always talking about it to the negroes, and told them that they were all damned fools to work, for that she would not, as freedom they were sure to get. That about a fortnight after New-year's Day, she said the negroes were to be freed on Easter-Monday, and the only way to get it was to fight for it, otherwise they would not get it; and the way they were to do it, was to set fire, as that was the way they did in Saint Domingo.[15]

The court records of former slave and free black conspirator Denmark Vesey reveal that the 1822 plot to seize and burn Charleston, South Carolina, had been partly inspired by events in the former French colony. According to Rollo, one of its leaders: "Denmark had told us it was high time we had our liberty. . . . He said, we must unite together as the Santo Domingo people did."[16] Jack, another leader, testified that Vesey frequently read "all the passages in the newspapers that related to Santo Domingo," as well as many others "that had any connection with slavery."[17] Michael Johnson has recently questioned this 1822 slave conspiracy, arguing that it was simply the result of local political machinations.[18] An older historical literature—along with recent rebuttals of Johnson's interpretation—remain persuasive on the existence of this major slave plot.[19] More important, Johnson's attempt to reduce it to slaveholder's political differences ignores the cross-national life of the leading protagonist who was born, raised, and worked in the circum-Caribbean, and sought to lead his followers to Haiti's promised land. In 1826, William Bowser led fellow slaves in a revolt on the *Decatur,* embarking from Baltimore to New Orleans with the intention of sailing to Haiti. They seized the ship, but their intentions were thwarted.[20] Three years after Bowser was hanged, one hundred slaves on board the *Lafayette* bound for New Orleans rose in revolt apparently inspired by the Haitian Revolution.[21] The Malê Revolt—also known as the Hausa Uprising and the Bahía Rebellion—in the port city of Salvador da Bahía, Brazil, in January 1835, involved several hundred slaves who nearly succeeded in seizing the city. This uprising was anticipated by dozens of slave revolts and conspiracies stimulated by the overthrow of French colonial slavery in St. Domingue.[22] In short, it is inconceivable that the Haitian Revolution failed to influence scores of slave rebellions and conspiracies throughout the Americas from the 1790s onwards.

Haiti's revolutionary example also inspired speeches, letters, and poems by numerous African American abolitionists and antislavery activists, especially from the 1830s onwards. My "Beloved Brethren," wrote Boston's free black antislavery activist David Walker in the second article of his *Appeal to the Colored Citizens of the World*, self-published in 1829, "remember the divisions and consequent sufferings of *Carthage* and of *Hayti*. Read the history particularly of Hayti, and see how they were butchered by the whites, and do you take warning."[23] He went on to remind his black readers that "Hayti, the glory of the blacks and terror of tyrants, is enough to convince the most avaricious and stupid of wretches" of the failure not to terminate this wretched system of slavery.[24]

In a speech comparing slave abolition in the French and British colonies delivered in 1838, black American physician and abolitionist James McCune Smith noted France's "first, most glorious example" of revolutionary republicanism followed by "immediate and entire emancipation," and acknowledged "the independence of Hayti."[25] Three years later, on February 26, 1841, Smith delivered *A Lecture on the Haytien Revolutions with a Sketch of the Character of Toussaint L'Ouverture* at New York's Stuyvesant Institute for the benefit of the Colored Orphan Asylum that was subsequently published as a small book.[26] Martin Robison Delany, fellow physician and originator with Frederick Douglass of the antislavery newspaper *North Star*, published a letter in the July 1849 edition addressed to the colored populace of Cuba evoking Haiti's example. "Let them," he wrote, "but remember the masterly and noble reply of Henry Christophe, one of the oppressed of St. Domingo, who in answer to general Leclerc, the able captain and brother-in-law of the emperor Napoleon said, 'It is needless to count on numbers or means. My determination to be a man and *freeman*, is the sum of my arithmetic!' But let them come to this noble determination and conclusion, and the colored races of Cuba are *free!*"[27]

There is no doubt that subsequent archival research will unearth more evidence of revolutionary Haiti's example and its inspiration for slaves and free blacks for freedom and equality throughout the nineteenth century. Matt Clavin, for example, has recently argued that African Americans seized upon the symbols of Toussaint and the Haitian Revolution to create a "subversive ideology" during the American Civil War.[28] Not only will such findings further undermine claims for a lack of conclusive evidence of Haiti's impact on the United States and elsewhere as argued by some historians, but they further buttress the critical point that Haiti's example continued for slaves and free blacks across the nineteenth-century Americas beyond the Age of Revolution.[29]

Moreover, the story of Haiti inspired freedom's first generation at Morant Bay, Jamaica, in October 1865. Black protesters rose against the continuation of poor economic conditions thirty years after colonial abolition after which they were brutally suppressed by the colonial governor. This rebellion is usually examined in British colonial terms.[30] There were, however, important hemispheric dimensions. In a letter published in the *Jamaican Guardian*, George William Gordon stated: "I was told by some of you that your overseer said that if any of you attended this meeting they would tear down your houses. Tell them that I, George William Gordon, say they dare not do it. It is tyranny. You must do what Haiti does. You have a bad name now, but you will have a worse name then."[31] There is some dispute as to whether Gordon uttered these precise words, but this former slave, landholder, political spokesman, and spiritual leader was executed for his role in the rebellion. His executioner was Governor Eyre, who was also aware of the impact of slave emancipation in his own bailiwick. In a letter written three months after the rebellion, he noted: "It must be borne in mind that the success which attended the efforts of the Haytians against the French [1804], and more recently of the St. Domingans against the Spanish [1865], afforded examples and encouragement which from the vicinity of those republics to Jamaica, were constantly before the peasantry of this country."[32] Despite its self-exculpatory context, Eyre's examples of inspirational emancipation cross-nationally in the 1860s echo those of his fellow countryman Buckingham's from the 1840s.

II. FREE GOVERNMENT OF BLACKS

The making of new republics from former colonies in the Western Hemisphere during the Age of Revolution presented powerful new beacons of liberty, especially in the continental Americas. "How joyfully," reported Brissot de Warville, on landing in Boston in 1788, "did I leap to ashore to tread this land of liberty!" "A refugee from despotism, I was at last to have the happiness of witnessing freedom." He was to be an enthusiastic supporter of the French Revolution.[33] Benedict Anderson's influential work on the role of "the originating Americas" as Creole pioneers of modern nationalism provocatively extends this notion of the exemplary republic globally.[34] These beacons of liberty, however, proved attractive to those who were already free rather than to those who sought liberty from an existing condition of enslavement. Many of the new republics and nation-states in the Americas contained powerful slaveholding political elites. The transatlantic slave trade continued for two decades after the founding of the United States and three decades after the independence of Brazil. Slavery continued in Spanish South America through the 1850s, while it expanded continentally in the U.S. republican and Brazilian dynastic empires. Slaves and their allies sought alternative beacons of liberty, especially places where slave systems had been terminated.

On January 1, 1804, Jean Jacques Dessalines proclaimed Haiti's independence. The former military commander under Toussaint assumed the mantle of emperor for the next three years before he was shot dead on October 17, 1806. Shortly thereafter, Haiti split into a northern state ruled by Henri Christophe who became King Henri I in 1811, and a southern republic under Alexandre Pétion, a light-skinned Creole born in Port-au-Prince in 1770 and elected president in March 1807. The civil war dragged on for more than twelve years until the death of Pétion on March 29, 1818, when Jean Pierre Boyer assumed control of the South followed by the whole of Haiti in 1820 after the suicide of Henri on October 31. Despite this long civil war, together with constitutional differences and contrasting land policies, both regions shared significant commonalities, including opposition toward reintroducing legal slavery as well as opposition toward the slave trade and slavery wherever these continued to be practiced.[35] During a period of retrenchment in wars of national liberation against Spanish America, Venezuelan military and political leader Simón Bolívar appealed for assistance from President Pétion. On January 2, 1816, Bolívar was welcomed to southern Haiti by Pétion. The latter provided six thousand rifles, munitions, supplies, naval transport, and money in exchange for a promise from the former to abolish slavery in the areas he liberated in Venezuela.[36] The Great Liberator was most appreciative: "In my proclamation to the inhabitants of Venezuela and in the decree that I shall issue, announcing liberty to the slaves, I do not know that it will be permitted me to demonstrate the real sentiment of my heart towards Your Excellency and to leave to posterity an undying monument to your philanthropy."[37]

President Pétion's reply expressed Haiti's commitment to liberty as well as an appreciation for the finer points of international diplomacy: "You surely must feel how ardently I desire to see the oppressed delivered from the yoke of bondage; but because of certain diplomatic obligations which I am under toward a nation that has not yet taken an offensive attitude against the Republic, I am obliged to ask you not to make [these arrangements known]."[38] Although Bolívar freed his own slaves, and offered freedom in exchange for military service to slaves, many other slaveholders and slaves were less responsive.[39] The final eradication of slavery in Venezuela did not occur until a generation after independence in 1854.[40] The central point, however, is that the Haitian leader's support for emancipation elsewhere in the Americas represented a clear example of state sponsorship of freedom for those who were enslaved. From the perspective of slave emancipation, the Great Liberator was Pétion rather than Bolívar.

President Pétion's protection of the rights of former slaves in the case of the *Deep Nine* further demonstrated the significance of this new free government. While visiting Haiti, British planter Robert M'Kewan saw "a great number, say from thirty to forty negroes [sic], who avowed themselves to be runaways from this island [Jamaica], and many of them were personally known to my own negroes [sic], who accompanied me up there."[41] Years earlier, British consul Charles McKenzie informed his colonial superiors in London that Port-au-Prince was home to a "large" number of "refugee slaves from the British colonies."[42] M'Kewan was visiting Haiti in search of the former black crew of the pilot schooner *Deep Nine* owned by his brother James M'Kewan. In early January 1817, the *Deep Nine* left Port Royal for eastern Jamaica to provide pilots to vessels. While anchored at Rocky Point, with slaveholder James gathering supplies ashore, the black crew took off with the schooner. The M'Kewan brothers suspected the slave pilots had steered for Haiti—about 170 miles northwest of Jamaica—a suspicion later confirmed once they visited the new black state and attempted to retrieve the slaves. The M'Kewans lodged an official complaint with President Pétion claiming "restitution of property that has been piratically taken from us."[43]

Since the slave pilots freed themselves and were not removed pirate-like, M'Kewan's claim was clearly fraudulent. The Haitian leader was unequivocal in his response: "I have just given directions for restoring to you the vessel, and every thing appertaining to her, but as to the men, they are recognized to be Haytians by the 44th article of the constitution of the republic, from the moment they set foot in its territory, and it is out of my power to restore them to you agreeably to your demand. Each country has its laws, as you must know, sir, and, fortunately for the cause of humanity, Hayti is not the only one where slavery is abolished."[44] Article 44 of Haiti's revised 1816 constitution stipulated: "All Africans, Indians, and their descendants and blood relatives, born in the colonies or foreign lands, who would come to live in the Republic, will be recognized as Haitian; but will only enjoy the rights of citizenship after a year's residence."[45] Moreover, Haiti had abolished slavery and—like any other nation—was bound to respect its own laws. With diminishing hopes, the M'Kewans called on intervention from Admiral John Douglas, head of naval forces in Jamaica.

President Pétion was as firm in his response to Admiral Douglas. The vessel had been returned and its articles were either to follow or be compensated for. The former slaves, however, were not only free but the protection of their new status was the duty of the government. The president then drew upon the example of England as a free soil nation: "England herself offers an example in the right of asylum, which she has so generously exercised during the revolutionary disturbance which agitated the world—that, if the persons claimed by Messrs. James and Robert M'Kewan had been able to set their feet in the territory of England, there, where no slavery exists, certainly the claim would not have been admitted."[46] Although not mentioned specifically, Pétion was referring to the 1772 decision that slaveholding within England (but not the British colonies) no longer had legal foundation. The point has been made that the original legal decision in the *Knowles v. Somersett* case was quite restricted, but abolitionists turned it into a broader attack on the institution of British slavery.[47] So did the president of Haiti in the case of the *Deep Nine*. In short, Haiti was free soil, and its government upheld the freedom of any slaves who reached its shores, as was the case in England, some northern states in America, and elsewhere, in accordance with the dictates of international law.

This new free government sometimes even sought to export emancipation in the Americas. President Dessalines once declared regretfully: "Unfortunate Martinquans . . . I am not able to fly to your assistance and break your chains [France reintroduced colonial slavery in 1802]. Alas, an invincible obstacle separates us. . . . But perhaps a spark from the fire which we have kindled will spring forth in your soul."[48] In February 1822, Haitian President Jean-Pierre Boyer spearheaded an invasion of 12,000 troops into neighboring Santo Domingo (now the Dominican Republic). The president's first major decision was to liberate around 4,000 slaves and promise them the redistribution of farmland. (It is also not unlikely that numerous slaves crossed into the free territory of Haiti before this 1822 abolition edict made such cross-border activity redundant.) We should not ignore the basic fact that emancipation was a consequence rather than a motivation for Boyer's invasion. The president was largely concerned with preventing a joint French-Spanish invasion of the island that might threaten Haiti's independence. At the same time, by the early 1820s Haiti and Santo Domingo represented an island of freedom in a Caribbean sea of slavery.[49] The key point about these actions was that they reflected a free government of blacks who were proven to be staunch allies of emancipation. The harsher realities of state policies toward ordinary Haitians in the generation following independence[50] does not alter the fact that the new black state symbolized freedom for slaves who wanted freedom, abolitionists who argued for the success of emancipation, and free blacks longing for a better way of life.

This black beacon in the Greater Antilles attracted free people of African descent who were denied civil liberties in their homelands. Mahommah Gardo Baquaqua, a Muslim from the Bight of Benin forcibly imported to Pernambuco in northeastern Brazil during the 1840s, eventually won his liberty. After deliberating whether to go to England or Haiti, he chose the latter because its climate was similar to his homeland and would better suit his "health and feelings." "When I arrived at Hayti," explained Baquaqua, " I felt myself free as indeed I was. No slavery exists there, yet all are people of color who dwell there."[51] It has been estimated that literally thousands of black seamen visited St. Domingue/Haiti between 1790 and 1830. For waterborne slave hirees like George Rayner, the black republic proved a lasting refuge. According to Jeffrey Bolster, most free black sailors took "justifiable pride in Haiti, delighting in their new-found ability to play off the Haitian state against shipmasters and consular officials."[52] A small set of refugees based in Santiago, Cuba, sought the rights of citizens in the new nation.[53] President Boyer encouraged black immigration from the United States. Those who came to Haiti, he noted, "being children of Africa, shall be Haytians as soon as they put their feet upon the soil of Hayti."[54] Around six thousand African Americans—mostly free but with some self-liberators—from major northern U.S. cities ended up walking this new soil during the 1820s.[55] Haiti's free soil was still enticing African Americans during the era of the American Civil War. Northern visitor William Nuel stopped at the home of free black woman Aunt Hagar located in southwest Georgia in 1861. Several black men asked him when he could take them and their children to St. Domingue.[56] After self-emancipating to Union lines in southeast Virginia, around five hundred former slaves left Hampton Roads, Virginia, for Île à Vache Island off the coast of Haiti during the first week of April 1863.[57]

Unfortunately, Haiti's promise failed for many of these freedom seekers. Free blacks in the 1820s returned to the northern United States because of poor lands, recurrent illness, and cultural alienation.[58] The search by self-emancipators in Civil War Virginia for improved conditions in off-shore Haiti proved abortive because of wretched conditions, and the survivors were forced to return a year later.[59] But these harsh realities must not overlook the original aspiration. People moved in *expectation* of greater freedoms even if these did not always work out. Most important, the establishment of a free government of blacks and its beacon-like qualities betokened a racial politics of solidarity around the first black state in the modern world. This was the logical consequence of many of the new state's actions—as well as a convincing explanation for its post-emancipation pariah status among America's new nation-states with powerful slaveholding elites. After trading successfully with Haiti for two years after its independence, the United States imposed a blockade on commerce with and immigration from the new state.[60] Moreover, Haiti served as a beacon of anti-enlightenment modernity, a racial symbol in sharp contrast to the recent claims of some scholars that its actions foreshadowed a modern agenda of human rights.[61]

III. A FRESH AND RECENT EXAMPLE

On Friday, August 1, 1834, the Abolition of Slavery Bill passed by the British Parliament a year earlier went into effect. A quasi-free system of apprenticeship was implemented with the objective of easing the transition from slave to free labor. Its specific objective was to train slaves to work for compensation and slaveholders to become employers in a new system of free labor relations. The apprenticeship period was scheduled to terminate after six years, but conflict between the new apprentices and their employers helped to terminate the system prematurely on August 1, 1838. Thus ended a centuries-long colonial system of slave trading and plantation production.[62] Three years later, Buckingham referred to this "fresh and recent" example of emancipation in the British West Indies before slaves in the U.S. South.

Slaves throughout the colonial Caribbean were quickly attracted to this new beacon of liberty. According to French aristocratic intellectual Alexis de Tocqueville, the British West Indies proved irresistible to slaves in the adjoining French colonies: "Already we know that on the English islands nearest ours, islands that were once French and are still populated by Frenchmen, there are recruitment companies whose purpose is to facilitate our slaves' escape. . . . How could it be otherwise? Here the black man is a slave, there he is free; here he vegetates in misery and hereditary degradation, there he lives in an opulence unknown to the European laborer. The two shores on which such contrary things occur face each other across a narrow channel that can be crossed in just a few hours and that every day is crossed by rivals who want to provide the fugitive with the means to break free from his chains."[63] Although Tocqueville's view that ex-slaves in the British Caribbean lived better than

European laborers is a dubious comparison (see chapter 6, below), he was correct that slave flight was facilitated by the close proximity of free to unfree soil. Martinique was only twenty-four nautical miles from St. Lucia and thirty-six nautical miles from Haiti. Guadeloupe was only thirty-three nautical miles from Haiti and twenty-four nautical miles from Antigua. "A good wind," wrote Tocqueville, "the cover of night, and the smallest boat are enough for part or all of a workshop to escape."[64]

Enslaved men and women in the Danish West Indies also headed for proximate English free soil. In May 1840, eleven slaves left Leinster Bay and Annaberg for Tortola, followed by four slaves a short time thereafter.[65] "We are informed," wrote *The Jamaican Royal Gazette*, "that in the months of April and May last [1842], there ran away from the three *Danish* Islands to Tortola, more than one hundred *Danish* slaves."[66] Karen Olwig estimates more than one hundred slaves left St. John mostly for the British free colony of neighboring Tortola some four miles distant during the 1840s. Some of these sea crossers made their escape by hollowing out big trees and using them as canoes previously employed by slaves in their fishing activities.[67] Neville Hall, a leading authority on slavery in the Danish West Indies, summarized this process and its implications with a clarity that deserves full quotation: "Externally, it was impossible to isolate the [Danish] colonies from the British decision to emancipate or from the ferment of its effects. British Tortola was practically within cannon shot of a poorly policed St. John and the narrows between could be swum by the intrepid, or negotiated by fishing boat and improvised raft. The British island held magnetic attractions for the slaves of St. John, particularly after 1840. . . . By 1845 there were instances of slaves escaping from the more distant St. Croix to Tortola. In the same year the futility of attempts at prevention was demonstrated by the simultaneous escape of 37 slaves from St. John."[68] These self-emancipators ceased their saltwater endeavors once systems of slavery were terminated. French colonial slavery ended as a consequence of the 1848 French Revolution and abolitionist activism. The Danish West Indies terminated colonial slavery in early July 1848 largely in response to a major slave uprising in Frederiksted, Saint Croix.[69] But we should not overlook possible connections between persistent saltwater crossings from French and Danish slave soil to British free soil, the increasing difficulty of managing colonial slavery from European metropolitan capitals, and the passage of colonial abolition laws.

Self-emancipators from the U.S. South also sought free soil across the sea.

In late July 1849, some three hundred slaves on the Georgia-Florida border planned to revolt, steal the steamboat *William Gaston*, and head for the British West Indies. The boat's delayed arrival exposed the plot, and the attempt was thwarted.[70] On November 2, 1841, a group of nineteen slaves led by Madison Washington en route from Hampton Roads, Virginia, to New Orleans seized the slave ship *Creole*. Washington opted for the U.S. colony of Liberia on the West African coast, but the lack of provisions dictated against his choice, and the rebels directed the ship toward the Bahamas. Slavery had been legally abolished in this British colony since 1833, and the slave rebels expected their freedom from the colonial authorities. The British authorities arrested the rebels, but they were soon released after a reported fifty boatloads of black Bahamians surrounded the *Creole* and threatened to free them by force. In a letter to the British governor, Francis Cockburn, the U.S. Consul John Bacon explained that upon boarding the *Creole* "I saw a large collection of persons on the shore nearest the vessel, and many in boats; and was, at the same time, informed that the moment the troops be withdrawn from the brig, an attempt would be made to board her by force."[71] The *Creole* was allowed to continue its journey on December 2, 1841, minus its slave cargo. Southern slaveholders were understandably peeved about the loss of their property as well as British intervention in an American affair—an unease shared by many other Americans who had not forgotten from whom they had won their independence, followed by frequent meddlesome actions on the high seas. In contrast, abolitionists were enthused over the actions of the British in supporting emancipation, while Madison Washington became an antislavery movement hero.[72] The key point to bear in mind is that these U.S. slaves were inspired by the example of British West Indies Emancipation, and black Bahamians supported their freedom-seeking efforts en masse.

Over the course of the 1840s and 1850s, abolitionists, antislavery activists, and self-emancipated slaves, especially in the northern United States, paraded the example of British abolition annually every August 1 across the Anglo-Atlantic world. What began as a small church thanksgiving service quickly blossomed into a major public event celebrating abolition in the British Caribbean in the past as well as mobilizing for the future termination of U.S. slavery. Large crowds would parade through the main streets of villages, towns, and cities, often led by brass bands, and accompanied from the late 1840s onwards by armed companies of black soldiers. After the parade, there would often be a repast and even a dance followed by speechifying by major abolitionist figures.

Funds were raised; self-emancipators were called upon to address the crowd; and propaganda against the evils of U.S. slavery was dished out in plentiful and colorful form. These annual events became known variously as West Indies Day, Emancipation Day, and August First Day, and were to become essential commemorative and mobilization events in the antislavery calendar between the late 1830s and early 1860s.[73]

These annual commemorative events were usually climaxed by a stirring antislavery speech by prominent activists designed to invigorate the ground troops for the grand struggle. During the 1850s, West India Emancipation events became much more organized and militant, reflecting the increasing regional polarization around the issue of slavery as well as preparation for more militant ways of abolishing the institution. This was reflected in the speeches. In August 1857, former slave and prominent abolitionist Frederick Douglass spoke at Canandaigua, New York. He discussed the changing times, the reasons for the commemorative event, and its importance. He also believed that West Indies Emancipation was the result of the hard work of "saints," "God," and the "British government."[74] "Nevertheless," Douglass added, "a share of the credit of the result falls justly to the slaves themselves." "They did not hug their chains," but "swelled the general protest against oppression." "What Wilberforce was endeavoring to win from the British Senate by his magic eloquence," thundered Douglass, "the Slaves themselves were endeavoring to gain by outbreaks and violence."[75] Moreover, while some may dispute the strategic effect of revolt for abolition, he concluded that the "answer is that abolition followed close on the heels of insurrection in the West Indies, and Virginia was never nearer emancipation than when General [Nat] Turner kindled the fires of insurrection at Southampton."[76] In other words, Douglass used the past commemoration of West Indies Emancipation in upstate New York to remind his listeners of the role of slave revolt in bringing about emancipation in the Caribbean. One can only speculate on the implications of Douglass's message for ending U.S. slavery, especially since he refused to join John Brown in his subsequent attempt to start a slave rebellion in the southern states at the federal arsenal of Harpers Ferry, Virginia, two years later in October 1859.

One year after Douglass's speech, visiting Methodist missionary Henry Bleby from Barbados addressed an August First Day gathering at the celebration of the Massachusetts Anti-Slavery Society, Island Grove, Abington, Massachusetts. He issued a trenchant statement linking slave revolt and abolition cross-nationally. Bleby told his audience he was an "eye witness" to the 1831–32 Jamaica insurrection that constituted "one of the principal events which hastened on the crisis of the movement for West Indian Emancipation, and constrained the British government to 'let the oppressed go free.'"[77] Slave and Baptist deacon Samuel Sharpe, who led the revolt, had "a mind worthy of any man" and "oratorical powers of no common order."[78] He was followed by around 50,000 slaves who engaged in the "insurrection" at Christmas, "claimed their rights as British subjects, and as free men, refusing to go to work on any terms, except on payment of their proper wages as free workmen."[79] The revolt was eventually brutally suppressed. The hanging of Captain Dehany, one of Sharpe's lieutenants, was a picture of "manly courage" that earned applause from the crowd listening to Bleby's speech.[80] About 2,000 slaves were slain, "either shot or hanged in cold blood."[81] The speaker reported seeing one slave shot in the head with the executioner putting his finger in the hole—"That is the kind of freedom we will give you, you black devils."[82] Bleby reported that he had conversed with Sharpe in jail and asked him why he had rebelled. "'Sir,' said he, 'in reading my Bible, I found the white man had no more right to make a slave of me than I had to make a slave of the white man—(applause); and I would rather go out, and die on that gallows, than live a slave' (Loud applause)."[83]

Reverend Bleby's August First Day speech delivered in Massachusetts in 1858 clearly depicts the heroic and noble slave resisting slavery. There is little doubt, for instance, his evocation of slave rebel deaths in Patrick Henry–like terms—give me liberty or give me death—struck a responsive chord with a New England audience conditioned by this kind of revolutionary republican ideology. All this is irrefutable. But Bleby's speech also highlights several links between the British West Indies and the U.S. South. He drew, for example, suggestive parallels between the proslavery press in Britain and the United States. The former "mislead the masses by asserting that the slaves were better off than they would be in freedom, that they were perfectly content with their lot, that they hugged their chains, and that it was, in brief, a condition very little short of the happiness of Paradise."[84] The former image of the happy slave in British proslavery argument was now the centerpiece of southern-planter proslavery ideology. One of Bleby's objectives was to refute this existing U.S. propaganda by drawing attention to the spuriousness of its British counterpart as exposed by the Jamaican slave revolt. Moreover, the climate of the late 1850s was much more rebellious and violent compared to earlier periods of antislavery agitation. For example, Bleby's 1858 speech fell between the 1857 Dred Scott decision and John Brown's raid on Harpers Ferry in 1859, both of which inflamed sectional tensions. What is most intriguing is Bleby's potential comparison. Was he simply suggesting that Jamaican slaves deserved their freedom because of the nobility of their uprising? Or was he implying that mass upheaval and its consequent success in ending British colonial slavery provided an object lesson for slaves and their abolitionist supporters to obtain emancipation in the United States? (Bleby and Douglass are strikingly similar in this regard.) We can ask the same question of Bleby's audience in their responses to his words. Were they applauding "manly resistance" because it resonated with an American tradition of armed struggle for national independence? Or were they acknowledging that armed struggle was now the only viable path to the abolition of slavery and the destruction of the slave power?

This brings us to the question of the impact of British emancipation on slaves in the U.S. South. According to Eugene Genovese, Kentucky ex-slave Lewis Clark "suggested that when the slaves in Kentucky had heard of the emancipation in the British West Indies, they became less militant because they considered their own emancipation a matter of time."[85] We can doubt the commonality of Clark's attitude as well as question the author's main argument that slave revolts in the U.S. South reveal a unique paternal slave mind compared to slaves in other New World slave societies. In contrast, Buckingham's contemporary observation encourages a more dynamic search for possible linkages among slaves between the two regions.

We should acknowledge that most work on slave revolts in the ante-emancipation South was originally produced by a pioneering generation of scholars including W. E. B. Du Bois, Joseph Carroll, Herbert Aptheker, Harvey Wish, Charles Wesley, Raymond and Alice Bauer, Lorenzo Greene, Davidson McKibben, and others, during the 1930s and 1940s.[86] They challenged the prevailing view that slaves hugged their chains by documenting a remarkable range of slave revolts, conspiracies, and various forms of collective and individual resistance in the face of overwhelming odds. Few of these scholars, however, paid much attention to the significance of the *timing* of these slave revolts and conspiracies. Having written a study of annual emancipation commemorations and mobilization in the Black Atlantic world every August from the 1830s through 1860s, I made the new realization on rereading these pioneering works that scores of slave revolts and conspiracies occurred during early August. Some are clearly explainable. Bell Wiley quotes a local Mississippian's view that slave violence and insubordination in Bolivar County, Mississippi, broke out because of the recent withdrawal of a military patrol from the area in August 1863.[87] The timing of many other episodes, however, remains unexplained. One example of English emancipation before U.S. slaves is a slave conspiracy from early August 1841 in the Mississippi Valley with possible Caribbean connections.

On the morning of August 13, 1841, readers of the antislavery newspaper *Herald of Freedom* in Concord, Massachusetts, breakfasted to the byline, "Intended revolt of the Slaves in the South":

> The New Orleans papers of the 23rd contain an account of the discovery of an intended revolt of the slaves in Louisiana and Mississippi, which has produced a great sensation. There was a systematized plan, it is stated, in which the negroes from Bayou Sara to Natchez were combined to rise and murder the whites. This plot, it is said, was accidentally discovered by an overseer who in the night overheard the negroes discussing the subject. This led to their examination next morning, when they confessed the fact, and gave information that led to the arrest of several others. The alarm was immediately spread abroad, arrests were made in various plantations, and it was found by the confessions that they all agreed in the main facts, that there was to be a general rise, and that the first of August was the day agreed upon.[88]

A subsequent letter published in the *New Orleans Picayune* reported that the court trial of the principal witness revealed nothing, the jailed slaves were liberated, and "the insurrection pronounced a humbug." Aptheker notes starkly that this slave plot was crushed in July.[89] McKibben uses this "incident" to exemplify the contradictions of newspaper reportage: sweeping exaggeration of a slave revolt followed by adamant denial.[90]

But this 1841 slave plot in the lower Mississippi Valley raises two other intriguing questions. To what extent was this outbreak part of a longer tradition of slave revolt in the region? A generation later, Union General Benjamin Butler, stationed at New Orleans, reported an "insurrection broke out among the negroes, a few miles up the river," in early August 1862.[91] During the same time, thousands of slaves self-emancipated toward Union lines in southern Louisiana.[92] A generation before the 1841 conspiracy, Charles Deslondes led a slave army on New Orleans.[93] In 1795, fifteen years earlier, a number of slaves had organized a conspiracy to rise and kill their owners at Pointe Coupee in lower Louisiana, of which fifty-seven slaves and three local whites were convicted, and twenty-three slaves hung and decapitated.[94] This suggests a tradition of slave revolt over generations in a coastal region linked to the Caribbean and broader Atlantic world.

Rural people have long memories, as suggested in diverse ways from interviews with American ex-slaves conducted during the 1930s to Edward Thompson's work on eighteenth-century English rural plebian culture.[95] Moreover, we should never underestimate the silence of the official record. My search of the prominent weekly economic journal *De Bow's Review*, based in New Orleans from 1846 through 1869, reveals zero references to slave revolts or conspiracies.[96] Yet we know protest occurred. Lawrence Dunbar, an African American graduate of Fisk University, wrote his doctoral thesis at the University of Chicago documenting at least 158 reports of riot, insurrection, and sedition in New Orleans newspapers between 1850 and 1860.[97] Winthrop Jordan's *Tumult and Silence at Second Creek* is not only a wonderful work of historical detection revealing a major slave plot in the Mississippi Valley that was hushed up by planters and the press for fear of contagion, but also raises the question of how many other slave revolts and plots were hushed up.[98] Indeed, an unlikely source for this tradition of slave revolt can be traced to early twentieth-century fantasy novelist Robert E. Howard of Texas—the author of Conan the Barbarian tales—whose short story "Black Canaan" published in 1936 depicts racial unrest as part of a long series of black uprisings in lower Louisiana.[99] One of the problems with listing slave revolts and conspiracies—apart from Winthrop Jordan's suggestive analogy that attempts to quantify slave whippings is like describing the weather by counting clouds,[100]—is that it ignores the connective tissue between the outbreaks and attempted revolts.[101]

The other important question is why was this 1841 slave plot timed for August 1? One reasonable explanation is that it drew from the "fresh and recent" termination of British colonial slavery in the British West Indies three years earlier in 1838. It is not unlikely that ships, sailors, and passengers both free and enslaved carried abolition news from the Caribbean to New Orleans through the lower Mississippi Valley. Moreover, such news could have been carried from the northern states because the annual public commemoration of West Indies Emancipation by white and black abolitionists was beginning to take off during the early 1840s.[102] Finally, we know that southern planters took very seriously the contagion of British emancipation during this period. This was exemplified in Texas's pursuit of statehood during the early 1840s.

We do not have time to narrate this intriguing story,[103] but the issue was succinctly put in a letter from Abel P. Upshur, U.S. secretary of state, to John C. Calhoun, South Carolina planter and future secretary of state, dated August 14, 1843: "There can be no doubt, I think, that England is determined to abolish slavery throughout the American continent and islands if she can. It is worse than childish to suppose that she meditates this great movement, simply from the impulse of philanthropy. . . . I can find no other motive than a desire to find or create markets for her surplus manufactures, and to destroy all competition with the laborers of her colonies. . . . The present attempt upon Texas is the beginning of her operations upon us."[104] Behind this comment lurk fresh fears about Britain seeking to win back its former colonies, the unrivaled sea power of the former colonial master, global free market domination by London, and the troublesome spread of slave emancipation into the plantation South. The previous year, David Turnbull, former British consul to Cuba and abolitionist, was expelled by the Spanish colonial authorities, accused of supplying arms and munitions to rebels and slaves during *La Escalera* (the Ladder), so-named after the instrument of torture for implicated slaves. This massive slave conspiracy that gripped the Spanish colony during the early 1840s occurred just two hundred miles southeast of the soon-to-be southern slaveholding state of Florida.[105]

IV. THEIR OWN NORTHERN STATES

An older historical literature on the early U.S. national period once argued that northern states quickly terminated the institution of slavery in the aftermath of the successful revolutionary war of independence. The reasons included the economic unfeasibility of slave-based agricultural production, the rhetorical impact of natural rights ideology, and Christian-based antislavery activism.[106] It is now more popular to argue that slavery ended gradually in the northern states over a long period of time and that the timetable of its demise varied according to region.[107] Vermont's constitution of 1777 was the first in the United States to outlaw slavery. It stipulated, however, that both the native-born and foreign-born "servant, slave or apprentice" must serve until twenty-one if male and eighteen if female.[108] Although slavery ended in New England during the revolutionary era, there were still examples of legally held slaves reported from Connecticut during the 1850s. Moreover, slavery died a slow death in the Middle Atlantic region. In 1810, New York and New Jersey contained more than 90 percent of the 27,081 slaves in all northern states.[109] The reasons for this delayed action had to do with the entrenched nature of the institution in the Middle Atlantic region compared to New England, especially the political organization of slaveholding interests concerned with the protection of private property. Although this revisionist view is more persuasive than its predecessor, the key point for our purposes is that southern slaves associated the northern states with liberty and abolition regardless of the speed or gradualness of slavery's termination, as well as the protracted methods by which it was ended.

Over the course of the next two generations, as southern slavery expanded into the southwest territories, the free-soil North expanded into the northwest regions. The new western states of Ohio, Indiana, and Illinois outlawed slavery in their constitutions in 1802, 1816, and 1818 respectively.[110] The 1820 Missouri Compromise added Maine to the Union as a free state. During the 1820s, Pennsylvania legislated against federal laws of fugitive return, making it harder for slaveholders to recover runaway slaves from the state.[111] In the aftermath of the 1842 U.S. Supreme Court ruling in *Prig vs. Pennsylvania* that the state's legal protection of free blacks from kidnapping contradicted the federal fugitive slave law of 1793, the Massachusetts state legislature passed the Personal Liberty Act of 1843 that prohibited state officials' compliance with federal fugitive slave laws. Personal liberty laws were subsequently passed by several other northern states including New Hampshire, Connecticut, Rhode Island, Pennsylvania, and Vermont.[112] It is doubtful if slaves cared much about the irony of southern states claiming federal privilege while northern states invoked states' rights. What inspired them was northern states' legislative action that increasingly demonstrated an antipathy to southern slavery and an unshakable commitment toward abolition.

No less inspiring was the emergence of the abolitionist movement in northern states from the early 1830s onwards. It included antislavery newspapers like *The Liberator* (Boston), *Emancipator* (New York City), *Freedom's Journal* (New York City), *Colored American* (New York City), *Anti-Slavery Bugle* (Salem, Ohio), *Frederick Douglass' Paper* (Rochester, New York), *Herald of Freedom* (Concord, Massachusetts), *National Anti-Slavery Standard* (New York City), and *Christian Recorder* (Philadelphia), among others. It included local and state antislavery organizations like the New England Anti-Slavery Society, formed in 1832 in Boston and growing within a year to several thousand members, and a dozen local branches, together with national antislavery organizations such as the American Antislavery Society with sixty-three delegates from ten states formed in Philadelphia in 1833, with its sweeping "Declaration of Sentiments."[113] It included scores of antislavery picnics held every August 1 in the groves, public halls, and public spaces of Massachusetts, northern Indiana, eastern Michigan, upstate New York, and Ohio's western reserve, from the early 1840s onwards. Thousands attended the antislavery picnic at Tranquility Grove, Hingham, outside of Boston in early August 1844, where they paraded under banners, listened to speeches, sang songs, raised funds, and partook of a hearty repast.[114] It included an array of celebrity abolitionists like William Lloyd Garrison, Charles and Lewis Tappan, Wendell Phillips, Frederick Douglass, Charles L. Remond, Samuel J. May, Sojourner Truth, Charles C. Burleigh, Samuel R. Ward, Maria Stewart, Henry H. Garnet, James L. Loguen, and others. It included a series of slavery causes célèbres such as the *Amistad* (1839), the *Creole* (1841), the *Pearl* affair (1848), the *Christiana* resistance (1851), fugitive Thomas Sims's return from Boston (1851), fugitive Jerry McHenry's escape to Canada (1851), fugitive Anthony Burns's arrest in Boston (1854), John Anderson's case (1860–61), and others. Historian Thomas Campbell estimates 156 fugitive slave cases involving around 300 slaves during the 1850s, while the Hortons calculate more than 80 well-publicized fugitive slave rescues and attempted rescues.[115] Many of these fugitive slaves were returned to slavery, while the abolitionist movement was small, isolated, and often factionalized. Still, this protest movement occupied a vital niche in the civil society of the antebellum North for more than a generation. The vital question is the extent to which this parade of northern exertions for abolition affected southern slaves.

It is not unreasonable to argue that southern slaves might have remained oblivious to all of these state laws and civil society actions throughout the antebellum northern and western regions. Fergus Bordewich points to the isolation and unawareness of southern slaves. The making of the U.S. antislavery movement during the 1830s occurred, he argues, "far beyond the narrowly circumscribed awareness of slaves isolated on Southern plantations."[116] And later he notes fugitives were mostly "woefully ignorant of what lay to the north."[117] But there is much evidence to question the validity of this assessment. Richard Newman's recent detailed study of the voluminous files of the Pennsylvania Abolition Society argues that, within a decade of the passage of Pennsylvania's Abolition Act in 1780, "both enslaved people and free blacks alike began envisioning Pennsylvania as a haven from slaveholders' national power."[118] White and black mariners circulated Walker's *Appeal to the Colored Citizens of the World* to slaves and free blacks in Savannah, Richmond, Charleston, and New

Orleans in 1829 and 1830. In August 1830, slave Jacob Cowan received two hundred copies from Walker with instructions to distribute them throughout the state. Later that same year, self-emancipated slaves were captured with copies in their pockets.[119] They surely were aware of external radical abolitionist exertions even though these never resulted in a revolutionary overthrow of southern slavery.

Moreover, slave narratives revealed that self-liberated slaves knew a great deal about freedom during their previous enslavement. Austin Steward wrote: "The more we knew of freedom, the more we desired it." Although Jim Pembroke, later known as the Reverend James Pennington, did not know the exact demarcation between slave and free soil, his direction was clear. "My only guide was the *north star*," he wrote, "by this I knew my general course northward, but at what point I should strike Penn, or when and where I should find a friend I knew not." Fugitive Jarm Logue learned in conversation that "All the negroes are free in Illinois—they don't have any slaves there."[120]

But perhaps the most powerful evidence for this awareness is that slaves kept taking off for these northern and western states in large numbers. We will never know the full extent of slaves' self-emancipation because of its clandestine nature. There are, however, some useful indicators of its proportions. David Ruggles's Committee of Vigilance, based in New York City, claims to have assisted 1,675 fugitive slaves in successfully escaping to freedom between the late 1830s through 1843, with 5,000 in total attempting to escape.[121] During the mid-1850s, the black Committee of Nine in Cleveland, Ohio, passed on 275 fugitive slaves to Canada, while the Detroit Vigilance Committee reported passing along 1,043 fugitive slaves. Thomas Garrett, Underground Railroad stationmaster at Wilmington, Delaware, claims to have assisted 2,750 slaves to freedom from the 1820s through 1860.[122] William Still is reported to have assisted around 900 escapees through Pennsylvania to Canada during the 1850s.[123] All we can say with some degree of certainty is that slaves self-emancipated themselves at a rate of at least 1,000 a year during the first three decades of the nineteenth century; that this number increased significantly with the formation of the abolitionist movement and the Underground Railroad from the 1830s onwards, climaxing to a much higher number per year by the 1850s, especially from the slaves states in the Upper South; and that these self-liberators were attracted to the North and West because of their association with liberty and abolition. Most important, these states delineated clear borders between slavery and freedom for self-emancipators.

Emancipation inspired slaves to act for freedom across borders in colonies, nations, and federal states. It expanded the temporal and spatial dimensions of the English abolitionist's schema. It also offered a more labile definition of revolt across borders. But there is one other brief consideration: to what extent did these examples have a cumulative impact, or, in Buckingham's terms, "increase the general *desire* to be free"?

In contrast to an older historiography, it is now firmly established that slaves wanted their freedom. Indeed, without this original impulse, these external forces would not have had much of an impact. In other words, slave revolts across borders "inspired" rather than created a general desire to be free. Moreover, this inspiration was multifaceted and prolonged. It drew from a variety of sources including slave revolts, free soil, free water, and state-sponsored abolitions over a long period of time. This was different from the impact of the French Revolution and Enlightenment ideas proposed by some scholars of slave revolts.[124] Finally, slave revolt across borders throughout the nineteenth century was cumulative in the sense that state crises frequently afforded opportunities for freedom. In other words, the mother of emancipation was fertile *between* as well as during wars of national liberation, civil war, and abolition.

The topic of slave revolt across borders is significant for several reasons. First, it demonstrates how slaves exploited the contradictions of slave and free soil on land and over water. Their actions point to pores in slave systems that might well have encouraged legal emancipation, especially in the Caribbean after the Haitian Revolution and British colonial emancipation. Second, Buckingham's "English" example suggests that slaves continued to be inspired by examples of abolition beyond the Age of Revolution as well as the Francophone Atlantic. At the same time, we must be careful not to exaggerate favorable connections between slaves seeking freedom and a British empire committed to legal emancipation after the 1830s.[125] British imperial liberties did not always match the ideals projected by traveling antislavery activists like Samuel Ward (see chapter 4, below). Third, slave revolt across borders contributed to imagined communities based upon common racial identity. When black Bahamians surrounded the *Creole* ship demanding the release of its incarcerated slave rebels and the emancipation of all other slaves, this was the politics of racial solidarity in action. An even more striking example was when the Haitian state protected escaped slaves, and insisted on their inviolable rights in the international arena. In contrast to some recent commentators who claim that such actions portended a modern human rights agenda born out of the eighteenth-century Enlightenment project, the argument here is that movement toward and protection of ex-slaves' freedom constituted a black beacon of anti-Enlightenment functioning as a flawed but significant historical counterpoint to modernity.[126]

Fourth, slave revolt across borders throughout the nineteenth century provides scholars with a more expansive understanding of the familiar notion that state crises frequently afforded opportunities for freedom. Fifth, it contributes to slave-revolt historiography. Older debates contrasting conservative maroons with revolting slaves, the paucity/infrequency of revolts in the U.S. South and Brazil compared to the Caribbean, the Haitian Revolution as a demarcation between rebellion and revolution, and so forth, are rightly being replaced by more detailed studies of individual revolts,[127] the role of African veterans in revolts,[128] and the cross-national dimensions of slave rebellions. Finally, the study of slave revolt across borders contributes to the conceptualization of emancipation and the African Diaspora with its focus on movement, homelands, and racial solidarity.

By the time of Buckingham's death in 1855, slavery had been abolished in several places in the Americas, including the French West Indies (1848), the Danish West Indies (1848), Ecuador (1851), Columbia (1852), Argentina (1853), Peru (1854), and Venezuela (1854). It took a bloody civil war to destroy the institution of American slavery a decade later in 1865. Only future research will reveal the extent to which other examples of abolition inspired slaves outside of their borders, and the consequences.

PART TWO
LIVES

Samuel Ward and the Making of an Imperial Subject

The boast of the Englishman, of their freedom from social negrophobia, is about as empty as the Yankee boast of democracy.
—SAMUEL R. WARD, 1851

Who wonders that we are among the most loyal of Her Majesty's subjects.
—SAMUEL R. WARD 1855

Had Republican America remained a colony of Great Britain, the firs[t] to August, 1834, would have emancipated every slave, and made us a nation of FREEMEN.
—*THE COLORED AMERICAN*, August 5, 1837

The American-born fugitive and prominent antislavery activist Samuel Ringgold Ward spent fifteen of his forty-nine years in Canada, the United Kingdom, and Jamaica. The significance of spending nearly one-third of his life on British soil removed from his native country, however, has attracted limited scholarly comment. These years and places are usually interpreted in one of three ways: exile from the United States, new vineyards for "Christ-like labors," or as masonry for the wall around U.S. slavery.[1]

In contrast, this chapter examines Ward's antislavery labors in Canada, the United Kingdom, and Jamaica between 1851 and 1866. It demonstrates the ways in which Ward was transformed into an imperial subject through the pursuit of personal and race-based liberty. This transformation is explained in four ways: Ward's physical relocation from unfree to free soil, his advocacy of legal equality for all people regardless of racial origin, his calls for emigration to the British Empire, and his commitment to the spread of Pan-African evangelical Christianity. The documentary evidence draws primarily from Ward's *Autobiography of a Fugitive Negro* published by John Snow in London in 1855. Although Ward's *Autobiography* resembled the form, function, and utility of many slave narratives, it was marked by one key difference: it was written by one who had spent some four years prior to publication living and working

within the British Empire and who used this knowledge to authenticate imperial liberties.[2] Samuel Ward's speeches and letters, together with newspaper
articles in the U.S., Canadian, and British press, are examined for details of
the last decade of his life in Jamaica from 1855 through 1866 not covered by
his *Autobiography*. Apart from providing the first critical evaluation of Ward's
transatlantic antislavery labors *in extenso*, this chapter further seeks to expand
the conventional nationalist framework (American, African American) of the
slave narrative.[3] Moreover, it transcends existing evaluations of traveling black
abolitionists beyond the notion of visiting other countries for fund-raising,
antislavery mobilization, and building diplomatic pressure on the United
States—the so-called abolitionists' "liberating sojourn." Its most urgent task
is to reveal the contradictions between liberty and empire, a tension that is
unfortunately overlooked in some recent historical literature.[4]

There are three current interpretations of Ward's relationship to Britain.
Some have dismissed the views of traveling black abolitionists like Ward,
Josiah Henson, and Frederick Douglass for becoming "almost intoxicated"
by their social mobility and acceptability in British social circles.[5] It is true
that Ward's *Autobiography* was full of laudatory praise for reforming lords
and ladies, but why should we find this strange given the necessity of woo-
ing a powerful constituency to the U.S. antislavery cause? Besides, Ward also
praised "the peasant" (English, Irish, and Scottish rural laborers) as well as
"the prince" (reforming aristocrats like lords Shaftsbury and Brougham) for
their "chord of sympathy" for his "suffering people."[6] A second interpretation
of Ward's relationship to Britain is that his consistent praise for the Empire
was never authentic; it was just a clever way of ingratiating himself with powerful patrons in order to achieve his aim of persuading Great Britain to pressure the United States into terminating slavery. One problem with this view
is that it fails to appreciate the historical specificity of antislavery struggles in
the Anglo-Atlantic world in which Ward and others were embroiled. A more
serious limitation is its imposition of an unchanging one-dimensional political
identity. In other words, black leaders are "authentic" when addressing black
people, but only clever strategists when dealing with whites. The reverse is
equally valid. Samuel Ward's attraction is that his multifaceted political agenda
within an imperial polity transcends such facile racial categorization.

Finally, a recent work has argued that Ward and other black abolitionists
who visited the United Kingdom were Anglophiles. Their fascination with
England, argues Elisa Tamarkin, "was part of a much larger cultural forma-

tion in American life." Samuel Ward, being the "'most loyal of her subjects'" continues Tamarkin, exemplified devotion to the English in texts produced by American writers.[7] This view fails on several fronts. It makes Ward an "American," but his movement within imperial circuits connecting Canada, Britain, and Jamaica defined his adult political life. Moreover, Ward was a political activist determined to end U.S. slavery, not some alienated American intellectual trying to work out his identity in the United Kingdom. Most importantly, Ward turned his back on his native land in contrast to many U.S. writers, including authors of prominent slave narratives such as Frederick Douglass.

A deeper documentary excavation of Ward and his times is warranted to refute superficial interpretations of Ward as a sycophant, nationalist, or Anglophile. Moreover, a wide range of historical evidence reveals fascinating contradictions rather than icing the cake of a pre-existing position—dupe, strategist, alienated American. Ward's fifteen years abroad were less exceptional than formative in making his transnational life and labors.

I. MOVIN'

Samuel Ringgold Ward was born a slave on October 17, 1817, on the eastern shore of Maryland.[8] He was the second of three boys born to slave parents Ann and William Ward. Under threat of sale, the family escaped to Greenwich, New Jersey, in 1820. After six years, fears of slave-catchers and kidnappers prompted the Ward family to relocate to the greater anonymity promised by New York City. These fears were serious enough for Ann to keep her son Samuel ignorant of his slave birth for many years. In a confidential letter to prominent abolitionist Gerrit Smith, Ward disclosed that "his mother placed facts in the possession of my wife" about his birth during the summer of 1842.[9] Ward attended New York's African Free School, a benevolent institution for the moral uplift of Africans founded in 1789 by the New York Manumission Society, after which time he was briefly employed by black activists Thomas L. Jennings and David Ruggles.[10] In 1835, Ward moved to Newark, New Jersey, where he taught school for several years. On August 1, 1838, Ward addressed a prayer meeting at the Colored Methodist Church in Newark commemorating emancipation in the British West Indies colonies.[11] Ward married Emily Reynoldson, and they had a son also named Samuel Ringgold. In May 1839, Ward obtained his license to preach in the New York Congregational Association. Over the next decade, Ward became a prominent minister in New York State. He preached to white congregations in South Butler from 1841 to 1843 and then in Cortland from 1846 to 1851. Ward's antislavery zeal got him appointed agent for the American Anti-Slavery Society in 1839. When it split the following year, he went with the American and Foreign Anti-Slavery Society. Ward was often critical of the limited anti-racist agenda of white abolitionists. Ward voiced his criticism in an 1840 letter to an antislavery newspaper editor about "too many Abolitionists" who "best love the colored man at a distance."[12] Furthermore, his belief in the limits of moral suasion and the need to propagate abolition resulted in his becoming a prominent campaigner for the Liberty Party, the nation's first antislavery political party, during the 1840s. Between 1849 and 1851, Ward edited the party's newspaper, the *Impartial Citizen*, from Syracuse, New York, a semimonthly concerned with antislavery, temperance, and reform movements. He also joined the Syracuse Vigilance Committee. It was in this capacity that Ward was to clash head-on with the national expansion of U.S. slavery that drove him across the border into British Canada.

The continental expansion of the American Empire brought with it the spread of slavery and demands for federal protection of personal property, especially fugitive slaves. On September 18, 1850, the Fugitive Slave Act received presidential approval. In legal terms, it provided federal protection for the pursuit, capture, and return of southern slaveholders' chattel. In human terms, it further betokened a legal assault on the pursuit of freedom by slaves in southern states, posed a massive new threat to self-liberators living in northern and western free states, and increased the potential for kidnapping those people of African descent who had been born free. In essence, it confirmed slavery as a U.S. institution.

In a speech on the impending bill delivered at the famous reform meeting place of Faneuil Hall, Boston, on March 25, 1850, Ward vigorously condemned slavery's national expansion betokened by the Fugitive Slave Act. He praised the antislavery sentiments of New York Senator William H. Seward, whose politics he did not share, "but when an individual stands up for the rights of men against the slaveholders, I care not for party distinctions. He is my brother."[13] At the same time, he expressed disgust with those northern supporters of the bill who "lick up the spittle of the slavocrats, and swear it is delicious."[14] This bill must be opposed at all costs, he continued, and such "crises as these leave us to the right of Revolution, and if need be, that right we will, at whatever cost, most sacredly maintain."[15] Seventeen months after delivering this speech, Ward enacted his own "right of Revolution" by helping fugitive William "Jerry" McHenry escape from Syracuse, New York, across the border to Canada West in violation of the recently passed Fugitive Slave Act.[16] Facing the risk of arrest and incarceration, Ward fled to Canada, colonized by the British since 1763, and free soil since the legal termination of colonial slavery in 1833. "I went," he explained, "and a month or two after, my family followed: since which time we have each and severally been, *con amore*, the most loyal and grateful of British subjects."[17]

The abolition of British colonial slavery encouraged others to relocate to its liberty-granting domains. In 1842, the American and British governments signed the Webster-Ashburton treaty, "consenting to none of th[o]se propositions" to extradite fugitives in Canada back to their former slaveholders in the United States.[18] Although former slaves had been relocating to British Canada since the late eighteenth century, their numbers increased after the legal abolition of colonial slavery during the early 1830s and the refusal of the British government to accede to southern slaveholder demands. The majority of Canada's "35,000 to 40,000 coloured people," Ward explained in his *Autobiography*, were "refugees from American slavery."[19] Their journeys were often difficult. Fugitive slave Andrew Jackson fought off five slave catchers with the aid of a hickory stick.[20] Upon boarding a ferry to cross into Canada, an unnamed fugitive was accosted by his former slave-owner who told the ferryman he would blow his brains out if he sailed. The fugitive seized a handspike and, "holding it menacingly over the ferryman's head, said, 'If you don't loose the boat and ferry me across, I'll *beat* your brains out.'" The ferryman obeyed the fugitive, who "sprang from the boat to the shore" and, "rising, took off his poor old hat, and gave three cheers for the British sovereign."[21]

After joining the Canadian Anti-Slavery Society and becoming one of its most successful agents, Ward was dispatched to the United Kingdom in April 1853 to "plead in behalf of my crushed countrymen in America, and the freed men of Canada."[22] He embarked from New York City because of "the risk of being apprehended by the United States' authorities for a breach of their execrable republican Fugitive Slave Law."[23] Over the next thirty months, Ward traveled extensively throughout England, Scotland, Ireland, and Wales. He described Great Britain as "a land of freedom, of true equality."[24] "I am here on this platform," he told an audience of the English Sunday School Union in London, "and elsewhere in the British Empire, just because it is not safe for me to be in my native country."[25] He pursued a variety of antislavery labors including preaching, lecturing, writing, and fund-raising. After ten months of this work, he had raised 1,200 pounds sterling (nearly $150,000 today) for the Canadian Anti-Slavery Society.[26] In late 1855, Ward left Great Britain and instead of returning to Toronto, Canada—his domicile according to the frontispiece of his *Autobiography*—he relocated to Jamaica, colonized by the British in 1655 and just entering its third post-emancipation decade. This was where he spent the remaining ten years of his life, preaching the word of God to freedom's first generation and espousing the advantages of settlement in the British Empire.

II. LEGAL EQUALITY?

As important as Ward's antislavery labors was his advocacy of post-emancipation citizenship and equal rights under the law. Although "Negro-hate" was prevalent in both the United States and Canada, Ward insisted on a crucial distinction between the republic and the colony. In the United States, he wrote, discrimination "is sanctioned by the laws and the courts, [while in Canada it] is not."[27] He claimed not to care too much about being excluded from the white man's table since "in many cases I would not reciprocate it."[28] Indeed, Ward projected quite an independent spirit. "I did not feel as some blacks say they felt," he wrote, "upon landing [in the United Kingdom]—that I was, for the first time in my life, a man. No, I always felt that; however wronged, maltreated, outraged—still a man."[29] Compare these words with the reaction of former slave and abolitionist Moses Roper upon reaching Liverpool in 1835: "my feelings when I first touched the shores of Britain were indescribable, and can only be properly understood by those who have escaped from the cruel bondage of slavery."[30]

What was crucial as far as Ward was concerned was equality under the law. "Happily for us," Ward writes, "we have equal laws in our adopted country [Canada]; and I know of no judge who would sully the British ermine by swerving from duty at the bidding of prejudice."[31] As an agent for the Canadian Anti-Slavery Society visiting the United Kingdom, he spoke on behalf of the rights of freedmen of Canada as well as slaves in the United States.[32] In the United States, he could not visit the capital of the nation because it was "slave-holding territory," and he might be fined, flogged, or arrested. But he was free to move about in London, had visited the "British senate" [House of Lords] with a personal invitation, and witnessed the passage of benevolent law for "the suppression and prevention of crime." "Who can blame a Negro for loving Great Britain?" he wrote; "[w]ho wonders that we are among the most loyal of Her Majesty's subjects?"[33] Wrapped in the protective mantle of imperial ermine, Ward was espousing equal rights under the law for all colonial subjects. Together with physical relocation, the pursuit of equality under the law in the British Empire—compared to its absence in the expanding U.S. Empire—was another aspect of Ward's transformation into an imperial subject.

This imperial vision of liberty under the law, however, was also short-sighted. Although Ward rarely missed an opportunity to sing the praises of liberty and equality under the Lion's paw, he appears to have ignored the plight and neglect of innumerable colonial subjects. He toured rural Ireland twice—in September 1854 and June 1855—only several years after the Great Potato Famine had claimed a minimum of 750,000 Irish lives between 1845 and 1849. Not only was his *Autobiography* mute on this terrible consequence of colonial abnegation; his writings make it unlikely that he would have attributed its causes—as well as the abject rural poverty that shocked him so—to the irresponsibility of British imperial stewardship.[34] Was Ward avoiding comment on a controversial subject in the name of what he considered to be his greater duty of soliciting British help to terminate American slavery? According to one recent scholar, Frederick Douglass's silence on the Great Famine during his travels to Ireland was due to a combination of "Atlantic ethical culture" and American "political identity in a transnational context."[35] This explanation might work for Douglass, but not for Ward, who expressed little American political identity in his work and writings by the 1850s.

Two decades after the Great Potato Famine, and one decade after Ward's relocation to Jamaica, Afro-Jamaicans exercised their "right to Revolution" at Morant Bay in October 1865. Baptist deacon Paul Bogle led about 400 black protestors in a battle after which 18 colonial officials and militiamen were killed and 31 injured. The colonial governor, Edward John Eyre, quickly mobilized the military and disaffected Maroons in eastern Jamaica, resulting in the suppression of the uprising and the deaths of over 400 Jamaicans, the flogging of 600 participants, and the destruction of a thousand homes. The draconian measures pursued by the governor of Jamaica resulted in his dismissal and the reversion of the colony to control by the British Crown after nearly three centuries of local governance. At the same time, the uprising reflected the extent to which some of freedom's first generation in western Jamaica continued to suffer from poor soil, poverty wages, and general deprivation.[36] These colonial subjects were far from content with their imperial liberties.

The forty-eight-year-old Samuel Ward—now resident in Saint Thomas-in-the-East—wrote a response to the 1865 rebellion called *Reflections Upon the Gordon Rebellion*, published in February 1866.[37] He offered this eight-page pamphlet as "a correct account" of "this most diabolical affair."[38] Ward condemned the "wanton and wicked outrage" of the revolt, as well as the "hellish designs" of the mob beyond Morant Bay.[39] But the real culprit in Ward's account was ex-slave, merchant, and assemblyman Mr. Gordon. "The origin of the Jamaica Rebellion of October 1865," declared Ward, "was nothing more nor less than the seditious and treasonable teachings of George William Gordon and his subalterns."[40] Furthermore, Ward defended the draconian actions of Jamaican Governor Eyre (who was subsequently recalled to London), arguing that undue severity had not been exercised in the suppression of the revolt because the "safety of the whole island as to property, order and life was endangered."[41] In short, blame for the "diabolical affair" rested "upon a mulatto and his confreres" not "semi-savage negroes as Paul Bogle."[42] The moral that Ward drew from the "Gordon Rebellion" was a paean to black loyalty to the British Empire: "if the black people of all grades, will cease once, and for ever, to follow bad mulatto leadership, to disloyalty, to the gallows, and to perdition, our beloved country [Jamaica] will remain quiet, and loyal, and peaceable."[43]

Had Samuel Ward changed his mind concerning the "right of Revolution" since his own physical actions during the "Jerry" rescue in Syracuse? Or was he convinced that mass expressions of Jamaican discontent would have fared better under his own leadership? Did Ward shift from a potential Toussaint in 1851 to a civilizing agent in 1866? These questions are impossible to answer with certainty because of the lack of evidence concerning the last decade of Ward's life in Jamaica. (We still do not know the whereabouts of his grave.) It is possible that Ward's opposition toward Gordon was partly fueled by intraracial tensions between lighter and darker leaders of African descent.[44] What is more certain is that Ward's 1866 pamphlet reflects the mind of a seasoned colonial loyalist who opposed ruffling imperial feathers. Throughout its eight pages, there is constant reference to the issue of "loyalty" to the British Empire, while nowhere is imperial stewardship ever seriously challenged. Indeed, such was Ward's commitment to the civilizing potential of the British Empire that there is little doubt that he would have approved of the new Crown status for Jamaica in 1866 even though he never lived to see it in operation.

Moreover, like other black abolitionist travelers to Great Britain such as Frederick Douglass, James Pennington, and Harriet Jacobs, Ward's own positive experiences led him to extrapolate that, unlike the United States, "anti-Negro hate" was absent from Britain and Europe more generally. In doing so, he overlooked the racial challenges facing domiciled people of African descent.[45] Ward's writings are conspicuously silent on marginalized groups in British ports, towns, and cities, where numerous people of African origin lived and worked.[46] Although more research beckons, the disproportionate representation of Irish Catholics and people of African descent in the ranks of the working poor suggests second-class citizenship because of religious and racial exclusion.[47] Paul Gilroy's 1987 publication 'There Ain't No Black in the Union Jack' critiquing racial and cultural oppression in 1970s Britain reminds us of its longevity.[48] This would have disappointed past advocates of post-emancipation legal equality like Ward.

III. CANAAN

As an immigrant who moved freely throughout the British Empire, Ward embraced his new home of Canada. On several occasions, he referred fondly to his adopted domicile. It was a "great moral lighthouse for the black people, free and enslaved, on this continent."[49] His identity as a British subject emerged from the fact "that that country [Canada] had become to me, in a sense in which no country ever was before, my own, and those people my fellow citizens."[50] He also promoted his new home for future settlement. "The banks of the St. Lawrence are cultivated to a considerable extent," he remarked, "and that cultivation both bespeaks the industry and the enterprise of the yeoman, and the profit of living on the great watery highway to the ocean, and near to large and populous growing towns." Samuel Ward was not alone in promoting the virtues of emigration to Canada. Henry Bibb, a fugitive slave from Kentucky who settled in Sandwich, started the Voice of the Fugitive in 1851, a bimonthly newspaper calling for the abolition of U.S. slavery, as well as temperance, educational reform, agricultural development, and black immigration to Canada.[51] The same year that Bibb began his newspaper saw the publication of A Plea for Emigration or, Notes of Canada West by Mary Ann Shadd, a free-born journalist and educator from Wilmington, Delaware, who eventually settled in Chatham, Canada West.[52]

While in the United Kingdom, Ward supported the economic development of the colonies. At an antislavery meeting convened at Castle Inn, Woodford, Essex, he "showed how, by developing the resources of our East and West-India Colonies, and by promoting the cultivation of cotton there, in Africa, Australia, and elsewhere, and thus augmenting the supply of free-labour staples, slave-holders would eventually be thrust out of the markets of the world by the more successful enterprises of free labour."[53] He also called for the emigration of free blacks and fugitive slaves to Jamaica. He told a Boston, Lincolnshire, audience about a fund-raising plan to "establish sugar and cotton plantations" in Jamaica to compete with slave-grown crops in America.[54] In early May 1858, Ward told a meeting in Kingston, Jamaica, that "the excellence of the climate, the rich and varied productions of the soil, the abundance of unoccupied land, and its social and political condition" promised equal opportunities for "a comfortable and respectable position in life, under free institutions . . . conferring the equal rights and privileges of British subjects."[55]

At the heart of Ward's promotion of imperial immigration was the freedom to farm independently. When the Ward family left the United States for Canada, they desired to "purchase a little hut and garden, and pass the remainder of our days in peace, in a free British country."[56] Along with a pleasant climate and bounteous soils, the "land is so excellent" because of its access to "the best markets" and it "is so cheap." "The Government sells the best lands in the country at six to eight shillings the acre, and allows ten years' credit at annual payments."[57] Moreover, black settlements like Dawn, Canada West, pioneered by those "who dared the perils of flight," were proving their worth. "The outlay of a little capital," Ward predicted, "the continuance of such energy as has brought the settlement to its present state, and the yet further increase of that energy . . . will make the 'Dawn,' as it is called, a very flourishing town not many years hence."[58] At the same time, Ward warned that the future prosperity of these settlements was in the hands of freedom's younger generation. Some of "the sons and daughters" of those who fled needed to accomplish more with "the plough and the axe, the scythe and the cradle" outdoors, and with "the needle and its accompaniments" indoors.[59] Thomas Holt estimates that in 1845 over 20 percent (66,000 people) of the former slave populace of Jamaica worked peasant freeholds of up to ten acres.[60] A decade later, Samuel Ward was encouraged to move to Jamaica by the offer of fifty acres in St. George's Parish gifted to him by British Quaker abolitionist John Candler.[61] We should not underestimate his love of the land: early in his *Autobiography* he remarks wistfully that he might have made something more of himself if he had "clung to the use of the hoe, instead of aspiring to a love of books."[62] Thus, the encouragement of emigration by people of African descent to the British Empire represented the third transformation of Ward into an imperial subject.[63]

At the same time, this promotion of imperial immigration contained some serious flaws. Harvey Amani Whitfield has pointed to the poor soils and poor climate and harsh conditions faced by earlier generations of black loyalists in Upper Canada that were replicated among later generations of self-liberators to Canada West.[64] This raises the question: was the British government encouraging emigration as a means to provide a cheap and ready supply of black labor to white farmers with fertile soil but lacking workers? Mary Shadd's biographer concludes that her 1851 *Notes of Canada West* "was an unabashed propaganda tract that exaggerated the benefits of the Canadian haven while ignoring many endemic problems."[65] Shadd's colleague Ward was guilty of similar hyperbole. Although he did not deny some problems of "Pro-slavery feeling" as well as "Negro-hate" in British Canada,[66] one wonders how attractive such an environment would have been to prospective black immigrants. Indeed, how is it possible to reconcile Ward's promotion of equal opportunities for black immigrants to Jamaica with the violent suppression of the popular uprising in 1865 revealing the brutal realities of imperial stewardship?

IV. ETHIOPIA

Samuel Ward's fourth transformation into an imperial subject was through the expanding lens of his religious understanding, especially his embrace of Pan-African evangelical Christianity. In May 1839, Ward obtained his license to preach in the New York Congregational Association. Over the next decade, he became a prominent minister in New York State, pasturing to white congregations in South Butler from 1841 through 1843 and in Cortland from 1846 to 1851.[67] What he described as this unusual "connection" was important for both the antislavery cause and for people of African descent. "If I should acquit myself creditably as a preacher," he explained, "the anti-slavery cause would thereby be encouraged. Should I fail in this, that sacred cause would be loaded with reproach. So, if I were successful or unsuccessful in this charge would *encouragement* or *discouragement* come to the people of colour."[68]

In short, Reverend Ward's tenure as a Congregational preacher in New York State during the 1840s was primarily concerned with local and regional religious duties and antislavery labors. While Ward was preaching to all-white congregations, the biblical verse that "Ethiopia shall stretch forth her hands unto God" assumed a profound importance as evangelical Christianity made its mark on the slave quarters and free households in the Atlantic world from the late eighteenth century onwards.[69] In particular, it became associated with the evangelical conversion experience promoted by black preachers. In his book *Jamaica: Its Past and Present*, published in 1843, English Baptist missionary James Phillippo called for black preachers to spread the word of God throughout Jamaica and beyond as a means to counter the revival of West African–derived Myalism that had reportedly infiltrated Christian places of worship and proved too pervasive for even the most seasoned proselytizers.[70] I don't know if the African American religious leader Alexander Crummell— New York City born, Cambridge University graduate, and Ward's colleague— ever read Phillippo's *Jamaica*, but this remarkable Episcopalian minister spent nearly twenty years of his life spreading the divine message as a missionary in the new nation of Liberia in West Africa before the earthly intervention of a *coup d'état* forced his reluctant return to the United States.[71]

Samuel Ward's cousin—Maryland-born escapee, antislavery activist, and Presbyterian minister Henry Highland Garnet—served as a missionary for the Scottish Presbyterian Church at Sterling, Westmoreland Parish, Jamaica, between 1854 and 1856. There is still some debate about who converted whom: did Garnet bring Christianity to the local people, or did the locals—slaves who had been liberated by British ships from illegal slave traders and dumped in Jamaica to begin life as free people—convert Garnet to a more Afro-centric worldly view?[72] What we do know is that Ward occasionally expressed a recognizable Afro-centric worldview. On August 3, 1852, Ward addressed an audience of more than one hundred black people at a West Indies Emancipation Day commemoration in Toronto, Canada. His main concern was "Who are we colored men?" in the past, present, and future. "The past was secure," he argued because "the acknowledged source of the world's civilization was Africa, was Egypt, was Ethiopia." This was an important statement on the African origins of Western civilization, a theme echoed by numerous contemporaries of Ward.[73] As to the present, Ward referred to travelers' accounts reporting "cities of much elegance and refinement" in Central Africa, as well as quite a list of educated black men in the United States—"lawyers, physicians, clergymen." What was at stake here was proving not only that contemporary Africa was civilized, but also that people of African descent were making a success of their freedom. This was aimed at those defenders of slavery who argued that Africans were fit for nothing but slavery.[74] As for the future, Ward asked his audience: could God have "disciplined this race with captivity and slavery . . . without a purpose"?[75]

In short, Ward stretched forth his hand unto God under the Lion's paw. In mid-July 1854, at the Old Meeting House, St. Clements, in the United Kingdom, Ward told the audience "that it was a cause for thankfulness that God had given to Great Britain such colonies [British Cape, India, etc.], through which we could reach the heathen world."[76] The penultimate page of his *Autobiography of a Fugitive Negro,* published the following year, was just as emphatic: "I am among those who believe that the British colonies are both the agency by which, and the medium through which, the gospel can, ought, *must,* be given to the heathen world."[77] Although there is little extant evidence, it is not unreasonable to assume that preacher Ward functioned as a civilizing agent bringing light to the darkness of poor benighted congregations in Jamaica after the mid-1850s. Just over a century later, during the auspicious dawn of de-colonization, African novelist Chinua Achebe's *Things Fall Apart* offered the most explosive rebuttal to the Reverend Ward's faith in Pan-African evangelical Christianity.[78]

The complexity of Samuel Ringgold Ward as an imperial and imperialist subject—as well as a North American of African provenance—is significant for several reasons. First, it provides us with an alternative way to think about black abolitionists visiting the United Kingdom to build an antislavery wall. Indeed, Ward's physical and political peregrinations within the British Empire contrast markedly with the more famous "liberating sojourn" of Frederick Douglass to the United Kingdom in 1845–46 and 1859. It also differed from the short and long-term missionary proselytism of Henry Garnet to Jamaica and Alexander Crummell to Liberia. Second, this notion of the imperial subject draws our attention to Ward's concern with post-emancipation rights—such as equality under the law, anti-racism, and economic independence as an important aspect of freedom—expanding our conventional understanding of Ward as an abolitionist. In short, Ward was concerned not only with gaining liberty for slaves but also making emancipation work successfully on free soil. This is the reason why, I think, he titled his memoir *Autobiography of a Fugitive Negro* rather than autobiography of a fugitive slave.

Third, Ward's experience as a former American slave who operated within the British Empire suggests that the notion of the figure of the "black loyalist" needs to be expanded. At present, we are familiar with the stories of those black soldiers who served the British faithfully during the American War of Independence being called black loyalists as well as those African Americans who patriotically served in the Union military during the American Civil War.[79] Samuel Ward's transformation into an imperial subject suggests greater temporal (1780s through 1860s) as well as spatial dimensions (Anglo-Atlantic) of the black loyalist for whom the pursuit and enactment of liberty was essential. Fourth, Ward's life and work offer some poignant insights into the shifting borders of unfree and free labor, racism, and prejudice, as well as contrasting empires in the Anglo-Atlantic world. Finally, the imperial subject draws our attention to an appreciation as well as over-appreciation of colonial freedoms. Samuel Ward's life and labors were less a paean of praise for the British Empire than a register of the potential and pitfalls of the peripatetic fugitive. He deserves our attention most of all because this Prometheus unbound labored to make imperialism subject to alternative understandings of liberty and freedom in the modern world. Sam would have appreciated the classical allusion.

CHAPTER 5

Freedwomen and Freed Children

An exercise in comparative history, however desirable, is not possible until the data for each country have been properly assembled.

—KEITH THOMAS

Every woman on the estate then [during slavery] worked in the field, now the case is altered; and as they get rich they keep their wives at home to take care of their houses or look after the children, who used all to be reared in the nursery of the estate; and for that reason at least half the female laborers have to be taken from the field and from the estate and applied to other purposes.

—BRITISH GUIANA PLANTER, 1848

An important 'meaning of freedom' for women and men—but above all for women—must have been the right to control one's own body, the right to be free of violation and abuse.

—BRIDGET BRERETON

It is to make women a focus of inquiry, a subject of the story, an agent of the narrative—whether that narrative is a chronicle of political events . . . or a more analytically cast account of the workings or unfoldings of large-scale processes of social change.

—JOAN SCOTT

One of the most dynamic developments in emancipation studies over the past two decades is its gender turn. Older categories of labor, race, citizenship, and politics have been reinterpreted regarding the various roles of black and white women as well as the social construction of sexual spheres of femininity and masculinity. Moreover, previous debates over ex-slave women's labor withdrawal have been replaced by examinations of the reconstruction of ex-slaves' households in which black women's agency is centered rather than marginalized. These new directions can be partially explained by the lack of attention to such topics in the past, along with the emergence of a generation of professional women historians attracted to the subject, together with the expansion of gender studies into new historical areas.[1]

This pioneering research has begun to generate comparative studies of gender and emancipation. We now have regional studies of the pan-Caribbean.[2] There are informative collections of essays comparing the lives and labors of free black women.[3] Two historians of emancipation recently assembled an international group of scholars to address the relationship between gender and emancipation in the Atlantic world. They state their argument and its spatial significance in the opening sentence of the subsequent published volume: "From Brazil to Cuba to the U.S. South, from Jamaica to the British Cape Colony, from Martinique and Haiti to French West Africa, gender was central to slave emancipation and to the making of the nineteenth-century Atlantic world."[4]

Much of this recent scholarship has opened our eyes to the enormous potential of international approaches to post-slavery developments beyond the nation-state. At the same time, there are some drawbacks. The exclusive focus on gender, for instance, precludes understanding the broader dynamics of post-emancipation societies. According to one reviewer: "This risks reproducing the very lack of balance characterizing the androcentric studies which the book's theme so rightly challenges."[5] More important for our purposes, the potential of comparative methodology for emancipation and gender studies remains unfulfilled. These collections invite the reader to make the comparisons through discrete chapters rather than either the contributors or the editors providing systematic comparative analysis. The contributions to the Scully and Paton volume, for instance, examine gender and emancipation across time and space, but none of them provide specific comparisons. The comparative method pursued in the editors' introduction is largely one of similarities: emancipation was gendered; men benefited more from emancipation then women; freedwomen's invisibility versus freedmen's visibility in the archives; freedwomen's commonality with working-class women in the new political economy of capitalist social relations of production, and so forth.[6] This emphasis on similarities broadens the spatial and temporal dimensions of gender and emancipation, but it is less clear what we are learning anew from the comparative method beyond gaining a greater cosmopolitan reach. Moreover, the Anglo-Atlantic world continues to serve as the epicenter of gender and emancipation, with other collective experiences in West and Central West Africa, Central and South America, and the Indian Ocean either peripheral or absent altogether.

This chapter provides an explicit comparative analysis of ex-slave women and children in the nineteenth-century Caribbean, United States, and Latin America. It makes two central arguments. First, a comparative treatment reveals compelling contrasts based on demographic and legal developments that get overlooked in local, national, and regional treatments. These differences consist of women and children gaining liberation *before* official abolition compared to men together with alternative understandings of freedom for ex-slave women and children within the household. The second argument is that freedwomen and freed children helped shape the emancipation narrative both as self-emancipators and more broadly as historical agents. In contrast to older studies that claimed exceptional democracy in the post-abolition United States that ignore the exclusion of women, as well as recent works that argue emancipation benefited men more than women because it excluded the latter from the political sphere, this concluding section makes a case for a more expansive definition of women's politicking. In particular, it traces a black woman's river of resistance that flowed into and beyond abolition. There are similarities, differences, and connections among women and children throughout nineteenth century post-emancipation societies in the Caribbean, North America, and South America. Our major objective is to steer between the rock of U.S. uniqueness and the rapids of universal gender categories.

Although the term "gender" is employed in this chapter, it is used primarily as an alternative to "women" and "sex." Our concern is less with "engendering history" than on the ways in which a comparative methodology can reveal new dimensions to the free lives and experiences of women and children.[7] Moreover, I share the view of those scholars who argue that ex-slave women were historical agents in social processes of abolition and post-emancipation societies even if the documentary archive reflects patriarchal domination. Some recent work on gender and emancipation argues that we can do little but speculate because of this archival bias. Patricia Scully thinks historians should "give up the search for clarity and rather expose the opacity of our understanding," while Madhavi Kale adopts a "postcolonial criticism of the category of labor" because of the silences in the British imperial archive concerning subaltern subjects.[8] This archival pessimism is unfortunate. Social historians, social anthropologists, historical sociologists, literary scholars, and others have produced rich studies of working-classes, slaves, women, American Indians, the colonized, prostitutes, gays, and so on, in spite of archival silences. Although representations of post-emancipation freedwomen and freed children must frequently be filtered through documents produced primarily by adult male chroniclers, we can still use these sources in rich and innovative ways. Besides, enslaved and freedwomen also produced documents.[9]

I. ANTE-EMANCIPATION EMANCIPATION

In many emancipation studies, there is a clear divide between the era of slavery and post-abolition. Thus, slavery ended legally through either national or colonial abolition. But in some slave societies, slaves became legally free *before* general emancipation. This was especially true for women and children. At the same time, there were important differences in this process best appreciated through comparative analysis.

Women predominated among free black populations in slave societies. Enslaved women were three or four times more likely to obtain their freedom in Brazil than enslaved men.[10] The largest population group in the province of Goiás in 1832 consisted of free women of color.[11] In two parishes of rural Bahia in 1835, women made up nearly 56 percent of all freed slaves.[12] In Rio de Janeiro, in 1828, a visiting English clergymen observed "negro men and women bearing about a variety of articles for sale." Although some were enslaved, "a large proportion . . . were free and exercised this calling on their own account."[13] Women were also more likely to attain their freedom than men in the Caribbean. In French Martinique and Guadeloupe between 1685 and 1848, there lived a class of slaves known as *libres de fait:* those manumitted by their owners without official documentation. The majority of these semi-free slaves were "young women who had close domestic associations with slave-owners."[14] Free women of color predominated among free blacks in St. Domingue's major port city of Cap Français during the 1790s.[15] In nineteenth-century Barbados, women represented more than 60 percent of all manumissions.[16] In 1871 Havana, Cuba, there were 1,247 female *cortadas* (women slaves who purchased their own freedom) compared to 890 males.[17] This gender imbalance also characterized slave societies in the Indian Ocean. Adult women predominated over adult men among free persons of color in Mauritius between 1780 and 1830. There were also more freedwomen than freedmen before the legal abolition of slavery in the United States. The majority of free coloreds in the U.S. South were women who inhabited major southern cities—Baltimore, Richmond, Charleston, and New Orleans. By 1860, they represented more than 58 percent of the free black population in the region's largest cities.[18]

How to account for this difference in gender and emancipation? There were important regional distinctions. In the U.S. South, Loren Schweninger argues, it was "because white men who took slave women as sexual partners sometimes provided them with deeds of manumission."[19] In the Caribbean, enslaved women earned money through domestic work and marketing activities to buy their freedom; they also obtained freedom as a "gift" for years of domestic service.[20] Penelope and her children were emancipated by merchant Jean Nicholas Martin Isnard in Cap Français, St. Domingue, "in exchange for the services she has performed for me."[21] In Latin America, there were numerous reasons why enslaved women were liberated, including buying freedom with money obtained from domestic services, marketing activities, and sex work, together with benefiting from personal relations with slave owners. In Mauritius, enslaved women were more frequently manumitted than enslaved men.[22] There is little doubt that sexual relations played a role in the emancipation of many slave women, although this explanation should not be automatically heralded over all those others. It also fails to explain the actions of those slaveholding women who freed enslaved women.

Moreover, the reasons for emancipation were not always clear. Ruth Hendrick of Halifax County, Virginia, wrote up a deed of manumission setting free all of her twelve slaves, consisting of three men, two women, and seven children. The two women—forty-year-old Hagar King and twenty-three-year-old Esther Robinson—together with the seven children—seventeen-year-old Alle King, twelve-year-old Abrian King, ten-year-old Sarah King, eight-year-old Tobitha King, six-year-old Edith King, four-year-old Lilinda King, and two-year-old John Robinson—were deeded to "be a free people and enjoy all the liberty and privileges that the laws of this country allow them." The manumission bill contains no explanation beyond "for divers causes," and the suggestion that Ms. Hendrick freed her slaves because she was "moving."[23]

While freedwomen represented the majority of the free colored population in the nineteenth-century Americas, there was a critical comparative difference. Free coloreds in general, and freedwomen in particular, constituted a smaller percentage of the total population in the United States compared to the Caribbean and Brazil. According to the 1860 U.S. Census, there were 488,070 free blacks in the United States: this amounted to one-tenth of 1 percent of the total U.S. population compared to 12 percent who were enslaved.[24] In 1860 Cuba, there were 225,843 free coloreds, amounting to 15 percent of the overall population compared to 43 percent who were enslaved.[25] In 1817–18 Brazil, there were 585,500 free coloreds amounting to 15 percent of the total population compared to 50 percent who were enslaved.[26] In other words, women were less likely to be freed *before* abolition in the United States compared to Latin America. The difficulties facing slave women (and men) seeking their freedom made the U.S. South an exceptional slaveholding society in comparative perspective.

Along with women, some children were liberated before the final legal termination of slavery. Throughout nineteenth-century Latin America, the passage of free-womb laws ended the enslavement of children in 1811 (Chile), 1813 (Argentina), 1821 (Peru, Ecuador, Columbia, Venezuela), 1825 (Uruguay), 1831 (Bolivia), 1842 (Paraguay), 1871 (Cuba, Puerto Rico), and 1871 (Brazil).[27] In all of these colonies and nation-states, slave children were liberated before their parents and elders were freed by national and colonial legislation outlawing slavery. Although there were numerous reasons for the abolition of child slavery, one of the most important ones was a political commitment to the eventual eradication of slavery. In contrast, enslaved children were emancipated together with their parents and elders with the legal abolition of slavery in 1833 (British West Indies), 1848 (French West Indies, Danish West Indies), and 1863 (Dutch West Indies). This simultaneous process of women's and children's emancipation also characterized wartime abolition in 1790s St. Domingue and the 1860s United States. In short, women and children often had an experience with emancipation different from that of men before the abolition of slavery, and the difference is best appreciated through a comparative methodology.

II. SELF-LIBERATORS

War was the mother of emancipation as slaves seized opportunities for liberation during political upheavals. This interpretation has become a hallmark of emancipation studies. What is less remarked upon is the extent to which enslaved women and children joined this barefoot plebiscite. Who were they? Why and how did they escape? And what were the consequences of their actions on systems of bondage and their reproduction?

Enslaved men were the most likely self-emancipators during the long night of slavery. Male runaways usually outnumbered female runaways in colonial Spanish America.[28] Men escaped more frequently than women in eighteenth century St. Domingue.[29] This was not least because they constituted a demographic majority as a consequence of the gender imbalanced Atlantic slave trade of two men for every one woman.[30] Alvin Thompson's examination of maroon communities across the Americas documents more male than female runaways.[31] Around 1,138 males compared to 142 females were reported in 1,500 notices for slave runaways in newspapers published from 1736 to 1801 in Williamsburg, Richmond, and Fredericksburg, Virginia.[32] Over three-quarters of newspaper advertisements for slave runaways during the 1730s in the colony of South Carolina involved men; while males predominated over females by three to one in subsequent decades.[33] Michael Mullin's comprehensive examination of 9,550 runaway advertisements in newspapers published between 1732 and 1806 for six plantation societies of Maryland, Virginia, South Carolina, Georgia, Jamaica and Barbados estimates 1,918 women runaways compared to 7,701 male absconders.[34] It has been estimated that more than 80 percent of fugitive slaves in ante-emancipation U.S. southern states were male.[35] Enslaved women did self-liberate. Harriet Clemens left her plantation in Mississippi "on 'count de Nigger overseers" who "kep' a-tryin' to mess 'roun' wid her an' she wouldn' have nothin' to do wid 'em."[36] But women were less likely to leave because men had greater mobility as skilled workers (watermen, carriage-drivers, factory operatives, seamen, and so on.) In addition, slave women bore greater domestic responsibilities for family and kin. Enslaved women were much more likely to abscond for shorter periods to avoid work, punishment, or in search of time alone.[37]

The advent of war and the prospect of abolition, however, transformed conditions and led to a remarkable rise in the extent and impact of enslaved women seeking their freedom. For the sake of clarity, we can divide their actions into three broad categories: women self-emancipators, female camp followers, and liberation by the sword.

Many enslaved women and their children sought personal liberty amidst political upheavals caused by military conflict. During the British occupation of St. Domingue in the 1790s, slave women and children departed from sugar plantations en masse. David Geggus generalizes that "where a mass exodus was possible the proportion of women was close to that of the men and this in turn entailed losses of children."[38] (From the perspective of the self-emancipators, of course, these losses were the gains of liberation.) The greatest swathe of women self-liberators occurred during the American Civil War. This was partly because of their sheer numbers—nearly 2 million enslaved women lived in the U.S. South according to the 1860 national census—as well as the extensive reach of invading forces into the farms, plantations, towns, cities, and coastal waterways of the slaveholding South. Some used the chaos of wartime conditions to abscond.

Octave Johnson, a self-emancipator who became a corporal in Company C, Fifteenth Regiment of Corps d'Afrique, testified that there were thirty runaways in his Louisiana parish in 1861 "of whom ten were women."[39] Many others steered for Union lines. In late May 1861, General Benjamin Butler, based in Fortress Monroe, southeast Virginia, informed General-in-Chief Winfield Scott: "Up to this time I have had come within my lines men and women with their children—entire families—each families belonging to the same owner.[40] Thousands of men, women, and children descended upon New Bern in tidewater North Carolina after its capture by Union troops in March 1862. A. E. Burnside, brigadier general commanding North Carolina, informed Edward Stanton, secretary of war, of their tenacity: "The city is being overrun with fugitives from the surrounding towns and plantations. Two have reported themselves who have been in the swamps for five years. It would be utterly impossible, if we were so disposed, to keep them outside of our lines, as they find their way to us through woods and swamps from every side."[41]

One scholar estimates that 290 slaves were involved in forty-two "separate black-initiated escape incidents" in wartime Georgia between 1861 and 1864. Women and children were reported in most of the escape parties.[42] Planters from Liberty County, Georgia, informed the local Confederate commander of "the number of Slaves absconded & enticed off from our Seaboard as 20,000 & their value as from $12 to $15 millions of Dollars." These self-emancipators included women and children.[43] More than 6,000 slaves left southern states for Wisconsin, Minnesota, and Iowa in the upper Midwest during four years of war, including many women and children. Rachel Weeden and Matilla Newbern took advantage of wartime conditions to depart the lower Mississippi Valley. Matilda Busey, together with her husband James and nine children, fled Kentucky for a Union camp in early 1862.[44] Josephine S. Griffing, a member of the freedmen's aid movement, reported the migration of a "host of miserable women, with large families of children, besides old, crippled, blind, and sick persons" to the nation's capital in 1865.[45] Indeed, many of the nearly 500,000 slaves who entered Union lines during four years of civil conflict were women and children.[46] In short, the crisis of slavery during wartime conditions facilitated the self-liberation of enslaved women and children to a far greater extent than during previous less tumultuous periods.

The second way in which enslaved women self-liberated was by following invading armies. Although historians describe runaway slaves regardless of their sex during the American War of Independence, it is not unreasonable to assume that enslaved women joined men in self-liberating toward British lines in places like coastal Virginia in 1775 and 1776.[47] According to Philip Morgan, the Virginia colony was approaching a balanced sex ratio of slave men and women by the 1730s, while in colonial South Carolina, "the number of slave men and women, boys and girls, approached parity in the last twenty five years of the colonial era."[48] A reasonable extrapolation from this balanced gender ratio was that women as well as men self-liberated during the subsequent anti-colonial struggle. When Argentine forces invaded the Banda Oriental (later Uruguay) in 1811–12 during the early years of the wars of independence in Spanish South America, several hundred women were reported to have fled their owners and joined the invading armies. Juliana Garcia and her children were only one of many families.[49] More than six decades later, enslaved women and children abandoned farms, plantations, and towns to join independence forces in Cuba's First War of Independence.[50] It remains unclear, however, whether the actions of these camp followers were affected by the passage of the Free Womb law passed three years earlier. In 1870, Spanish abolitionist politician Segismundo Moret introduced a bill for the gradual abolition of slavery to the Cortez in Madrid, proposing the freeing of all slaves turning sixty as well as children born of enslaved mothers since September 1868. This law was designed to solicit loyalty from slaves toward the Spanish colonial regime, and might well have discouraged women and children from following insurgent troops because the freedom of the latter was now guaranteed by the state. Perhaps the single largest instance of enslaved women and children following an invading army occurred during General William T. Sherman's march through central Georgia to Savannah during the latter stages of the American Civil War. It has been estimated that about 19,000 slaves followed the Union Army during the fall of 1864, including many women and children.[51]

A third route to freedom for slave women and children was by liberation from invading armies. In the months following the outbreak of slave revolt in the northern province of St. Domingue in August 1791, slave insurgent armies led by Jean-François Papillon and Georges Biassou destroyed plantations and farms, liberating slave men, women, and children from the sugar and coffee plantations of the region.[52] After Lincoln's Emancipation Proclamation of January 1863, the Union Army assumed the mantle of federal deliverer as slaves were freed whenever they showed up in their vicinity. In Alabama, former slave Gus Askew recalled federal soldiers marching through town to "set us free," while ex-slave Jim Gillard remembered "how de Yankees come to Spring Villa."[53] Georgia ex-slave James Bolton recalled: "Jus' befor' freedom comed 'bout 50 Yankee sojers come through our plantation and told us that the bull-whups and cow-hides was all dead and buried."[54] Although insurgent troops sometimes only liberated male slaves for fighting purposes during Cuba's First War of Independence, they often liberated women and children as well.[55]

These various routes to freedom, however, did not come without problems, some of which were severe. During the early years of the American Civil War, self-emancipators were often turned away or returned altogether. A woman who served as a cook in the private mess of Major George E. Waring Jr. was "claimed by one Captain Holland as the fugitive slave of his father-in-law." The major, reluctantly complying with orders from above, noted "she was given up to him."[56] Camp followers of armies often paid a heavy price for seeking their freedom. Hundreds of slave followers of Sherman's army died through malnutrition, neglect, and abandonment to avenging Confederate forces.[57] The Spanish wars of liberation during the early nineteenth century proved no less grisly for camp followers.[58] Military liberation could also be dangerous. Insurgent leaders Jean-Francois and Biassou are reported to have sold women and children who could not fight to the Spanish in Santo Domingo for military supplies.[59]

The comparative significance of examining women self-emancipators is several-fold. First, enslaved women's barefoot plebiscite on the institution of slavery during social upheavals made them agents of their own liberation much like their male counterparts. The term "women self-emancipators" is a more accurate reflection of their belief-system than "fugitives" or "runaways." The latter two terms reduce them to criminals and hide their sex, while the former conveys a better sense of what they were after. Second, those who sought their freedom during wars and abolition struggles were just as likely to have been women and children as men. This stood in sharp contrast to ante-emancipation periods when male self-liberation predominated. Third, slave women and children seeking opportunities for liberation during political upheavals represented a similar phenomenon across the nineteenth-century Americas. In other words, they contributed to the unfolding of a large-scale historical process of abolition and emancipation *as* women and children beyond narratives dominated by male protagonists.

The exodus of women and girls from plantation slave society transformed production and reproduction in a unique way.[60] After the abolition of the Atlantic slave trade to the United States in 1808, the system of American slavery expanded through biological reproduction. Young enslaved women, together with the potential breeding of girls, became essential to the reproduction of slavery. Young enslaved women and girls who absconded took their labor *plus* their potential reproductive capacities and breeding worth. When young enslaved men left, they only took their labor and their value as existing property since age, health, and skill level determined their market price. Once women and children left, slave societies that had stopped participating in the Atlantic slave trade and relied upon the biological reproduction of the slave system through the enslaved woman's womb were doomed to extinction. When these women and children either removed themselves or were removed from slave societies that relied on reproduction through female pregnancy and children's labor potential, they were terminating such societies. In addition, the exodus of children from plantation slave society had an additional long-term impact. When young children left, they did not take their existing labor with them, but their future investment for either work or market sales.

III. FREER BODIES

Although slave-owners denied it, abolitionists implied it, and the evidence remains elusive, enslaved women were frequently the victims of various forms of domestic violence and sexual exploitation by slave-owners, overseers, drivers, and even non-slaveholders. The category of "mulatto"—either in official census returns or as a racial descriptor in civil society—throughout slave societies in the Americas testified to slave-owners' power over the bodies of slave women. Elizabeth Fox-Genovese's description of social relations in the plantation U.S. South has a broader spatial and temporal relevance: "Despite occasional examples of tenderness and loyalty between masters and slave concubines, the masters' unchecked power over their slave women brought into the center of the household that public violence against which white women were protected."[61] Although some scholars have argued for "pronounced differences" between slave women in North America and the Caribbean, suggesting that not all concubines were sexually exploited in the latter region, it remains the case that the bodies of slave women were the legal property of slave-owners in all slave societies and as such could not be sexually abused under existing laws.[62] Eddie Donoghue's study of enslaved women in the Danish West Indies insists that relationships between black women and white men were "coercive" and "pervasive" rather than "consensual" and "romantic."[63]

The prevalence of slave women's sexual abuse across the nineteenth-century Americas is exemplified by three experiences. Mary Prince was enslaved in the British Caribbean, after which her owners brought her to London in 1827. With the aid of white abolitionist benefactors, she narrated her memoirs, subsequently published as *The History of Mary Prince* in 1831. The memoir is full of brutal beatings, savage whippings, and the incessant physical abuse of enslaved women in Bermuda and elsewhere. The descriptions of domestic violence are plentiful but less so concerning sexual abuse. Mary Prince refers to scenes in which her owner Mr. D. "had an ugly fashion of stripping himself quite naked and ordering me then to wash him in a tub of water." This seems tame, but she adds: "This was worse to me than all the licks."[64] A generation later, Linda Brent (née Harriet Brent Jacobs) published her memoir *Incidents in the Life of a Slave Girl* in the United States. In chapter 10, "A Perilous Passage in the Slave Girl's Life," Jacobs is a little more overt than Prince in her discussion of how her owner Dr. Flint would "whisper foul words," and "pollute my mind with foul images."[65] This testimony to slave women's sexual abuse, however, is rather subtle, perhaps reflecting the mores of slave narratives designed to rally but not offend a bourgeois readership.

Such subtleties were absent in a court case in Recife, Brazil, during the early 1880s. Slave-owner Henrique Ferreira Pontes was accused of "deflowering" his slave Honorata, her age estimated anywhere between twelve and seventeen. The defendant did not deny "he caused the deflowering," but challenged "the right of the court to take action in a case concerning a slave woman deflowered by her master, and therefore claiming that the inquiry should not have been opened and the public prosecutor should not have entered a complaint against him." After physical examinations revealed that acts of copulation had taken place, and that the "victim" was very young, Pontes was found guilty. Upon appeal, however, he was exonerated with the court deciding the "trial was null and void." One of the judges clarified his ruling: "I am among those who believe that as long as slaves exist in our country and as long as our legislation concerning them remains in force, masters cannot commit any crimes against their slaves other than those resulting from their authoritative power over them and from their right to punish, and that aside from these exceptions, masters cannot commit crimes against their slaves."[66] There is little doubt that these rights of property in slave women were exercised across the slave Americas, even if not all slave-owners chose to exercise them.

The advent of legal abolition did not curtail women's sexual abuse. According to Peter Blanchard, rape "was used as a weapon to terrorize and punish the female population in Venezuela" during national wars of liberation.[67] Some ex-slave women who ended up in Union lines during the American Civil War were the victims of sexual abuse by federal soldiers, although the evidence remains elusive.[68] The family of freedman Wesley Edward was attacked in Pittsylvania County, Virginia, sometime in August 1868. The attackers, reported Edwards, "threatened the life of his wife who was sick in bed and then ravished his daughter."[69] Roda Ann Childs informed a local Freedmen's Bureau agent in 1866 Georgia that she was "called upon one night" while her husband was absent and whipped while tied to a log. "Then a man," she added, "supposed to be an ex-confederate Soldier as he was on crutches, fell upon me and ravished me."[70] Between 1870 and 1899, there were 206 reported rape cases in Trinidad, many of these by ex-slave men on ex-slave women.[71] But the abolition of the rights of property in slaves removed the slave-owner's "authoritative power" over the bodies of slave women and girls. Sexual predators like Pontes, Flint, and "D" no longer had the law behind their molestations. The changed nature of this relationship was dramatically illustrated in the British Cape colony during the 1830s. Enslaved women were often sexually abused when working in settler-owner farms. With the advent of emancipation, however, freedwomen and freedmen decided that the former should leave domestic employment and work in their own homes to avoid "former slaveholder's sexual abuse" that they had once had to endure.[72]

Along with new control over their bodies, freedwomen benefited from greater control over their families. Motherhood was consistently shaken, undermined, and occasionally destroyed by slave sales. Slave families were constantly separated while slave mothers faced random acts—transporting urban slaves to plantations, free-born children sold as slaves, and so forth—in nineteenth century Cuba.[73] The inter-regional slave trade in nineteenth-century slave societies proved to be particularly destructive.[74] In Brazil, it has been estimated that some 200,000 slaves were forcibly relocated from one region (mostly the older sugar-producing Northeast) to other regions (the central and southwest coffee zone) between 1850 and 1881. Since the gender ratio was about two men to every woman, this resulted in female majorities in northern provinces and male majorities in coffee areas, with divided slave families everywhere. H. Augustus Cowper, the British consul at Recife, Brazil, reported family break-ups in heart-breaking terms: "Children are torn from their parents, parents from their children, the tie of husband and wife, which

no man is 'to put asunder,' is severed like the Gordian knot."[75] The destruction
of families was no less brutal in the U.S. South. Walter Johnson estimates that,
of "the two thirds of a million interstate sales made by the [slave] traders in
the decades before the Civil War, twenty-five percent involved the destruction
of a first marriage and fifty percent destroyed a nuclear family—many of these
separating children under the age of thirteen from their parents."[76] When he
was interviewed in 1937, ex-slave Samuel Walter Chilton still recalled those
times more than eight decades earlier when little "babies was taken from deir
mothers breast while nursin' some time dat mouth would be holin' tight but
they snatched him away." Chilton added "Sometimes dey sell your mother an'
leave you."[77]

This division of slave families and interregional trading, however, appears
to have slowed down in the years immediately preceding legal abolition. As
we have seen, slave families self-liberated together during the American Civil
War. Moreover, slave-owners would often "refugee" their slaves to safer environments away from invading Union troops without breaking up families
as had been the case during the ante-emancipation decades. According to
one account, the Brazilian Parliament abolished "the separation by sale of
a husband from his wife or a child under fifteen from his mother" in 1869,
two decades prior to legal abolition.[78] With the advent of emancipation, ex-
slave families were reconstructed around the household economy. And those
who left the farms and plantations for work in urban areas in the cities of
the New South like Atlanta and Durham often went as families.[79] This was in
marked contrast to the system of individual slave hiring to urban areas in the
ante-emancipation decades. In short, emancipation wrought greater physical
empowerment of freedwomen. It also brought greater cohesiveness to the ex-
slave family. This was particularly pronounced in those ex-slave societies in
which families emerged as a consequence of natural reproduction and more
balanced sex ratios.

IV. FAMILIAL RECONSTRUCTION

The role of slave men as primary workers in cash-crop production—such
as sugar, tobacco, cotton, rice, indigo, wheat—is familiar to students and
general readers. It is also incomplete because women and children labored
prodigiously in the fields. On sugar estates in the British Caribbean, for
instance, children aged between five and twelve years worked in the third
gang, and those between twelve and eighteen worked the second gang.[80] Slave

women were major agricultural workers in slave societies. Most historians of Caribbean slavery agree that slave women had become the leading cash-crop producers on plantations in the British and French West Indies by the early part of the nineteenth century. Enslaved women did much of the work on sugar plantations in late eighteenth-century St. Domingue.[81] In Jamaica, sugar employed nearly 50 percent of the enslaved population, the majority of whom were women.[82] More generally, slave women dominated sugar production throughout the other ante-emancipation British Caribbean colonies.[83] Although the Spanish slave trade landed more men than either women or children in Cuba, and the former predominated in plantation production over the latter, it was also the case that "black female slaves on all the estates [shared] the harsh tasks of the plantation with their male partners."[84] The predominance of female agricultural workers was due to a sexual division of labor in which slave men were favored for supervisory roles such as drivers and overseers as well as skilled positions like boilers, watchers, carpenters, blacksmiths, and coopers.[85] It continued until legal abolition.

Enslaved women also labored throughout the plantation regions of the ante-emancipation U.S. South. By the 1850s, women worked alongside men in the tobacco and wheat fields.[86] The region's major cash crop knew no sexual division of labor. It has been estimated that enslaved women over sixteen worked an average of 11–13 hours a day (12–14 hours for men), and between 261 and 284 days per year (between 268–289 days for men) in the cotton fields during the 1850s.[87] Although enslaved men's selection for skilled work explains why enslaved women performed agricultural work throughout the plantation Americas, the major factor in the U.S. South was biological reproduction of the slave populace after the abolition of the Atlantic slave trade in the United States in 1808. We cannot date precisely when enslaved women began to play such a prominent part in cash-crop production in regional economies throughout the U.S. South, but it was probably after the ending of the transoceanic slaves trade and the development of a more equal sex ratio among slaves. The critical point about the working roles of enslaved women and children in the ante-emancipation period was their coerced contribution to the reproduction of the slaveholder's household economy.

The advent of abolition to slave societies was to transform the nature of slave household production dramatically. A frequent complaint by planters, bureaucrats, and travelers after the termination of slavery was that women and children stopped working in the fields. What is striking is the ubiquity of this complaint. Reporting from the coffee fields in southern Brazil in 1891, Pedro Dias Gordilho Paes Leme lamented: "Immediately after the emancipation act 50 percent of the laborers, the part represented by women, stopped working."[88] According to one white Georgian, the difficulty of obtaining women field workers in the postwar cotton region meant the loss of "a very important percent of the entire labor of the [U.S.] South."[89] Freedwomen's participation in full-time plantation labor fell from 70 percent to 33 percent between 1866 and 1868 in Georgetown, South Carolina.[90] Freedwomen were reported to have stopped working in the tobacco fields of Virginia. "As a general rule," wrote Frank G. Ruffin, planter and editor of the *Southern Planter and Farmer* based in Richmond, "I know hardly an exception—women and children do no farm work."[91] Lieutenant Edwin Lyon, Freedmen's Bureau official in Charlotte County, was only slightly less bemused than Ruffin. "One of the strangest developments of negro character under the free system is their indisposition to work their wives and children." He was amazed that "even the most industrious freedmen encourage their wives and daughters in idleness, so that field labor is materially affected thereby." "Very few women," concluded Lt. Lyon, "work in the field, and very few have any work to do indoors, so that in cases where there are large families, there is a degree of poverty where there should be plenty."[92] Observers of emancipation in the Dutch West Indies after 1863 noted a strong reduction in the supply of wage labor provided by ex-slave women and children.[93] A British special magistrate in Berbice wrote in 1840: "we find the number of women and children occupied in agricultural employment to be considerably, I may add, alarmingly, diminished."[94] In the immediate aftermath of abolition, women and children withdrew their labor from sugar estates across the British Caribbean, much to the chagrin of former slaveholders, planters, and British colonial officials.[95]

This contemporary testimony provides both accurate and inaccurate descriptions of existing conditions. On the one hand, these reports were correct in that many freedwomen did withdraw from cash-crop production. One influential study of the postbellum U.S. southern economy estimates that the supply of labor offered by former slaves declined between one-fourth and one-third of its previous levels and that this was largely the consequence of the withdrawal of female and child labor.[96] Moreover, the take-off of Asian indentured servitude to key sugar-producing colonies in the post-emancipation British West Indies was directly traceable to the withdrawal of ex-slaves from cash-crop production, many of whom were women who had been so important in the waning ante-emancipation decades.[97] On the other hand, this testimony was largely hostile because many of its reporters bemoaned the fact that ex-slaves no longer worked in old ways. For them, slaves had worked prodigiously and ex-slaves should labor the same way but were no longer doing so. The problem, however, was not that the ex-slaves—especially women and youngsters—were not working in agricultural production. Rather, it was the biased standard of comparing free with slave productivity that characterizes so much of the evidence. As such, we have to be skeptical of the accuracy of the evidence as an accurate indicator of what ex-slaves wanted. When planters and bureaucrats complained that the ex-slaves did not work as well in the new system as the old system, we must never forget that their measurement of the failure of emancipation was based on a questionable comparison with the past.

One of the leading values of ex-slave women and children was the pursuit of alternative ways of living removed from coerced cash-crop production and toward familial reproduction. Many ex-slave women were central to this process of familial reconstruction, especially in the ways in which they sought to reconstruct the family away from the reproduction of the slave family for slaveholders and towards their own means of self-reproduction. Between 1806 and 1809, former slaves cultivated family plots on land once owned by French planters in the Republic of Haiti. They turned their backs on sugar production and pursued a mixed farming economy of cereal crops, coffee, and livestock for home consumption as well as local markets.[98] Two decades after Haiti's independence and the abolition of slavery, at least one-third of Haitians worked their own land as well as someone else's. Although a myriad of alternative labor arrangements emerged—including sharecropping and day laboring— many ex-slaves pursued family strategies. After the abolition of slavery in adjoining Santo Domingo in 1822, many farmers turned to cultivation of tobacco on small family homesteads.[99] From St. John, it was reported that ex-slave women continued working provision grounds after the abolition of slavery, while their household economies monopolized the pig-farming industry.[100]

A central component of ex-slave life in the British Caribbean was a "gendered strategy" in which women and children pursued domestic production and marketing while men exchanged their labor or skills for cash wages. Some children were encouraged to attend school; some boys were taught trades; some girls worked in the home. One planter from British Guiana described this switch from the old system to the new one and its family strategy a decade after abolition. The ex-slaves, he reported, "keep their wives at home to take care of their houses, or look after the children, who used all to be reared in the nursery of the estate; and for that reason at least half the female laborers have been taken from the field and from the estate." Although this testimony has its ambivalence much like that reported from the Virginia tobacco fields—was this ex-slave strategy paternalistic or was it the consequence of spousal agreement?—the shift toward an alternative form of life and labor was unmistakable.[101]

The family household economy was also prevalent in the post-emancipation U.S. South. This is certainly the consensus of social historians who have studied the region. Ex-slaves rejected the forced pace of the slave regimen for a "family-based system of labor organization" along gender lines, argues Jacqueline Jones.[102] The rise of tenant farming, writes Eric Foner, "made each family responsible for its own plot of land, [and] placed a premium on the labor of all family members." Although women performed household work, and children attended school when they could, "they frequently engaged in seasonal labor." This was especially the case in the former slave plantation regions of cotton, tobacco, and wheat production.[103] These older and more general treatments of family economies have been confirmed by more recent local investigations into the U.S. South's post-emancipation economy. A special investigation prepared by a local Freedmen's Bureau official based upon a questionnaire to seven planters in Charlotte County, Virginia, reported that, although some freedwomen did not return to the tobacco fields, others did either full- or part-time, while some "wives and daughters work in the field when called upon in the busy season of planting."

Many of these freedwomen pursued domestic activities, including housework, child rearing, "a little spinning," and sundry other chores.[104] Sharon Holt and Laura Edwards make a persuasive case for the transformation of freedwomen's household economy in the northern tobacco-belt counties of North Carolina, where freedmen engaged in wage labor in the fields, while freedwomen earned wages through various domestic activities—washing, cooking, marketing, and so forth. These were major rather than minor contributions to ex-slaves' household economies.[105] Leslie Schwalm argues that freedwomen withdrew their labor in post-abolition South Carolina "because their own survival and that of their families depended on doing so." They "were no longer willing to perform double duty in domestic production for their employers."[106] Despite a bewildering array of labor arrangements and postwar contracts between planters and freedpeople in 1860s coastal South Carolina that defy easy categorization, Julie Saville makes a persuasive case for the "reconstitution of family households . . . through whose development ex-slaves pursued economic independence."[107]

Many former slaves who emigrated from the U.S. South to Iowa during and after the American Civil War pursued similar family strategies. Black women would work at home and hire out during the higher-wage-paying season. Matilda Dandridge would "take the children and go out into the fields and hoe and pull weeds from around the plants" while her husband hired out as a day laborer on local farms. Rufus Dandridge worked on the farms of Lee County in the day and plowed his own crops by candlelight at night. Other black women worked as domestic servants, laundresses, or took in borders. Poorer families relied on children's "outwork" as a supplement to the household economy. Black men would work as laborers. This cash economy was no doubt important to household economies.[108]

The Mitchell household provides a good example of a family strategy in the post-emancipation South. In 1903, the sixty-two-year-old farmer and veteran of the 128th United States Colored Infantry owned fifty acres of land "all paid for" worth $250 in Jacksonboro, South Carolina. "My wife & daughters & I work the place & we make one to two bales of cotton," explained Kit, for which the family received between $30 and $50. They produced "from 50 to 100 bus[hels] of corn & from 30 to 60 bus[hels] of potatoes." They also had a garden and two horses. Mitchell's son-in-law lived with them and "works another place." Mitchell's "wife never did do any of the ploughing, she just does a little chopping now & then, and very little of that—She looks after the garden." Mitchell's "daughter helps since with the chopping & with the cotton picking."[109]

Mitchell's testimony merits additional comment. The information came from a deposition by a black Union veteran who was requesting a pension from the federal government. The nature of the evidence—a legal record—reveals a male head of household; but this should not exclude the possibility that the Mitchell household was consensual among the adults when it came to economic concerns. In addition, we cannot underestimate the changed nature of the family economy: the pooling of labor and resources was for the reproduction of the Mitchell family and not for the profits of Mitchell's previous slaveholder and his family.[110]

In post-abolition Cuba, there also appears to have been gender stratification among freedwomen and freedmen. Women pursued wage work, by either moving to towns or working seasonally when wages were highest, or both. One manager reported fourteen years after abolition: "During the harvest I give the negro [*sic*] women preference, and pay them the same salaries as the best male labor. They are the most constant, their work is usually well done, and each one keeps her man straight, which is an appreciable item." The men often worked on estates and plantations. One assistant manager of the ingenio [sugar plantation complex] *Soledad* reported: "Most of the laboring men, if they have families, when they are paid off, go away for a day or day and a half and take their money to their families, and then come back to work." In addition, freedwomen performed household work—including washing, mending clothes, and cooking—as well as overseeing small livestock farming.[111] In 1890s Vassouras, Brazil, freedwomen withdrew from year-round agricultural production and returned seasonally to pick coffee beans when they could earn the most for their labor. Also, sharecropping was adopted as a family system of labor in this regional economy. Freedwomen and their children would help at certain times, with the latter expected to perform additional household duties.[112]

In short, freedwomen and freed children did not simply withdraw from agricultural labor. Rather, they pursued alternative means of reconstructing the family in contrast to the reproduction of the slave family. For most slave societies prior to the early nineteenth century, slave work was reproduced through a lucrative transoceanic slave trade. After the abolition of the transoceanic trade, work was reproduced through transcontinental slave trades as well as the biological reproduction of slaves.[113] Slaves worked for slaveholders, whether they were men, women, or children. The slave family was largely defined by its ability to work and reproduce profits for slaveholders. This changed as ex-slaves reconstructed old and new families toward a very different understanding of life and labor after abolition. Freedwomen worked for themselves, breast-fed their own children, fed their families, sewed their own clothes, took care of family members when they were sick, and so forth. They were spared the violent and predatory actions of their former owners. Freed children worked for the household in a variety of capacities and sometimes were even schooled. It was the measurement of how well they achieved freedom—not how much women and children worked in the fields, not how economically rational ex-slaves were, and not how much the freed family approximated the typical (whatever that might be) household unit—that represented an important new feature of women and children's emancipation.

V. POLITICAL AGENTS

In their introduction to *Gender and Slave Emancipation,* editors Patricia Scully and Diane Paton make the comparative generalization that "emancipation tended to benefit men more than women." Freedwomen were excluded from the "political sphere," they argue, especially masculine forms of "military participation" and "nationalism," which tended to favor ex-slave men.[114] Politics was a male arena from which women were barred because of their gender. In post-emancipation societies, freedwomen's exclusion from the body politic, compared to freedmen, made their emancipation less beneficial. One suggestive comparative contribution here is its further undermining of the notion of U.S. exceptional emancipation since freedwomen in the American South were as excluded from the official political sphere of voting and representation as much as ex-slave women in the post-abolition Caribbean and Latin America.

But this gender comparison in the political sphere is debatable for several reasons. First, it assumes *ipso facto* ex-slave men's civic incorporation because they fought for the *patria.* However, ex-slaves' access to political power was often short-term, always contested, and never a *fait accompli* simply because male slaves had battled against slavery. Second, it offers a very narrow definition of what is political. A normative definition of politics—people are only political when they register, petition, campaign, vote, and so forth—would deny most subaltern people (including women) *any* political role in much of modern history. The logical consequence of this definition is that enslaved women were also apolitical, an interpretation strongly at odds with much historiography over the last generation.[115] Third, and most important, it ignores the collective activities of freedwomen, especially in the realm of political mobilization. Despite being excluded, these women resisted their marginalization. Their activities were important because they transcended individual strategies and suggest that emancipation wrought new collective forms of action in which women played considerable roles. These outward public politics by freedwomen varied enormously across time and space and cannot be reduced to one simplistic formula. We can, however, identify two major political arenas for these freedwomen's activities: struggles for social justice in the post-abolition workplace, and various forms of collective mobilization.

The transition from slavery to freedom in plantation societies wrought new forms of productive relations, organization of work, and types of compensation. Freedwomen were no less vociferous than freedmen in demanding that the new system not replicate the iniquities of the old. During the busiest months of the 1867 agricultural season, Colonel J. W. Jordan, a leading Freedmen's Bureau official in Virginia's central piedmont, provided a glimpse of their values. Some of the former slaves, "especially among the females," wrote Col. Jordan to his superior in Richmond, "do not comprehend the new relation they sustain to the white man." These "females" were "influenced by impractical and exaggerated ideas of freedom" that "cause all classes serious annoyances." They "go about poisoning the minds of the colored people against the whites—by gross misrepresentations—circulating dangerous rumors—interfering with contracts—and generally disturbing the relations between the races."

It is likely that these freedwomen were not satisfied with the ways in which labor contracting in the early post-abolition years was implemented injudiciously by landowners and employers as well as unfairly adjudicated by legal authorities like the Freedmen's Bureau.[116] Ex-slaves' island police squads opposed to the restoration of lands to former owners in coastal South Carolina during late 1865 and early 1866 were followed by collective demonstrations led largely by freedwomen. Bureau agent Erastus Everson got caught up in one on the Sea Cloud plantation on Edisto Island: "I was beset by the women on this place in a very serious manner, and was obliged to use decisive measures for the preservation of the property as well as for my own head." After explaining the need to return the land, Everson reported the freedwomen "said they would not make any arrangement whatever, for me or anybody else; that they cared for no United States officer: the Govt brought them to the island & 'they would burn down the house before they would move away' or 'farm it themselves until put out.'"[117]

Freedwomen in the post-emancipation Caribbean were no less political. Étienne Polverel, French commissioner for western St. Domingue, legally abolished slavery in the western and southern regions in October 1793. This was followed by the implementation of a "new" plantation system in which ex-slaves worked for wages, remained on former plantations, and worked for former masters in old ways. Many freedmen either worked unproductively or left the plantations altogether. Freedwomen were paid only two-thirds the pay of their male counterparts. Carolyn Fick summarizes their grievances thus: "Why should we receive less pay than the men? Do we come to work later than they? Do we leave earlier? They might have added: Do we not receive the same punishments as the men for refusing to work? Simply stated, the women saw themselves as individual and equal workers."[118]

The post-abolition British Caribbean witnessed collective protest by freed-women, especially against the new system of apprenticeship regarded as little more than a new form of enslavement. Hundreds of former slaves marched on Government House, Port of Spain, Trinidad, to protest the apprenticeship system inaugurated after legal abolition in 1833. "*Point de six ans, point de six ans*" (no six years, no six years) they chanted. It was reported that freedwomen were especially vocal in their protest.[119] There were scattered violence and major disputes over working hours and conditions at the sugar plantations of Belvedere, Gibraltar, Golden Grove, Pusey Hall, and Leith Hall in Jamaica during 1835 and 1836. According to Thomas Holt, these were "collective griev-ances" rather than individual acts of revenge. Not only did these protests re-flect the "solidarity of the workers," but a striking feature was the "prominence of women among the activists and leaders." Catherine Stanford and Diane Clark downed tools at the Leith Hall estate. They were joined by nine other women who said "they would not cut another cane; that they would die on the treadmill first." They carried on their strike for a few days before they were jailed. Louisa Beveridge was to perish from injuries sustained on the treadmill.[120]

Together with these struggles for social justice, ex-slave women and chil-dren also mobilized collectively.[121] Their activities were not new but part of a longer river of protest. The shipboard revolt aboard the *New Britannia* in Janu-ary 1773 began because some Africans "had conveyed on Board, by some of the black Boys, some of the Carpenter's Tools, wherewith they ripped up the lower Decks, and got possession of the Guns, Beads, and Powder." In 1721, the En-glish ship *Robert* lay anchored offshore from Sierra Leone. An unnamed woman obtained weapons and led an attack killing three of a five-man watch. The revolt was put down, and the woman was tied up, whipped, and slashed with knives until she bled to death.[122] During the long night of slavery, enslaved women participated in slave revolts, while social crises often saw women and children liberate themselves or even engage in military actions.[123] These ac-tions continued after the legal termination of slavery. Freedwomen reportedly participated in political rallies during elections in 1848 Martinique.[124] Black women, including those formerly enslaved, played a role in public leadership and political protest in the generation following emancipation in Jamaica.[125] For instance, a by-election in St. David in 1851 and a mayoral election in Kingston in 1853 both provoked riots in which women played roles. One judge thought it "a pity to see females mixing up with elections, but yet such is the case, and [in] every riot women are sure to be included."[126] Melanie J. Newton suggests that, despite being denied civic life beyond charitable and religious works in post-abolition Barbados, it "may be that women were present at civil rights meetings," but either were not permitted to speak or their presence went unrecorded.[127] Despite a rich historical literature on the Haitian Revolution, we still await a detailed study of gender, slavery, and emancipation that might highlight the political activities of slave/ex-slave women.

Studies of freedwomen in the post-abolition U.S. South have also revealed a rich pattern of political activism. In Virginia, freedwomen "joined secret societies affiliated with the Union Leagues, conducted fund-raising activities to support black organizations, encouraged their men to vote, and used their influence to pressure wavering black men to stay solid for black rights."[128] Freedwomen in Reconstruction Georgia marched in parades and attended conventions, voted resolutions up or down at public meetings, organized their own societies, encouraged their men folk to vote, and absented themselves from work during election day. One newspaper reported about the October 1872 election: "The Negro women, if possible, were wilder than the men. They were seen everywhere, talking in an excited manner, and urging the men on. Some of them were almost furious, showing it to be part of their religion to keep their husbands and brothers straight in politics."[129] In low-country South Carolina, women guarded guns at public meetings; while "wives and lovers wielded sanctions of bed and board on behalf of political action."[130] In short, freedwomen were political agents in a variety of ways in post-emancipation societies. Ex-slave women in the U.S. South were less part of an exceptional expansion of national democracy than political actors who shared common forms of mobilization against social injustice and for political redress with their sisters in other post-abolition societies.

Ex-slave women and children in the nineteenth-century Caribbean, United States, and Latin America were more likely to obtain their freedom than men before the legal abolition of slave systems outside of the United States. Wartime abolition provided more enslaved women and children with a chance to obtain their freedom in the United States and St. Domingue than anywhere else. Women and girls were less likely to experience sexual abuse from white men after abolition, although they were never completely free from sexual predators. Freedwomen played a similar role in reconstructing household economies around new understandings of familial liberty. Most significantly, ex-slave women were political agents who helped to shape the emancipation narrative. Of course, these comparisons are by no means comprehensive. The institution of child apprenticeship has been examined by several scholars of post-abolition societies but has yet to be systematically compared.[131] The mapping of political and ideological connections among freedwomen across borders still awaits the ambitious scholar.[132] But this chapter is long enough already. What remains to be done is to sketch a broader picture of the comparative experiences of the earliest generation of ex-slaves in the post-emancipation African Diaspora.

CHAPTER 6

Freedom's First Generation

The negro was not as good a laborer in the new as in the old system.
—BENJAMIN W. ARNOLD

I like to think of people having land wherever they are born. To me, they are more stable and much more secure when they have a foundation of their own. If not, you will keep paying, and even if you own a million dollars, you don't own anything.
—ST.JOHNIAN, born in 1880s

[Brazilian abolition] was part of a general program of economic modernization that entailed coercing freedmen into specific sectors of employment.
—KIM D. BUTLER

New forms of labor control in ever-larger areas of the world had replaced the efforts of slaves in the southern United States.
—SVEN BECKERT

Robert Engs's *Freedom's First Generation: Black Hampton, Virginia, 1861–1890*, first published in 1979,[1] offers an examination of a post-emancipation southern community through "longer time frames," the search for "elusive evidence," and the application of "different standards of measurement."[2] Building upon these alternative chronological, evidential, and measurement criteria, this chapter compares the generational experiences of ex-slaves in hemispheric terms. Emancipation is pursued in longer chronological sections of two to three decades beyond the usual decade or so. Thus: Haiti from 1804 through 1820s, the British West Indies from the 1830s through 1860s, the U.S. South from the 1860s through the 1890s, and Cuba/Brazil from the 1880s through 1910s. Moreover, the search for new evidence is less important than demonstrating new dimensions of ex-slaves' experiences through expanded, alternative, and linked approaches gleaned from existing evidence. Finally, freedom's meaning is pursued from the perspective of the ex-slaves rather than colonial officials, local politicians, removed philanthropists, or visiting missionaries, many of whom were quite hostile to freedpeople's choices and behavior. In short, we examine the first generation of ex-slaves in post-abolition societies through a comparative methodology of similarities, differences, and connections.

I. FREEDOM CROP INDEX

My dissertation-turned-publication on the political economy of emancipation in the tobacco region of the U.S. South argued that many ex-slaves withdrew from cash-crop production, especially in the tobacco and wheat fields of central Virginia, and that their withdrawal constituted an approximate indicator of economic freedom from former coerced forms of labor. In other words, emancipation in the tobacco fields could be statistically measured by the decline in labor-intensive tobacco production from the days of slavery compared to the days of freedom. In an early burst of comparative enthusiasm, I took the argument further to suggest that this labor withdrawal in tobacco Virginia resembled the free-labor struggles of other ex-slaves in post-abolition societies in which staple-crop production dropped markedly after emancipation. I called this process—ex-slave labor withdrawal and cash-crop decline—the *freedom crop index*. Only one book reviewer picked up on the concept.[3]

Subsequent reading, research, and reflection on the socioeconomics of post-emancipation societies have obviously inspired several qualifications to this point. First, tobacco was a special labor-intensive crop that required careful cultivation and attention all season long. This contrasts with cash crops like sugar, cotton, rice, indigo, and wheat that are far less labor-intensive. In other words, the concept squashes important differences in the extent of labor output: withdrawal in some crop calendars was far more extensive than in others because of the nature of the productive process. Second, the notion failed to differentiate between post-abolition and pre-abolition declines in agricultural production. The traditional regions of sugar production in northeastern Brazil, as well as older colonies of Barbados and Jamaica in the British Caribbean, experienced serious declines in sugar production *before* the advent of emancipation. Thus, the sugar decline in these regions cannot be attributed to ex-slaves' actions but rather to broader market forces in operation during slavery.[4] Third, there was not a sharp decline in the major coffee-producing region of southern Brazil after abolition in 1888. During the 1891–92 season, coffee production in the southern Brazilian state of Rio de Janeiro was estimated at more than 97 million kilograms. Despite soil exhaustion and depressed market prices, it still reached 60 million kilograms four years later. Over the next generation, coffee never failed to fall below 40 percent of total Brazilian exports. Finally, some ex-slave regions such as Trinidad and British Guiana actually experienced an increase in cash-crop production.[5]

Despite these qualifications and corrections, however, the *freedom crop index* remains a useful comparative tool for comprehending connections between cash-crop decline, ex-slave labor withdrawal, and the socioeconomics of freedom across the post-abolition Americas. Behind the dry-as-dust statistics—and negative appraisals offered by agricultural specialists like Benjamin Arnold—were real people who made conscious decisions not to work in old ways based upon their values with significant consequences. Former slaves sought their own pathways to freedom in the face of protests and criticisms by many contemporary planters, ex-slaveholders, and politicians. Most important, this concept provides an opportunity to compare post-emancipation production outcomes and their consequences in meaningful ways. This crude index will no doubt fail to satisfy the strict models of economic historians of emancipation, but as *Freedom's Seekers* has argued, ex-slaves were not *homo economicus* and were driven by different criteria. For them, success was not measured in terms of productivity returns or marketplace efficiency.[6] In researching the transformation of the post-emancipation U.S. tobacco region during the 1990s, I was struck by the extent to which cash-crop production declined in most former slave societies, that this seemed a remarkable development, and that local, regional, and national studies could not provide a satisfactory comparative explanation. This research question remains germane.

One of the most striking socioeconomic developments of post-abolition societies across the nineteenth-century Americas was the rapid decline in cash-crop production. For centuries, African and American slaves had forcibly cultivated cash crops on plantations and farms in the Western Hemisphere for consumers throughout the Atlantic world, resulting in large profits for planters, merchants, and political elites.[7] This matrix of slavery, profits, and economic expansion was to change relatively quickly with the advent of abolition. Many slave societies experienced a rapid decline in the production of major cash crops of sugar, rice, tobacco, wheat, cotton, indigo, cacao, and coffee in the decades immediately following the termination of slave systems. In 1791, St. Domingue exported more than 80,000 tons of sugar, 34,000 tons of coffee, and 3,000 tons of cotton. Fourteen years after abolition, Haiti was exporting only 1,000 tons of sugar, 10,000 tons of coffee, and less than 200 tons of cotton.[8] During the seventeenth and eighteenth centuries, Barbados and Jamaica were among the leading sugar-producing colonies in the world. Six years after the abolition of slavery in the British West Indies, this traditional empire of sugar production accounted for less than 14 percent of global returns.[9] Between 1824 and 1833, Jamaica's average annual sugar production reached 68,465 tons. By the later 1850s, this average was down to 25,168 tons.[10] After the abolition of slavery in the British colony of Mauritius in the Indian Ocean, sugar cultivation ground to a virtual halt as former slaves moved to the capital city, St. Louis, and its environs away from plantation production.[11]

Sugar production also declined in the post-abolition French Antilles. In 1847, Martinique produced more than 31,337 tons of sugar; two years after emancipation, this had fallen to 15,000 tons. Guadeloupe's decline proved to be even more precipitous: from nearly 38,000 tons to under 13,000 tons in three years.[12] In the Danish West Indies colony of St. John, land planted in sugar cane fell from 839 acres in 1846 to 126 acres by 1870, and ceased altogether around 1880, about a generation after emancipation in 1848.[13] In Suriname, Dutch West Indies, although sugar production fell marginally from 27 million pounds in the year of emancipation in 1863 to 25 million pounds in 1873, this was the not the case with other cash crops. During the same post-emancipation decade, coffee production fell from 281 million pounds to 71 million pounds and cotton cultivation dropped from 374,155 pounds to 143,835 pounds.[14] Sugar production in Guayama, the major slave region in southern Puerto Rico, was halved as a consequence of colonial abolition in 1873.[15] One of the most remarkable declines in sugar production occurred in post-emancipation Cuba. In 1870, Cuban cane sugar accounted for over 40 percent of world production. Two decades later (six years after abolition in 1886), it accounted for less than one-fourth.[16]

This fall in cash-crop production was equally spectacular in former slave societies north of the Caribbean. Rice production in the South Carolina Low Country plummeted from more than 77 million pounds of clean rice in 1860 to less than 31 million pounds by 1890.[17] In the Old Dominion, wheat production declined from 11 million bushels worth $15 million in 1860 to 7 million bushels worth $6 million in 1890; while tobacco fell from 122 million pounds worth $6 million in 1860 to 64 million pounds fetching $3.8 million in 1890.[18] King cotton was also affected by abolition. South Carolina sea-island cotton fell from more than 47,000 bags in 1858 to under 8,000 bags by 1886, while cotton production across the U.S. South fell from more than 5 million bales in 1860 to 3 million bales a decade later.[19]

How to explain this massive drop in cash-crop production in post-abolition societies?[20] Adverse climatic conditions did play a part. Severe drought devastated tobacco-crop production in late 1860s Virginia and sugar production in Puerto Rico during the mid-1870s.[21] Hurricanes destroyed sugar production in Danish St. John in 1867 and rice production in the coastal Carolinas in 1893.[22] An earthquake in Cap Français, St. Domingue, in 1793 probably had a deleterious impact on the local economy.[23] But natural disasters can only explain seasonal disruption in the short term: they are less satisfactory explanations for production declines over the period of a generation. According to a recent tourist brochure describing the Hofwyl-Broadfield plantation in coastal Georgia, produced by the State Parks and Historic Sites, hurricanes contributed to the fall of the region's rice empire by 1915.[24] But hurricanes cannot explain the long-term decline of rice production in the region. Besides, natural disasters do not account for cash-crop declines in those post-abolition areas that did not experience severe climatic conditions.

The devastation wrought by wartime conditions also fails to provide a persuasive explanation for agricultural decline. Within days of the outbreak of the slave uprising in St. Domingue, more than two hundred sugar plantations and hundreds of coffee plantations burned.[25] There is little doubt that the subsequent dozen years of slave revolt, colonial invasion, and anti-colonial resistance had a destructive impact on agricultural production. Similarly, the state of Virginia was a major theater of military operations from the first battle of Bull Run in 1861 through the surrender at Appomattox in 1865 during the four-year American Civil War. The destruction and loss of livestock and farming implements was especially prominent in parts of the Old Dominion.[26] According to testimony to the Southern Claims Commission, the Union Army was responsible for devastation and destruction of property throughout the region.[27] On the other hand, wartime destruction—much like adverse weather conditions—lasted for only a short period of time, followed by gradual economic recovery. The Georgia tourist pamphlet also mentions war as a contributing factor to the fall of rice production, yet one wonders how the scars of war—including Sherman's devastating march to the sea in late 1864—explain the decline of rice production over two generations between the 1860s and the early twentieth century.[28] On top of which, wartime devastation does not explain production declines in those areas that did not experience military conflict such as the British Caribbean during the 1830s, the French Antilles during the 1840s, the Dutch Caribbean during the 1860s, and Puerto Rico during the 1870s.

The most persuasive explanation for the long-term decline in major cash-crop production across the post-abolition Americas was the withdrawal of freedom's first generations away from the "slave" crop toward alternative means of lives and labor. This shift was prominent in the former slave colonies in the French Caribbean. Months after the 1791 uprising began in St. Domingue, former slaves took over abandoned plantations and began to cultivate crops independently.[29] After independence in 1804, former slaves converted old sugarcane plantations into subsistence-crop family farms cultivating coffee, cacao, and tobacco.[30] After abolition in French Martinique and Guadeloupe, ex-slaves turned to mixed subsistence-marketing farming of yucca, potatoes, yams, plantains, peanuts, and beans, along with livestock rearing.[31] This shift from sugar to food crops in the post-abolition French Antilles can be seen clearly from the increase in the number of small holdings devoted to subsistence farming. Between 1845 and 1865, the area of Martinique under food crops increased from 11,714 hectares (1 hectare = 2.4 acres) to 12,822 hectares, while the number of personal holdings went up from 1,984 to 5,478. In Guadeloupe, 6,611 hectares for food crops with 1,638 holdings increased to 8,678 hectares with 5,169 holdings.[32] In St. John, the Danish West Indies, former slaves replaced sugar production with the growing of cereal crops, the raising of livestock, and fishing.[33]

Former slaves also transformed the old plantation economy into subsistence family plots in the British West Indies, albeit with greater and lesser degrees of success. In Barbados and Antigua, former slaves remained tied to the plantation economy because the combination of high population density and small land size prevented the development of alternative means of agricultural living. Even though newer colonies like Trinidad and Guyana continued to export sugar at a fair rate, former slaves proved successful in withdrawing from the plantation economy and establishing subsistence family plots.[34] In post-emancipation Puerto Rico, former slaves moved from the sugar plantations on the plains to coffee production in the mountains.[35] In the Low Country of South Carolina, as well as coastal Georgia, former slaves shifted away from rice production toward a subsistence economy that better reflected "a nonmarket appreciation of leisure and time away from labor."[36]

In the major agricultural regions of post-abolition Brazil, freedom's first generation pursued two alternative paths to cash-crop production. In the older sugar belt, they expanded subsistence farming. In Bahia, most of the existing population of 130,000 former slaves sought access to land to make food for household consumption as well as crops that could be sold locally, including sugar, manioc, coffee, and tobacco on small plots of land. These ex-slaves shifted from gang labor on plantations to family labor with mixed-crop production.[37] The other option pursued in the newer coffee regions by numerous ex-slaves was to walk away from cash crop production altogether. In the major coffee-producing region of Vassouras in southern Brazil, former slaves flocked to Rio de Janeiro during the 1890s in search of higher-paying jobs as domestics and factory workers. They took "foot along the dusty roads in carts, on mules or horses, and by train," as they abandoned a past of "discipline, overwork, [and] servitude."[38] At about the same time, a younger generation of people whose parents had toiled in Virginia's tobacco fields for ages also turned their backs on older rural rhythms for higher-paying cash earnings in southern and northern urban areas.[39]

This decline in cash-crop production in post-abolition societies—together with former slaves' pursuit of alternative means of production and reproduction—represents a crude productive measure of the distance ex-slaves put between their former coerced plantation production and their alternative semi-independent and independent forms of existence. This relationship between reduced production and economic alternatives in the post-emancipation countryside was the *freedom crop index*. In other words, the economic magnitude of emancipation is measured in terms of the productive distance traveled from slave cash-crop production to independent productive activities. In comparative terms, this decline in cash crops was not an isolated case in local regional economies but rather a commonality throughout post-emancipation societies. It was the direct consequence of decisions made by former slaves not to work in old ways and was invariably opposed by planters, capitalists, and political elites. This post-emancipation general strike had profound implications for the nineteenth-century global economy in cash crops in terms of stimulating new markets, carving out new zones of productivity, and transforming older social relations of production.[40] Many economic historians evoke the wonders of the free market as the determinant of economic decision-making in most human societies. In contrast, this comparative analysis of cash-crop production and the reason for its general decline in post-abolition societies highlights the positive actions of freedom's first generations.

II. LAND, LAND, LAND!

One of the most important alternatives to cash-crop cultivation sought by ex-slaves was access to landholdings. Scholars have compared and contrasted ex-slaves' landownership in post-abolition societies in two key ways: proto-peasants and the land-labor ratio. During the early 1960s, social anthropologist Sidney Mintz introduced the key concepts of proto-peasantry and reconstituted peasantry in Caribbean historiography. He argued that slaves' dual roles as plantation laborers and subsistence producers led to the formation of independent peasantries after emancipation. Subsequently, many scholars of Caribbean societies have sought the roots of Afro-Caribbean peasantries in the slave past. One of the key features of this past was continual access to small amounts of land rooted in slavery and carried over into the post-abolition decades.[41] Mintz's interpretation became popular among numerous Caribbean historians from the 1970s onward and even influenced historians of colonial/independent Brazil as well as the U.S. South.[42]

The other comparative approach to ex-slaves' landholding concerns the land-labor ratio in the British sugar colonies. Seeking to explain the origins of a peasantry in the post-abolition British Caribbean, scholars have often depicted a continuum of islands regarding land size and availability of labor. Small islands with high population densities saw planters retain control of former slave labor and the continuation of plantation production. These places included post-emancipation Antigua, St. Kitts, and Barbados. Large islands with low population densities witnessed the flight of former slaves from the sugar estates and the establishment of a black peasantry. This occurred in Jamaica, Trinidad, and British Guiana. All other British colonies—St. Vincent, Tobago, Grenada, Nevis, Montserrat, St. Lucia, Dominica—saw both retention as well as flight and fall somewhere in the middle of the continuum. Although this land-labor ratio has sparked heated debate, it is frequently used to explain contrasting post-abolition outcomes in the British West Indies.[43]

Drawing upon the strengths and weaknesses of these two approaches, the following section employs a comparative methodology for examining the redistribution of land across the nineteenth-century post-abolition Americas in three ways. We begin with an examination of the extent of black landholding. Scholars continue to unearth more and more examples of ex-slaves' landholdings in post-abolition societies. At the same time, it is unclear how such local excavations provide the basis for comparing and contrasting broader landholding patterns. We then turn to a comparison of the ideological meanings of obtaining land for ex-slaves in various parts of the post-abolition Caribbean as well as the U.S. South. Although scholars often make the point that ex-slaves wanted land, the actual meaning of land to those who were once enslaved only makes sense through specific contextual understanding. At the same time, a comparative analysis reveals the limitations of regional and national explanations for such meanings. The third section looks at the significance of land accumulation for ex-slaves as well as more broadly for post-emancipation societies. As we work through this comparative analysis, we must not lose sight of the *freedom crop index.*

We should begin with the undeniable fact that most ex-slaves in the nineteenth-century Americas became rural proletarians because they were denied fair and legal access to landownership. Planters and political elites wanted continued plantation production, and recognized that the sale of land to ex-slaves would contribute to labor shortages and a rise in labor costs. Former slaves sought new forms of freedom, especially independence afforded from access to landholding. The post-emancipation economy points to the continuation of neo-slave forms of domination as many former slaves became mired in unfree labor practices through the rise of debt peonage, and either non-compensation or under-compensation in the post-emancipation plantation Americas.[44] In a recent historical overview, one of the leading economic historians of the Caribbean concludes that, after abolition, "many [former slaves in the British colonies] became proletarians who were forced by economic necessity to return to the plantations as salaried workers."[45] The same process operated in the post-emancipation Spanish Antilles. After the abolition of slavery in Puerto Rico in 1873, one scholar suggests that "the majority of *libertos* [former slaves] stayed working for their former owners and worked in agricultural labor" in one of the colony's three major sugar-producing regions.[46] In the major slave and sugar-growing region of Matanzas in central Cuba, the vast majority of former slaves remained landless, with only their labor to sell, and company stores controlling their mobility, thus constituting a "true rural proletariat."[47] It was hunger, want, or limited employment prospects elsewhere that resulted in large numbers of freedpeople remaining on the sugar estates in post-abolition Peru during the 1850s and on the coffee estates in post-emancipation southern Brazil during the 1890s.[48] In the post-emancipation U.S. South, the passage of crop-lien laws by virtually every state legislature, together with legal distinctions between tenants and laborers that favored landholders, attempted to shackle free labor to the land with its profits directed to landlords and employers.[49] Emancipated Mende slaves in the British protectorate of Sierra Leone were reported to have just "sat down" with their former owners after abolition on January 1, 1928, because of their limited options.[50]

The implementation of these new forms of domination upon former slaves, however, should not blind us to the emergence of new alternatives out of the social upheaval wrought by emancipation.[51] Recent research into post-abolition societies has revealed a remarkable degree of ex-slaves' partial or complete access to landholdings in contrast to their previous landless condition. According to the leading scholar of the British occupation of western and southern St. Domingue between 1793 and 1798, "very little cane was either planted or cut." Most slaves turned to "their gardens, and livestock . . . fashioning a new life." Others were engaged in "planting vegetables along the plantation paths and selling them to buy clothes and bananas."[52] In the southern republic of Haiti, numerous ex-slaves cultivated family plots on lands once owned by French slave-owners.[53] By 1820, surviving veterans of the Haitian Revolution were allocated between five and twenty-five *carreaux* (sixteen to eighty acres) for services rendered to the nation.[54]

Following the abolition of slavery in the French Caribbean colonies of Martinique and Guadeloupe in 1848, freedpeople settled upon vacant lands to plant yucca, potatoes, yams, plantains, peanuts, and beans, while others raised livestock.[55] Six years after the final abolition of colonial slavery in the British Caribbean, 19,000 freedpeople had purchased land in Jamaica, establishing sixty-eight free villages. A year later, in 1845, there were 20,724 legally registered properties of up to ten acres that might have embraced 66,000 Afro-Jamaican freedpeople, or one-fifth of the total populace. Afro-Trinidadians also accumulated land. In 1846, around 5,400 freedpeople had founded free villages; by 1859, a visiting U.S. journalist estimated that over 80 percent of former plantation workers owned ten acres or less. By 1860, over 10,000 freedpeople had become peasant landowners in St. Vincent, Grenada, St. Lucia, and Tobago. This land redistribution proved long-term: by 1895, there were 95,942 peasant households under five acres and 16,015 peasant households between five and forty-nine acres growing ginger, cacao, pepper, oranges for market as well as family consumption in Jamaica.[56]

The post-abolition Spanish Caribbean reflected regional diversity in patterns of landownership and usage by freedom's first generation. A recent detailed study of the notarial records in Guayama, one of Puerto Rico's three major sugar and slave regions, reveals only 24 cases of land transactions involving *libertos/as* (freedmen/freedwomen), amounting to a mere 366 *cuerdas*. Indeed, most black landowners in the region appear to have obtained their land as manumitted slaves *before* abolition in 1873.[57] This paucity of ex-slave landholding families was also replicated in the major sugar and slavery province of Matanzas in central Cuba. According to the 1899 census, only 2 percent of the "colored" agriculturalists (that is, "Blacks, Mulattos, Asians") either owned or rented their landholdings; while their acreage of 189 caballerias (1 caballeria = 33 acres) equaled less than 4 percent of the province's arable land. This was in contrast to the province of Pinar del Rio in which 1,775 "colored" owner and renter families (17 percent) held 11 percent of all arable land. These families pursued mixed farming of cash crops of tobacco and coffee for market and sweet potatoes, and *malangas* (yam/potato tubers) for home consumption. The eastern province of Santiago de Cuba was home to the largest landed class of Afro-Cubans: its 8,783 "colored" owners and renters worked small plots of land to produce cacao and coffee for the market, together with bananas, Indian corn, and sweet potatoes for home consumption. Altogether, these farmers constituted 30 percent of the province's agriculturalists who worked 26 percent of its arable land.[58]

The movement from plantation and farm to independent cultivation also occurred in the British colony of Mauritius in the Indian Ocean after colonial abolition. It has been determined that, except for 4,000 ex-slaves who contracted for one year's work on sugar plantations for the 1838–39 season, the majority pursued a series of independent strategies including occupying Crown land, creating small villages, and buying land. Many earned their living through fishing and subsistence agriculture. Others sold vegetables at low cost because their material needs were minimal.[59]

Although the post-emancipation U.S. South has often been depicted as a backward region of sharecroppers, poor tenant farmers, and neo-slavery, recent research reveals that freedom's first generation gained land in impressive numbers. In Charles City County, tidewater Virginia, established free black landholders like the Brown family of Ruthville broke up their holdings and sold small plots to former slaves out of a sense of civic duty.[60] In 1870, 121 freedpeople in Elizabeth City County, Virginia, owned 240 acres worth $52,000; by 1896, 735 black people owned nearly 3,000 acres worth $149,217. Although white Virginias still owned most of the land—and theirs was more valuable than that belonging to black Virginians—the latter were gaining, not losing, land in the post-abolition decades.[61] In Louisa County, Virginia, there were 1,317 black landowners in 1900; this meant that three-fourths of free-dom's first generation lived and labored on their own land. According to one optimistic estimate, Afro-Virginians fully or partially owned more than one million acres with farms and buildings worth a combined total of nearly $13 million by 1900.[62]

Freedpeople also became landholders in South Carolina. According to Edward Atkinson, a leading Massachusetts cotton industrialist who settled in coastal South Carolina during the early War years, former slaves desired their own land even before the advent of official emancipation:

> The most hopeful sign in this experiment [free labor on Union-oc-cupied plantations in post-1862 coastal South Carolina] has been the great desire of the freedmen to become freeholders, and this desire many have already realized. In some instances, several freedmen united their small earnings of the year 1862, and purchased the plantations on which they belonged at the tax sales; in others, small sums were loaned them by their employers for the same purpose. These men may be said to have become rich; there are some among them who have already accumulated from one to two thousand dollars, and at a recent sale of town lots and houses in Beaufort they were large purchasers.[63]

About 1,980 African American families owned 19,040 acres of land in Beau-fort County, St. Helena Island, by late 1867.[64] Between 1871 and 1876, around 14,000 black families—70,000 people in total—had acquired land from the South Carolina Land Commission. Although a few white families were to eventually predominate as owners of these lands, black families still owned over 44,000 acres of this land by 1890.[65]

In adjoining coastal Sapelo Island, Georgia, three former slaves—William Hillery, John Grovner, and Bilally Bell—organized the Hillery Land Company in 1871, purchasing 1,000 acres of land. The company went on to parcel out twenty plots of 33 acres to families on Sapelo Island to establish homesteads.[66] The acreage owned by blacks in Georgia increased from 339,000 acres in 1874 to 1,252,000 acres in 1903.[67] Black landownership was not restricted to the southeast Atlantic states: around 15 percent of all black Mississippians owned some land in 1910.[68] By the late nineteenth century, it has been estimated, between 20 and 25 percent of all black southern farmers owned land.[69] This was quite impressive given the recent stage of enslavement together with the hostile environment faced by black landowners in the U.S. South. Generations of black families would continue to own land throughout the region well into the twentieth century.[70]

Thus, many former slaves gained partial or complete access to landholdings in the Caribbean and the U.S. South. This similarity, however, tells us little about the ideological and cultural meanings of owning land for ex-slaves. These ran the spectrum from African-derived notions of communality to proto-peasant notions of markets and provision grounds to ideas of property rights and surplus extraction in modern capitalist societies. To review this large historical literature is less germane than pursuing a comparative analysis that illustrates the ways in which this spectrum transcends local, national, and regional frameworks.

African notions of communal ownership motivated some former slaves in post-abolition societies. After emancipation, many surviving ex-slaves in Haiti withdrew from plantation production to family plots according to African customs and land values that were either held by surviving African-born freedpeople, or were remembered because they were so recent in historical memory. According to one influential account of revolutionary southern Haiti, Congolese ethnic groups who predominated in the transatlantic slave trade during the final decades before the Haitian Revolution largely shaped peasant lifestyles, modes of social organization, and kinship ties to the land. This vision of freedom contrasted markedly with French notions of liberty and equality as well as revolutionary leader Toussaint Louverture's strict productive economy in the name of making a modern state out of a former slave colony.[71]

Similar notions of communal solidarity shaped by an African past characterized the life and labor of freedom's first generation in Mobile, Alabama. In July 1860, the slave ship *Clotilda* illegally deposited 110 enslaved African men, women, and children in Mobile. These Africans were mixed: some were Nupe, others were Dendi, but most were Yoruba. After five years of captivity, these West Africans gained their emancipation and in 1866 established African Town in northern Mobile. The men worked in shipyards and mills while women pursued truck farming. They pooled their resources to buy fifty-seven acres of land that became the basis of the new settlement. The housing pattern, political system of chiefdom, judicial system, and schooling all drew from traditional cultural mores. Conversion to Christianity, as well as intermarriage with Afro-Alabamans, did not dampen the original settlers' desire for family reunification as well as African homelands. Cudjo Lewis, one of the original settlers, later told Zora Neale Hurston that "he wishes at times to return to his native land, but he realizes that he would be a stranger there."

Over subsequent generations, their way of life developed into a remarkable expression of West Africa in coastal Alabama.[72]

Scholars have drawn upon the notion of a proto-peasantry to argue for the origins of a Caribbean peasantry in the transition from slavery to freedom. One of the problems with this regional focus, however, is that some post-abolition societies in the Caribbean did not have early black peasantries. According to the most recent study of slavery and freedom in the sugar plantation belt of southern Puerto Rico, ex-slaves were proletarianized early on because access "to land and subsistence production by slaves and *libertos*, both before and after emancipation, was weak, and the possibilities for ex-slaves peasant class formation were slim."[73] The same was true of slaves/ex-slaves in Danish St. Croix whose struggle for freedom and independence was curtailed by a harder work regimen together with the absence of a semi-autonomous system of food production and marketing.[74]

Another problem with this Caribbean focus is that it privileges one region over others by ignoring the existence of proto-peasants elsewhere, especially in mainland slave societies. Michael Mullin, for instance, argues that provision grounds in the Caribbean provided the basis for market relations in contrast to their absence in the U.S. South, with far-reaching implications. The "modern internal marketing system in the West Indian islands," he writes, had no "equivalent development [occurring] in the American South, where generally slaveholders, not their slaves, controlled surpluses including livestock and did not allot provision grounds anywhere close to the size and distance from the home plantation that were the case in the Caribbean."[75] This blanket contrast repeats an older regional dichotomy between the proto-peasant Caribbean and the non-proto-peasant U.S. South. Moreover, the comparison ignores those parts of the U.S. South that more closely resembled the proto-peasant existence in the Caribbean. In coastal South Carolina, the rice economy encouraged a task system of labor, together with communal productive activities, in which a former slave population continued to work the system in the old ways but without producing for former slaveholders.[76] In the sugar belt of ante-emancipation Louisiana, slaves worked for themselves, paced their own labor, organized their own productive activities, and controlled "the disposal of and profiting directly from the fruits of their labor," with important implications for the post-abolition era.[77] In short, proto-peasants occupied regions outside of the Caribbean, while not all parts of the Caribbean were inhabited by proto-peasants.

Along with notions of African community and proto-peasant consciousness, a third major ideological and cultural meaning of land concerned property rights. This appears to have been most developed throughout the U.S. South, presumably because of the unfettered development of propertied relations of production and capital accumulation during the nineteenth century. Rejecting older views of slaves' economy and communities that posit either the dialectic of accommodation versus resistance or cultural survivals versus acculturation, Dylan Penningroth examines the duality between property accumulation and kinship networks to make an argument for the meaning of slave property ownership within a capitalist society. His examination of some 250 claims by ex-slaves for property lost or stolen during the Civil War in Mississippi, Alabama, upcountry South Carolina, and Georgia concludes that "the claims of kinfolk involved both people's use of social networks to claim property and the often more powerful claims that social networks exerted on people."[78] This bred notions of greed and competition as well as solidarity and collectivity. Implicit within this analysis of social property ownership, however, resides a critique of individual accumulation that was socially unjust due to misappropriation.

Throughout the post-abolition U.S. South, many former slaves valued the land upon which they had worked for years in moral terms derived from the Bible and the labor theory of surplus value. The Bible was the most-read book in the slave quarters and provided many enslaved people not only with coping and belief systems but also with a set of moral values by which to live. Moreover, slaves worked for little compensation in a dynamic capitalist society that equated labor with compensation and social mobility. The slaves understood this. When freedom came, it was not only embraced, but also drew upon these pre-existing moral terms. Freedman Bayley Wyat provided an eloquent expression in his justification for why ex-slaves had a right to squat on land in tidewater Virginia: "We has a right to the land where we are located. For why? I tell you. Our wives, our children, our husbands, has been sold over and over again to purchase the lands we now locates upon; for that reason we have a divine right to the land. And den didn't we clear the land, and raise de crops ob corn, ob cotton, ob tobacco, ob rice, ob sugar, ob everything. And den didn't fem large cities in de North grow up on de cotton and de sugars and de rice dat we made? . . . I say dey has grown rich, and my people is poor."[79]

Generations of slave families had paid dearly for the land. This entitled their descendants to access to the same lands. The labor of slave families had transformed this wilderness into productive farmland. Not only did this benefit the economy of the region; it also helped spur urban growth nationally. And yet, some had grown rich, while freedpeople were poor. The labor theory of surplus value was on the minds of other former slaves too. After land auctions in the South Carolina sea islands, freedman Uncle Smart wrote to a former teacher: "Do, my missus, tell Linkum dat we wants the land—dis bery land dat is rich wid de sweat ob we face and de blood ob we back."[80] After fighting for the Union Army and helping to terminate slavery and save the Union, former slave soldiers who gained access to land simply could not understand why they were required to vacate land that they had worked on and fought for and over which they had risked their lives.[81] This explains, I would argue, why the roots of exploitation and racial inequality run deep in the collective consciousness of contemporary black America. They find less fertile soil in proto-peasant or African communal environs.

Finally, what is the comparative significance of ex-slaves' access to land-holding in post-emancipation societies? Three key points require emphasis. First, ex-slave landownership patterns are much better understood beyond national and regional categories. Landholding was prevalent among blacks in post-abolition Virginia, Georgia, South Carolina, Jamaica, Trinidad, eastern Cuba, and southern Haiti, but less so in Puerto Rico, central Cuba, Barbados, Antigua, and much of the U.S. South. Such a typology makes it hard to view the United States as exceptional. Second, although black landholding was comparatively similar across post-abolition societies, the meaning of owner-ship did not derive from some common experience of racial oppression and enslavement. This emerged from various cultural contexts, conditions of en-slavement and emancipation, and can only be truly understood in these terms. The statements that ex-slaves wanted land because they lived in the country-side or because they thought they deserved it are simplistic formulas rather than persuasive comparative explanations. Third, a comparative approach suggests that these different cultural contexts do not fit easily into national frameworks: there were proto-peasants in the coastal U.S. South as well as Ja-maica; African-derived values were promoted among Haitians and Alabamans; and property rights and their accumulation were important among African Americans but were by no means ubiquitous.

III. UNFREE GENERATIONS

Whenever I teach classes on slavery and emancipation to a younger genera-tion of undergraduates in the United States, I come across student papers that assume the inevitability of New World slavery's termination. After abolition in Haiti, they write, slavery was doomed to failure in one slave society after another throughout the nineteenth-century Americas. These students are in good company. Christian abolitionists thought that slavery was destined to fall consecutively—mainly because it was God's will. The more secular-minded university youngsters of today embrace the domino theory: after 1804 emancipation in Haiti, slavery fell in Spanish America (1810s–50s), the British West Indies (1830s), the Danish and French West Indies (1840s), the Dutch West Indies and the United States (1860s), and Cuba and Brazil (1880s). Once that first big push was made at the dawn of the nineteenth century, the rest were bound to follow, until the system finally toppled over by century's end.[82]

One obvious reason for thinking this way is that our knowledge that things have already happened tends to make them seem inevitable. (Presumably this is the picture we seek to complicate in the history classroom, not always with success.) Furthermore, students often see processes of abolition in linear terms because historians often present the transition from slavery to freedom in similar ways. The abolition of transatlantic slave trades, for instance, led ineluctably to the abolition of slave systems. Here's one example: "The abolition of slavery in the British West Indies was achieved incrementally, as abolitionists were forced to pass legislation that eroded the institution [1808 legislation] but fell short of complete emancipation until 1834."[83] Here's another: "During the nineteenth century, outside forces, especially from Great Britain, pressured Spain to end the transatlantic slave trade within its empire as a step toward the abolition of slavery."[84]

It is probable that the abolition of the Atlantic slave trade resulted in improved material conditions for many slaves in the British West Indies and the U.S. South after the first decade of the nineteenth century. But this was not the same thing as the abolition of systems of slavery. Once the transoceanic trade had been outlawed, planters, merchants, and statesmen developed regional slave trading systems in which generations of slaves were moved from older cash-crop plantation areas to newer, more lucrative areas of production. Slaves were exported from older sugar regions in the British West Indies (Barbados, Jamaica) to the newer colonies (Guiana, Trinidad) after the legal termination of British participation in the slave trade in 1808. In the ante-emancipation U.S. South, slaves were moved from older tobacco areas of Maryland and Virginia down to the dynamic expanding cotton regions of Mississippi, Alabama, Arkansas, and Texas. In Brazil, slaves were moved from older sugar-producing regions of the Northeast (Bahia, Maranhão, Pernambuco, Alagoas) to center provinces (Minas Gerais, Rio de Janeiro), and the newer coffee regions in the Southwest (Sao Paulo, Rio Grande do Sul).[85] Besides prematurely killing generations of slaves engaged in cash-crop production, these second middle passages had tremendous implications for destabilizing families and communities. More generally, the abolition of the Atlantic slave trade did not lead inevitably to the abolition of slavery in the British Caribbean, the United States, and Brazil, but resulted in the prolonged existence and expansion of slavery among those who were already enslaved as well as younger generations born into servitude.

Moreover, the passage of emancipation in place was frequently connected with the emergence of various forms of dependency and losses of freedom in other areas. We shall focus on three particular connections: the impact of the abolition of slavery in Haiti for the development of cotton and slavery in the U.S. South as well as sugar and slavery in the Spanish Antilles, the termination of slavery in the British West Indies and the importation of Asian indentured servants, and the global consequences of emancipation in the cotton economy of the U.S. South. These connections between freedom and unfreedom operated within the unfolding dynamics of a global marketplace and capitalist productive relations. The central connection was between ex-slaves' withdrawal from cash-crop production, their pursuit of subsistence farming as an alternative means of living, and the development of new forms of coercive and dependent labor in an expanding global marketplace. Thus, progress toward freedom was not linear, inevitable, or universal during the nineteenth century. It was not simply movement from slave societies to free societies with legal abolition as the watershed. A cross-national comparative approach reveals that benefits for former slaves in one area could lead to negative consequences for free people elsewhere. In short, emancipation wrought new forms of dependency, exploitation, and loss of freedom internationally. These links remain invisible in local, regional, and national approaches toward abolition as well as in historical narratives of progress.

The Haitian Revolution had a profound impact on the expansion of unfreedom in the young U.S. republic. In 1802, the French First Consul Napoleon Bonaparte reintroduced colonial slavery to the Caribbean and mainland colonies. This meant that slavery was to begin again in French Louisiana after a hiatus of nearly a decade. The loss of St. Domingue, together with a large part of Napoleon's army, however, forced the French dictator to reluctantly sell the Louisiana Territory to the United States under the presidency of Thomas Jefferson. The Virginia slave-holding president saw opportunities beyond the low price tag. Fugitive slaves were more easily captured and returned within one's own national borders rather than having to deal with the French (or the Spanish in Florida, the British in Canada, and so forth). Moreover, the entire Mississippi Valley westward was now potentially open to the expansion of southern slaveholding. Despite geographical limits eventually agreed upon by the U.S. Congress in 1820, hundreds of thousands of men, women, and children were enslaved as a consequence of this territorial expansion. The origins of this unfree generation are to be traced directly to the success of the Haitian Revolution.[86]

The Haitian Revolution also helped to create unfree generations in the Caribbean. The abolition of slavery in Haiti resulted in freedom's first generation turning their back on cash-crop production for alternative forms of life and labor. This left a lacuna in the sugar market as demand remained high after the world's major producer went into decline. Into the breach stepped planters in the British colonies. Before the 1790s, sugar exports from Jamaica to Europe amounted to around 60 percent of those from St. Domingue; by 1805–6, these exports were greater than those from the French colony in 1790.[87] But it was the Spanish Antilles, especially Cuba, which really filled the gap. Over the next generation, Cuba was transformed into the leading sugar and slave colony in the Americas. It has been estimated that over 25,000 refugees from Haiti crossed the fifty-mile sea stretch to Cuba by 1808. They brought expertise in coffee, citrus, indigo, tobacco, cacao, and cotton production.[88] They also transported slaves away from emerging Haitian freedoms toward an imminent slave society.[89] Moreover, around 780,200 African slaves were imported to Cuba between 1791 and 1870; while sugar cane production rose from 13 percent of the world's supply in 1820 to 42 percent by 1870.[90] As Franklin Knight summarizes: "The collapse of the sugar industry in St. Domingue, and the exhaustion of the soils in the leading British West Indian islands, provided part of the powerful initial impetus to the Cuban sugar cane grower."[91] Without the Haitian Revolution and former slaves' withdrawal from sugar production, it is hard to envision the reproduction of younger generations of slaves in the new colonies of the British West Indies before colonial abolition during the 1830s together with a loss of liberty for hundreds of thousands of Africans in the Spanish slave trade.

The decisions of freedom's first generation were also linked to the rise of

Asian indentured servitude throughout the post-emancipation Caribbean. After the abolition of slavery in the British Caribbean, former slaves withdrew from plantation production. Planters and their supporters used this reduced production—that is, the *freedom crop index*—as an argument to urge new forms of labor from overseas. Between 1837 and 1917, more than 430,000 men and women from India participated in the state-supervised system of indentured migration to the British Caribbean.[92] Although scholars debate the extent to which indentured servitude represented either a new system of slavery in the Caribbean or an opportunity to escape from the harsh realities of life in Asia,[93] there is little doubt that the process of indenture exposed workers to a whole new set of oppressive conditions and relations of dependency. Between 1856 and 1857, 707 of 4,094 passengers died on ships bound from India to the British Caribbean. This mortality rate of 17.27 percent approximated the gruesome percentage of the Atlantic slave trade.[94] On the plantations, Indian indentured workers labored on sugar estates once worked by slaves, were controlled by penal labor laws reminiscent of slave codes, and suffered from poor health conditions. Unlike their predecessors whose status as chattel property restricted their movements, indentured servants were often controlled by strict pass laws as well as through a system of debt peonage.[95] According to one petition written on behalf of indentured workers in 1864, laborers lived in appalling conditions in Jamaica, with the men earning four pence and the women and boys two pence daily. Many had feet infested with chiggers, requiring amputations. Others begged in the streets, several committed suicide, and some murdered their wives.[96] One major consequence of the landing of these new indentured laborers from India was the revival of sugar plantation production in parts of the post-abolition British Caribbean. Between 1834 and 1838, Trinidad's average annual sugar production was 15,227 tons. By the late 1850s, it had reached 26,564 tons. In British Guiana, the same period saw a rise from 51,278 tons to 61,284 tons.[97]

Asian indentured labor also replaced freedom's first generation in the French Caribbean. By the early 1880s—a generation after abolition—over 25,000 Indians had been shipped to Martinique and more than 41,000 to Guadeloupe. These immigrants helped to revive the colonial sugar industry. They were also exposed to harsh conditions and abuse.[98] But the toughest form of unfree labor was reserved for post-abolition indentured African workers. Between 1854 and 1862, around 18,518 indentures from Northwest and West Central Africa arrived in French Guiana and the French West Indies. Most of these workers were recruited through *repurchase*: merchants in African markets bought captives and liberated them in exchange for ten-year contracts to be served in the French Caribbean. French visitors described their wretched condition upon arrival: "In 1861 in Martinique, I witnessed the landing of a convoy of these poor devils, ironically called free workers. They were parked on the Savane in Fort-de-France, numbering about five hundred men, women, and children, naked, with serial numbers on plates of tin around their necks, trembling at the uncertain fate before them. They waited to be parceled out."[99] Once these indentured workers were assigned to planters, they worked out their terms. The advantages to employers were quite obvious. During the 1850s, the average daily wage of indentured Africans was 30–40 cents, which remained fixed for the length of contract. In contrast, farm workers earned from 1.00 to 1.50 francs.[100] In short, the choices of freedom's first generation contributed to the making of a bonded first generation across empires.

In addition to the French and British Caribbean, indentured labor replaced ex-slave workers on sugar plantations in Latin America and the Indian Ocean. Between 1890 and 1939, an estimated 33,000 Javanese workers were moved to the Dutch colony of Suriname to work on the sugar estates. Some of these indentured immigrants were women. Pieter Emmer argues that such migration served as a "vehicle of female emancipation." In contrast, Rosemarin Hoefte's detailed study of the labor mechanisms used to control contract laborers on the Marienberg plantation in Suriname, one of the largest sugar mills in the world, concludes that, while a few "may have gained some freedom by emigrating to Suriname," the "economic freedom women gained was at best quite limited."[101] The post-abolition decline in sugar production in the British West Indies similarly saw the rise of alternative sources for colonial sugar production in the British-controlled western Indian Ocean. The abolition of slavery saw the flight of ex-slaves from plantation production in Mauritius. By the end of the 1860s, there were some 313,000 Indian indentured laborers working the single-crop economy. Between 1812 and 1860, sugar exports from British Mauritius increased from 500 to 134,000 tons, making it one of the leading world sugar producers during the mid-nineteenth century. This remarkable leap in production was achieved through the extension of the plantation system of sugar estate work, penal labor laws, appalling work and health conditions, and debt peonage.[102] In short, the decisions of freedom's first generation in the British Caribbean led to the making of a new generation of unfree workers in the British colony of Mauritius in the Indian Ocean under a colonial umbrella.

This global transformation—especially former slaves' emancipation from plantation production and their replacement by new sources of bonded, indentured, and dependent labor—was replicated in the cotton economy. By the late 1850s, slaves in the U.S. South produced 60 percent of cotton consumed in the German Zollverien, 77 percent in Great Britain, 90 percent in France, and 92 percent in Russia. The onset of the American Civil War virtually ended production and resulted in what became known at the time as the "cotton famine." Textile factories, merchants, and proletarians were starved of the valuable white stuff. Consequently, rural cultivators in other parts of the world filled the breach. In India, cotton production increased from 986,000 bales in 1861 to 1,398,000 bales in 1864. This largely came from the three major regions of Gujarat, Deccan, and Mahratta in Western India. Here, peasant cultivators quickly shifted from subsistence production to cotton production. In the Bombay Presidency, cotton acreage doubled from more than one to two million acres between 1860 and 1865. In the northwestern provinces, it also doubled. Although one scholar claims this shift benefited peasant cultivators through improved living standards and reduced indebtedness,[103] it should not be forgotten that short-term gains from high market prices were made at the expense of long-term decline, especially the reduction in subsistence production and independent food cultivation.

Peasant cultivators in Egypt also reacted to the cotton famine by turning to production of the precious white stuff during the American Civil War. Between 1860 and 1866, cotton exports multiplied nearly fourfold from 50 to 178 million pounds. By 1864, it has been estimated that 40 percent of the fertile soil of the Nile Delta region in Lower Egypt was devoted to cotton production.[104] That same year, the price for cotton on the Liverpool market exceeded 31 pence per pound, a record market price for the Egyptian fiber according to statistics published between 1824 and 1870.[105] As economic historian David Landes describes the process in Egypt: "everyone connected with the cultivation or trade of the new white gold was working a bonanza." Merchants made a fortune selling cotton on the market, while the state reaped its reward from taxation. The peasant cultivators also reaped much of the estimated 40 to 50 million pounds earned by cotton sales during these years to eat white bread and meat, invest in dowries, make the pilgrimage, build houses, and buy silks, silver, pipes, and furniture. One consequence of this newly found prosperity was the expansion of enslavement as cultivators bought slaves. These new bonded laborers worked in the fields and performed *corvee* (unfree unpaid labor for the state). Others, including Circassian concubines, became status symbols.[106] Another result was the expansion of cotton production at the expense of food crops. Egypt—the granary of the Roman Empire, a nation that had always shipped beans and grains through its Mediterranean port city Alexandria to the outside world—now had to import food in order to feed its people![107] This paralleled earlier slave societies and their preoccupation with cash-crop production over local food production in the Caribbean and the U.S. South.[108]

The virtual cessation of cotton production in the U.S. South also inspired peasant cultivators in Brazil to pursue the valuable fiber. Brazilian cotton exports rose from 21,467,552 pounds in 1860–61 to a record 92,449,368 pounds in 1865–66. Most of this cotton was grown in the northeastern provinces of Pernambuco, Maranhão, Alagoas, Pará, Ceará, and Bahia, formerly the nation's sugar and slavery heartland. The major producers were small growers who cultivated cotton "in little patches on the edge of the great sugar-cane plantations," with little capital or technological investment. Even though cotton was considered the poor man's crop (*lavoura de pobre*), market prices made its cultivation highly attractive for a short while.[109]

One key explanation for this long-term transformation must be sought in the refusal of former slaves in the U.S. South to engage in working the slave crop.[110] This became evident as early as 1862 as former slaves in Union-liberated regions such as coastal South Carolina refused to grow cotton and turned to the cultivation of food and subsistence crops. Edward Atkinson, treasurer and agent for cotton manufacturers of Boston as well as one of the leaders of the Port Royal Experiment in South Carolina, argued that free labor was cheaper than slave labor in the production of cotton. Indeed, Atkinson was full of praise for freedmen who moved "from a state of utter destitution and ignorance to absolute prosperity and partial education" between 1862 and 1864. But many former slaves working in these new liberated zones rejected cotton cultivation for truck farming, raising vegetables, and fishing, the proceeds of which they sold to Union soldiers.[111] Their actions represented a rehearsal for the *freedom crop index* as former slaves turned their back on cash-crop production once emancipation was legally confirmed after 1865.

The return of the U.S. South to cotton cultivation brought a decline in market prices as the new producers were edged out of the global marketplace. In India, the quality, cleanliness, and price of the cotton product could not compete with the superior U.S. product preferred by the English textile industry. On top of which, the switch from food to cotton production resulted in the rise of dependency among peasant cultivators. By 1891, 30 to 40 percent of inhabitants of the major cotton region of Berar, India, had become landless laborers.[112] The same process of lost markets and increased dependency was also the unfortunate lot of peasant cultivators in Egypt. When prices fell toward the end of the 1860s, cotton merchants were left with a surplus product that they could not sell, while peasants had lost their income but were still required to pay taxes to the Egyptian state. Many cotton cultivators in these new production areas became increasingly enmeshed in sharecropping, debt peonage, and market dependency. Consequently, many forfeited their rural independence by giving up the land, as reported by the British Consul to Cairo in 1872: "Many of the poorer classes of natives, calculating that they could not obtain from the produce of the land sufficient to pay the increased demands, offered their lands gratis to any person who would relieve them of it and pay the newly imposed tax. Some wealthy persons accepted the land of their poorer neighbours on those terms, others paid nominal sums of 1 [pound], 2 [pounds] or 3 [pounds] an acre for it."

Although it is difficult to estimate exactly how much land was lost by peasant cultivators, one specialist in cotton and the Egyptian economy estimates the amount to have been more than 30,000 feddans (1 feddan = 1.038 acres) in three Lower Egyptian provinces during the reign of the Khedive Isma'il Pasha (1863–79).[113] By 1907, one contemporary estimated that 37 percent of all agriculturalists in the lower Nile Valley were landless workers.[114] Indeed, there is little doubt that the modernization of the nineteenth-century Egyptian economy inaugurated forms of socioeconomic dependency in the countryside that remained in place throughout the era of British imperial control from 1882 through 1952 until the inauguration of reforms in the post-independence era.

This cycle of cotton and dependency boomeranged back to the U.S. South. By 1891, southern farmers cultivated twice the amount of cotton produced in 1861. But the key difference was that white farmers who had traditionally remained outside the cotton economy now became caught in its web of debt, unpredictable market forces, and dependency.[115] By the 1890s, cotton's new retainers stretched from the Indus to the Nile to the Mississippi and were linked directly to freedom's first generation. As Sven Beckert summarizes, American emancipation wrought new forms of labor control globally.[116]

These sorts of global linkages in the cotton and sugar economies were mirrored in the impact of the abolition of slave trading and systems of slavery upon Africa. The abolition of the Atlantic slave trade during the early nineteenth century resulted in a build-up of slaves in the Asante and Gold Coast.[117] More generally, there was a spur to inward slave trading. By the late nineteenth century, slave societies in the Americas were a thing of the past. At the same time, the major European powers expanded upon an unprecedented wave of imperial aggrandizement, especially in Asia and Africa. Most general studies of emancipation in the Americas and neo-colonialism in Africa deal with the topics separately. But there were connections. Pioneers of abolition in the New World projected new forms of colonial domination through ideological justification of crusading against the slave trade in African societies.

Moreover, there were connections between the decline of slavery in the Americas and slavery's expansion on the African continent at the same time during the nineteenth century—between freedom's first generations in the New World and slavery's latest generations in the Old World. William Gervase Clarence-Smith, for instance, argues for a dramatic "resurgence of slavery" on the African continent during the nineteenth century that was "driven by the production of export commodities, drawing Islam closer to New World models of servitude."[118] Robin Blackburn insists "the spread of European rule in Africa in the late nineteenth century led to a horrendous expansion of slavery and forced labor in the newly acquired territories as the new rulers and their favored enterprises recruited labor for public works, plantations, and mines."[119] Paul Lovejoy argues for the massive expansion of slave-based production on the African continent during the nineteenth century.[120] Indeed, the complicated connections between the beginnings of the "scramble for Africa" and the final abolition of New World slavery during the same decade of the 1880s have yet to be fully researched.[121] But let us not forget our major aims: to reveal cross-national connections between freedom's first generation and the making of unfree generations, to be skeptical of narratives of progress and inevitability, and to be wary of "[D]omino[']s"—a tasteless U.S. pizza chain rather than a persuasive historical explanation.

Freedom's Seekers Today

*It is time to free ourselves from all the authoritarian regimes and their ruling
tyrants, it's time to free people's souls from slavery.*
—APRIL 6 YOUTH MOVEMENT, 2011

Freedom's Seekers has argued for the indispensability of comparative methodology for emancipation studies. More specifically, it demonstrates there
were moments and people that were inherently transnational, and that their
experiences and lives can therefore be best understood through comparative
approaches. The key protagonists were self-emancipators, slave soldiers, black
abolitionists, freedwomen, freed children, and freedom's first generation,
whose world was the nineteenth-century African Diaspora together with the
Indian Ocean. This book demonstrates the utility of the comparative method
to scholars, disciplines, and institutions interested in emancipation studies; encourages Anglophone scholars to draw upon non-Anglophone studies
of emancipation; and expands African Diaspora theory beyond slavery and
homeland studies. In particular, I hope that my comparative methodology
toward emancipation reveals more about the role and impact of Diaspora Africans and provides a recognizable and coherent set of parameters that prove
as efficacious as comparative slave studies.

We conclude with an extended comparison between the past and the present: freedom's seekers in contemporary societies in the light of past struggles.
Yesterday's self-emancipators are today's modern slaves seeking refuge in free
soil. Modern nation-states continue to argue over cross-border movements
and their potential impact. The United States and the United Kingdom are no
less ambivalent in their welcoming of political asylum-seekers and economic
refugees. Women and children remain central to household economies as they
were in post-abolition societies. Domestic violence and sexual abuse of women
and children continues to ravage many modern societies. Racial consciousness
sparked by the Haitian Revolution and West Indies Emancipation has become
a shadow of its former self in today's world organized around modern nation-
states, but international solidarity is far from moribund. Meanwhile, freedom's

seekers' latest generation on the global stage are Arab-speaking, share a Muslim faith, and seek to topple generational geriatric autocracies and patriarchal dynasties. If they succeed, they will transform a region and the world in ways pioneered by their nineteenth-century predecessors.

Any discussion of today's freedom seekers must begin with globalization. Trays of ink, together with countless hours of computer typing, have been devoted to its explication. Some argue that the last two decades have inaugurated a profound shift in the human condition in which everything has become interconnected, the nation-state is much less cohesive, everything is in flux, and representation and spectacle supersede material reality. Others reject this view altogether, claiming that globalization represents little more than the latest stage of a historical process of international capital, labor, and market flows that began five centuries earlier with the European colonization of the Americas and was enhanced two centuries ago with the advent of industrial capitalist economies and the making of modern nation-states and citizenship.[1] The logical consequence has been American imperial hegemony in Afghanistan, Iraq, and elsewhere during the last decade as simply the most recent unleashing of the conventional dogs of war.

The truth probably lies somewhere between the two: we are undoubtedly witnessing remarkable transformations, especially in science and technology, lightning-fast international movements of capital and information, and unprecedented levels of organization globally. Industrial manufacturing has expanded tremendously in the BRIC nations (Brazil, Russia, India, China) over the last two decades. On the other hand, industrial capitalism continues in older states: nearly one-fifth of the labor force in the United States and the United Kingdom works in industry while one-quarter of French workers are in the industrial sector.[2] The nation-state continues to operate as the defining political reality for most people, with South Sudan becoming the world's youngest nation-state on July 9, 2011.[3] Global power remains disproportionately in the hands of political and corporate elites in a select handful of Western nations, much like the 1890s. Just compare the seven current members of the G7, the world's most powerful financial group—Canada, France, Germany, Italy, Japan, United Kingdom, United States—with the leading colonizing nations a century ago—France, Germany, Italy, Japan, United States, United Kingdom.[4] The spectacular economic growth of the People's Republic of China since the late 1990s, however, along with the rise of Brazil, India, and Russia betokens some significant global shifts in the coming decades.

One aspect of globalization that has remained unchanged is the compatibility of free with unfree labor. This simultaneity first emerged during the expansion of colonial plantation slavery and the take-off of early industrial capitalism during the eighteenth century.[5] Recent scholarship suggests that slave labor remains an important component of the modern global economy. At the end of the 1990s, U.S. social scientist Kevin Bales estimated 27 million slaves in the world today. The largest group includes bonded laborers in India, Pakistan, Bangladesh, and Nepal. They are defined as slaves because they "give themselves into slavery as security against a loan or when they inherit a debt from a relative." Other groups include workers in extractive industries in South America, especially Brazil, agricultural workers in Southeast Asia and western Africa, domestic workers in capital cities, and sex workers globally. Collectively, Bales defines these workers as modern slaves primarily because they are absolutely controlled through violence, not compensated beyond basic subsistence, and economically exploited.[6] In 2012, a U.S. government report estimated 42,000 adults and children in forced prostitution, labor, slavery, or armed conflict, with around 800,000 people trafficked across borders annually.[7]

The awful extent of today's slavery lies somewhere between these contrasting poles. Anti-Slavery International, the world's oldest international human rights organization, which traces its origins back to the British antislavery movement during the 1840s, regularly reports cases of modern slavery. The winter 2012 edition of its monthly newsletter notes that, between 1995 and 2011, more than 41,000 workers were rescued from slavery in Brazil according to that nation's Labor Ministry. During 2011, some 2,270 workers from rural farms, plantations, and cattle ranches were liberated from debt bondage in Brazil.[8] The struggle for emancipation remains unfinished until all of these modern slaves are liberated from exploitative practices and ideological rationalizations propagated by predatory businessmen, political elites, and well-heeled consumers.

Many women and children are trapped in this modern global economy of bonded labor. Globalization has proven to be a double-edged sword. On the one hand, it has opened up opportunities for women and children to engage in wage work either close to home or across national borders. This has not only helped contribute to the household economy; it also reflects a new degree of freedom for women and young workers who are no longer tied to older forms of patriarchal control. On the other hand, there is little doubt that globalization has contributed to the making of a new category of exploited workers, many of whom are women and children. An industry of domestic servitude proliferates in which women and children from the poor world work for wealthy households in Paris, London, New York, Los Angeles, Zurich, Madrid, Rome, Toronto, Berlin, Tokyo, and numerous other rich global cities. A recent report prepared for the Human Rights Council of the United Nations asserts that "domestic servitude was rooted in entrenched patterns of gender discrimination and discrimination on the basis of race, ethnicity, and caste." The solution to these problems, concludes the same report, was to implement the commitments agreed to at Beijing, the Peoples Republic of China, and Durban, the Republic of South Africa, as well as to require political and civic leaders to both publicly recognize the value of domestic work as well as the "equal" human worth of domestic workers.[9]

One of the most disturbing features of this global economy of bonded labor concerns the exploitation of women and children in the sex industry. As argued in chapter 5, above, emancipation wrought more control over women's bodies away from the predatory actions of planters, slaveholders, and others. Globalization and mass tourism, however, have seen the re-emergence of new forms of sexual exploitation. Kevin Bales estimates about 1.5 million prostitutes in Thailand, of whom around one in twenty is enslaved. Moreover, a number of Thai women and girls end up as sex workers across borders in Southeast Asia, Japan, Switzerland, and Germany. Enticed as domestics, they pay large fees to employment agencies and end up as sex slaves caught in debt bondage.[10] This cross-border trafficking of women into the sex industry is prolific. In December 2008, four women from Eastern Europe who were forced into prostitution in the United Kingdom were compensated more than 140,000 pounds ($230,000).[11] Other women experience sexual abuse and exploitation, either as chattel slaves from slave-owners in places like Mauritania, West Africa, or as brick workers from employers in Pakistan.[12] The solution to this global problem of sexual abuse and violence toward women and children consists of a combination of more forceful police practices nationally, the ratification of international agreements that criminalize such activities, and the mass education of young and older males. The emancipation of women and children's bodies from these abuses remains unfinished.

At the same time, some of these modern exploited workers seek to escape their oppressive conditions. Both Temrazgint mint M'Bareck and Fatma mint Souleymane escaped slavery in Mauritania.[13] Talak, an ethnic Wahaya from the

Tahoua region of central Niger in West Africa, spent many years enslaved in northern Nigeria before she escaped across the border to Zongon Ablo. This village housed several hundred former Wahaya who had also self-emancipated from modern-day slavery.[14] These modern self-emancipators cross borders in search of new lives of self-control and human dignity.

More broadly, the forces of globalization have both pushed and pulled the working poor across national borders. Mexican and Central American workers cross daily into the United States in search of employment, higher wages, and greater opportunities. They are pulled by the massive dynamic economy of North America; they are pushed by poverty and unemployment in their homelands. These modern cross-border travelers offer a stark contrast to slaves in the U.S. South who crossed the Rio Grande in search of personal liberty in post-abolition Mexico. Contemporary Haitians flee their poverty-stricken—and now earthquake-devastated—native soil in search of decent living conditions in southern Florida, New York City, and elsewhere along the U.S. Atlantic seaboard. They are the reverse of slaves and free blacks from the eastern U.S. cities seeking liberties in post-independent Haiti several generations earlier.

Unlike self-emancipators who crossed from slave to free soil during the nineteenth century, there is no common explanation for these modern migrations. Some are fueled by economic push and pull factors. Others are sparked by political crises. North Africans in Tunisia, Egypt, and Libya, flee the political turmoil and economic disruptions resulting from the Arab Revolution and cross into southern Europe. Others are motivated by a combination of the two, such as Cuban emigrants. In short, most of this modern cross-border movement has been fueled by a combination of deregulated markets, labor ebbs and flows, and political instability. But what is similar is that these modern-day refugees seek alternative freedoms denied them in their birthplaces. It is a situation slave self-liberators would have understood.

These contemporary cross-border movements have fueled heated debates both within as well as between nation-states. The key issues include the motives of these new workers for leaving their homelands, their civil status in the country of arrival, and the implications of their relocation for existing societies. Both Republican and Democratic politicians in U.S. federal and state legislatures continue to lead campaigns against the entry of some 11 million illegal aliens and the granting of civil rights to undocumented workers. In Arizona, there have even been attempts to turn local police forces into quasi-immigration officials with the power to stop, arrest, and remove those without the proper documentation.[15] Meanwhile, supporters of Caribbean emigration to the United States criticize what they correctly interpret as a double-standard between the embrace of Cuban emigrants as "political refugees" from Communist Cuba compared to Haitian emigrants who are screened and often returned because they are considered "economic refugees." The reasons, of course, are because of a powerful anti-Cuba lobby in southern Florida in contrast to a lack of organized support for Haitians in U.S. politics. At the same time, it is hard to deny that Haitians are more deserving of political asylum than Cubans since many more of the former than the latter have perished under autocratic regimes supported by the United States during the last several decades.

These debates over cross-border immigrant movements in the New World are mirrored in the Old World. In 1998, member states of the European Union signed the Schengen Agreement that basically created a passport-free zone covering twenty-five European nations. Although the free flow of peoples across borders has been welcomed, some critics argue that it has created a European Fortress designed to keep out non-Europeans. These tensions manifested themselves in the reaction of some European Union nations to the influx of North Africans after the outbreak of the Arab Revolution in early 2011. Within a few months, some 27,000 North Africans turned up in Italy. The response of the Italian state was to issue travel visas to North Africans with the aim of encouraging them to move. Many ended up relocating. Recent outbursts by French and British officials against this Italian policy of immigrant removal reveal the contentiousness of immigration issues underlying the original treaty. It should also not be forgotten that the 2008 Global Crash has further exacerbated cross-border tensions in the Americas as well as Europe. This is beginning to find political voice in conservative and anti-immigration parties and policies in the United States, France, the United Kingdom, and elsewhere.[16] Much like self-emancipators moving from slave to free soil across the nineteenth century Atlantic Americas, freedom's seekers today inhabit a world in which national borders open as well as close.

The United Kingdom has proven to be especially opposed to the spirit of cross-border movement. In a trip to France in early June 2011, British Home Secretary Teresa May spoke of the need for "impenetrable borders" in the face of the recent upsurge of migrants from Tunisia and Libya to southern Europe.[17] Fortress Britain draws from a long tradition of anti-immigration policies that deny domestic residency to the families of African, Asian, and Caribbean workers.[18] It contrasts markedly with the imperial protection afforded self-emancipators and refugees after Britain had abolished domestic slavery in the 1770s, the slave trade in the early 1800s, and colonial slavery in the 1830s. What is different, however, is the origin, culture, and motivation of these new cross-border emigrants. When I grew up in London during the 1960s and 1970s, the immigration divide was primarily between whites who opposed the entry of blacks into Britain, and Asian, Afro-Caribbean, and West African people born and raised in their homeland of the United Kingdom. I still recall some of the bigots' charming expressions: "Go black home," "Keep Britain white," and "Wog a matter, all browned off, nigger mind, be all white in the morning." Second and third generations of British-born Asian, Afro-Caribbean, and African people have consistently and vigorously challenged the racist assumption that they are not British because they are not white.

Since the 1990s, however, there has emerged a new divide in which racial difference is compounded by religious differences. The Church of England replaced Catholicism as the nation's predominant organized faith nearly five centuries ago. Other faiths either fled the new religious orthodoxy or remained to be tolerated as "non-conformist" religions. Great Britain remains a predominantly Anglican society with some 17 million Church of England members in a population of around 60 million. The second largest faith is Islam, with some 7 million adherents. This religious divide widened during the 1990s, but especially after the September 11, 2001, attacks on the United States and the July 7, 2005, bombings in London.[19] Christian England under threat from radical Islam has unfortunately became the latest barrier between "them" and "us" in this (dis)United Kingdom. I still recall a minor but not insignificant example of this divide among my own family. At my grandmother's church funeral in the East Midlands town of Kettering in February 2005, my mother's brother-in-law wanted to know what a mosque was doing in his English hometown? The response, of course, is that not all British people are Christians.

Questions of homelands, emancipation, and national identity were central issues in nineteenth-century slave and free societies. It was because of such ambiguities that slaves, abolitionists, and freedpeople often imagined communities beyond the nation-state. Recently, we have witnessed some key moments of international racial solidarity reminiscent of past racial solidarities. The release of dissident Nelson Mandela, the electoral success of the African National Congress, and the destruction of the racist apartheid system in 1990s

South Africa inspired Africans, people of African descent, and their advocates around the world. The election of Barack Obama as the first African American president of the United States in 2008 sent waves of pride, consciousness, and hope across borders, inspiring Africans—especially Kenyans—inspiring Americans—especially of African descent—and many others.[20] The Haitian earthquake in January 2010 galvanized communities of color across the United States and elsewhere in the Western Hemisphere to support the survivors of that appalling tragedy.[21] Countless millions around the world—especially Africans, people of African descent, and underdog supporters—willed on Ghana to triumph in their quarter-final match against Uruguay in the 2010 World Cup Finals in South Africa. Not only were they the sole surviving African nation, but they symbolized the hopes and aspirations of the poor world against the might, resources, and reputations of the dominant football teams from the rich world.

But what is striking two generations after the winning of independence by African and Caribbean nations, together with the successful de-racialization of democracies in the United States, Brazil, and South Africa, is the rarity of these moments of international racial solidarity. This is not to deny continuing cultural connections through music and media, but it is to recognize the limitations of transnational racial solidarity compared to national and ethnic identities. Recent crises on the continent suggest that the African Union rarely acts beyond the particular interests of its national members.[22] The Caribbean lacks serious regional integration, a weakness symbolized perhaps by the withering away of the West Indies Cricket Team from its winning ways during the 1970s and 1980s. African Americans bond with people of African descent in the United States; but they also often resent the success of African and Afro-Caribbean immigrants. The tension between street vendors, taxi drivers, and other workers of African, Caribbean, and American origin is palpable on the streets of the nation's capital. African and Caribbean people bond with black Americans in the United States, but they also have major differences. Afro-Brazilians are the largest group of African-descended people in the Western Hemisphere, but their struggles are largely contained within national parameters primarily because of their poverty. Hegemonic national identity is one of the key challenges facing those committed to international racial solidarity in today's world, a challenge met by earlier generations of people of African descent against colonialism and for independence, contra slavery and pro freedom.

Perhaps the closest contemporary parallel we have to forms of international solidarity around slave revolts and black beacons in the Western Hemisphere can be found in political waves emanating out of mainland Latin America. For some post-abolition Haitian leaders, emancipation became state policy designed to influence regional events. The mainland equivalent was Simón Bolívar and his dream of a continent of interconnected independent republics. After the 1959 Cuban Revolution, Fidel Castro sought to offer a beacon of liberation to the region and globally. The fall of the Berlin Wall in 1989 and the inability of Cuba to come to terms with changes in the global economy served to restrict its message to one of survival. The Cuban beacon has been flickering off and on for a long time. The mantle of hemispheric change—especially sticking it to the leviathan in the North—was picked up by Venezuela under the leadership of President Hugo Chavez, insisting on spreading socialism regionally and even across the hemisphere Bolívar-like. In contrast to the ideological ghosts of Haitian emancipation or Cuban socialism, however, we should never forget that it is the material reality of high revenues accrued from Venezuela's oil riches that is driving this latest transnational project. For example, Venezuela sends *gratis* 100,000 barrels of oil daily to Cuba worth ninety U.S. dollars each.[23] These modern bonds are slick.[24]

This brings us to freedom's next generations. It is quite clear that the battle for political participation and legal citizenship in post-abolition societies has largely been won. The descendants of former slaves vote, represent, and politick throughout Latin America, the Caribbean, and North America in the early twenty-first century. This was primarily due to the success of mass protest movements for de-colonization and independence in the Caribbean (as well as Africa and Asia) during the 1940s–50s. The de-racialization of democracy in the United States during the 1960s was also the consequence of mass popular mobilization with the Civil Rights Movement and the passage of the 1964 Civil Rights Act and the 1965 Voting Rights Act. One measure of this electoral success is the contrast between older methods of blatant exclusion and denial of the ballot to African American citizens and more elaborate means of denying modern electorates access to political power through laws of voter identification, congressional redistricting, reduced numbers of polling stations, and so forth.[25] The de-racialization of democracy in South Africa during the 1990s was also the result of prolonged mass mobilization and coherent leadership by the African National Congress and its liberal and Communist allies, although we cannot ignore the impact of a successful international boycott together with the fall of the Berlin Wall and the end of the Cold War.

The battle for racial equality in post-abolition societies, however, remains unfinished. Why is it that people of African descent in former slave societies continue to bear disproportionate burdens of poverty, ill health, broken families, and lack of economic opportunities compared to white citizens? The right to freedom has been won, but the right to equality is about fair employment, decent housing, good education, better health care, and social justice. This is the battle for freedom's future generations in the twenty-first century not just in the New but also in the Old World. France has an estimated five million Muslims, many of whom hail from former French colonies in North and West Africa. Recent revolts by youth in the *banlieue* (working-class suburbs) were less motivated by jihadi politics than social problems around unemployment, poverty, illegal immigration, organized crime, and family breakdown.[26] The London riots in August 2011 were also a stark reminder that racial inequality continues to stalk urban areas of the United Kingdom.

The Arab revolution of 2011 provides us with the latest historical installment of the struggle for human freedom and dignity by freedom's next generation. Inspired by the popular uprising in Tunisia that saw the removal of an unpopular dictator, ordinary men, women, and children throughout the Arab world have mobilized to remove unpopular dictators and create more democratic forms of governance. There have been moderate successes in Tunisia, Egypt, and Libya, but failures in Yemen and Bahrain, while Syria remains in a bloody flux as I write. There are signs of progress—the removal of autocratic regimes—and failure—emigration because of severe economic crisis caused by political turmoil. There has also been a huge loss of life. By December 2011, the death count exceeded 20,000, ranging from 46 in Bahrain to 15,000 in Libya.[27] By the spring of 2013, the United Nations estimates the human toll in the revolution in Syria to be a staggering 70,000. This death count recalls the high numbers of those who fought and died to destroy racial chattel slavery in the nineteenth-century Americas. Another similarity between past slaves and present Arabs is the shibboleth that their liberty was gifted them rather than something for which they fought and died. This resurgence of the Arab street has called for greater social equality, including more decent-paying employment for qualified youth, increased tolerance toward non-Islamic faiths, and greater gender equality for women. Unlike political events, these social questions are much deeper and take longer to resolve. It is unclear where much of this is headed. But the most important lesson for freedom's future generations is the measurement of what ordinary people want versus the wants of those who have political power. This region could not provide us with a clearer modern demonstration of the fundamental disconnect between the dictates of political elites and the wishes and aspirations of men, women, and young people in the streets. Most troubling of all, the world's major powers—whether the superpower of the United States or the collective will of states embodied in the United Nations—continue to pursue their own diplomatic agendas over the needs and desires of ordinary citizens. Earlier generations of freedom's seekers would have recognized the dilemma.

NOTES

PREFACE

Epigraph One. Fritz Redlich, "Toward Comparative Historiography," *Kyklos* 11 (1958): 379.

Epigraph Two. J. E. Harris, "The African Diaspora Connection," in *Slavery in the South-West Indian Ocean*, ed. U. Bissoondoyal and S. B. C. Servansing (Moka, Mauritius: Mahatma Gandhi Institute, 1989), 3.

Epigraph Three. Thomas C. Holt, "Slavery and Freedom in the Atlantic World: Reflections on the Diasporan Framework," in *Crossing Boundaries: Comparative History of Black People in Diaspora*, ed. Darlene C. Hine and Jacqueline A. McCleod (Bloomington: Indiana University Press, 1999), 39.

Epigraph Four. En Vogue, *Free Your Mind*, www.youtube.com/watch?v=9tIYpvlQP_s

1. Anonymous reviewer's report, "The Great Emancipators: How Slaves Destroyed Slavery in the Americas," for *The Journal of American History*, enclosure in Edward T. Linthal, editor, to Jeffrey Kerr-Ritchie, January 19, 2011.

2. For a model study of transnational history in a global context, see Sugata Bose, *A Hundred Horizons: The Indian Ocean in the Age of Global Empire* (Cambridge, Mass.: Harvard University Press, 2006).

3. Paul E. Lovejoy, *Transformations in Slavery: A History of Slavery in Africa* (1983; New York, Cambridge University Press, 2012), 137.

4. Ira Berlin, *Generations of Captivity: A History of African-American Slaves* (Cambridge, Mass.: Harvard University Press, 2004), table 1; Robert Conrad, *The Destruction of Slavery in Brazil, 1850–1888* (Malabar, Fla.: Krieger Publishing Co., 1993), 210 (figure is for 1864); Franklin Knight, *Slave Society in Cuba During the Nineteenth Century* (Madison: University of Wisconsin Press, 1970), 86.

5. For the conceptual distinction between slave societies and societies with slaves that has strongly influenced slaves studies, see Moses I. Finley, *Ancient Slavery and Modern Ideology* (1980; Princeton, N.J.: Markus Wiener, 1998).

6. George Reid Andrews, *Afro-Latin America 1800–2000* (New York: Oxford University Press, 2004), 40.

7. Samuel Ward deserves a thorough biography. I thought of doing one myself, but other projects intervened. Chapter 4, below, serves in lieu.

8. Kim Butler's "Introduction: Brazil and the Afro-Atlantic Diaspora," in *Freedoms Given, Freedom Won: Afro-Brazilians in Post-Abolition Sao Paulo and Salvador* (New Brunswick: Rutgers University Press, 1998), 1–15, outlines a diasporic framework for emancipation, but we still await

her major comparative contribution. For a taste, see Butler's "Abolition and the Politics of Identity in the Afro-Atlantic Diaspora: Toward a Comparative Approach," in *Crossing Boundaries*, ed. Hine and Jacqueline McCleod, 121–33. I should add that Kim's project began as a master's thesis at Howard University.

INTRODUCTION

Epigraph One: Julie Greene, "Historians of the World: Transnational Forces, Nation-States, and the Practice of U.S. History," *Workers Across the Americas: The Transnational Turn in Labor History*, ed. Leon Fink (New York: Oxford University Press, 2011), 12.

Epigraph Two: Robert Gregg, *Inside Out, Outside In: Essays in Comparative History* (New York: St. Martin's Press, 2000), 5.

Epigraph Three: Matthew Pratt Guterl, *American Mediterranean: Southern Slaveholders in the Age of Emancipation* (Cambridge, Mass.: Harvard University Press, 2008).

1. Frederick Saunders, ed., *Our National Centennial Jubilee* (New York: E. B. Treat, 1877), 52, 191, 215, 352. The bargain referred to by Armitage was 20 million pounds in compensation to slaveholders as one of the key terms of the 1833 British Abolition of Slavery Act.

2. Ian Tyrell, "American Exceptionalism in an Age of International History, *American Historical Review* 96 (October 1991): 1031–55; Tyrell, "Making Nations/Making States: American Historians in the Context of Empire," *Journal of American History* (December 1999): 1015–44; George Frederickson, "From Exceptionalism to Viability: Recent Developments in Cross-National Comparative History," *Journal of American History* (September 1995): 587–604; Gregg, *Inside Out, Outside In*.

3. C. V. Woodward, "Emancipations and Reconstructions: A Comparative Study," International Congress of Historical Sciences (Moscow: NAUKA Publishing House, 1970), subsequently republished as "The Price of Freedom," in *What Was Freedom's Price?* ed. David G. Sansing (Jackson: University of Mississippi Press, 1978), 93–113. All references are to the 1970 edition.

4. Eric Foner, *Nothing But Freedom: Emancipation and Its Legacy* (Baton Rouge: Louisiana State University Press, 1983).

5. George Fredrickson, "After Emancipation: A Comparative Study of the White Responses to the New Order of Race Relations in the American South, Jamaica, and the Cape Colony of South Africa," in *What was Freedom's Price?* ed. Sansing, 71–92. This was subsequently republished as "White Responses to Emancipation: The American South, Jamaica, and the Cape of Good Hope," in George Fredrickson, *The Arrogance of Race: Historical Perspectives on Slavery, Racism, and Social Inequality* (Middletown, Conn.: Wesleyan University Press, 1988), 236–53. All references are to the 1988 edition.

6. Frank Tannenbaum, *Slave and Citizen: The Negro in the Americas* (New York: Vintage, 1946); Stanley Elkins, *Slavery: A Problem in American Institutional and Intellectual Life* (Chicago: University of Chicago Press, 1959); Eugene D. Genovese, ed., *The Slave Economies: Historical and Theoretical Perspectives* (New York: John Wiley, 1973), vol. 1. For a useful comparative study of slave societies (although its treatment of the United States is the weakest), see Laird W. Bergad,

The Comparative Histories of Slavery in Brazil, Cuba, and the United States (New York: Cambridge University Press, 2007).

7. Woodward, "Emancipations and Reconstructions," 155–56.

8. Ibid.

9. Foner, *Nothing But Freedom*, 2.

10. Eric Foner, *Reconstruction: America's Unfinished Revolution* (New York: Harper and Row, 1988).

11. Frederickson, "White Reponses to Emancipation," 236–37.

12. Woodward, "Emancipations and Reconstructions," 159.

13. Ibid., 172.

14. Frederickson, "White Reponses to Emancipation," 251.

15. Foner, *Nothing But Freedom*, 6.

16. Ibid., 3.

17. Frederickson, "White Reponses to Emancipation," 247.

18. Woodward, "Emancipations and Reconstructions," 172; Foner, *Nothing But Freedom*, 3.

19. Andrews, *Afro-Latin America*; Peter Blanchard, *Under the Flags of Freedom: Slave Soldiers and the Wars of Independence in Spanish South America* (Pittsburgh, Pa.: University of Pittsburgh Press, 2008); Ada Ferrer, *Insurgent Cuba: Race, Nation, and Revolution, 1868–1898* (Chapel Hill: University of North Carolina Press, 1999).

20. Andrews, *Afro-Latin America*, 80–83.

21. Bergad, *Comparative Histories*, 21.

22. Alex Dupuy, *Haiti in the World Economy: Class, Race, and Underdevelopment Since 1700* (Boulder, Colo.: Westview Press, 1989), 54; Laurent Dubois, *Avengers of the New World: The Story of the Haitian Revolution* (Cambridge, Mass.: Harvard University Press, 2004), 302. Patrick Manning, *The African Diaspora: A History through Culture* (New York: Columbia University Press, 2009), 149, suggests that battlefield losses and massacres in St. Domingue make "the revolutions in the United States, France, and the Latin American nations appear as gentlemanly disagreements in comparison."

23. Eric Hobsbawn, *The Age of Extremes: A History of the World, 1914–1991* (New York: Pantheon Books, 1994), 26.

24. The Taiping Rebellion against the Manchu ruling dynasty claimed many hundreds of thousands of Chinese lives between 1850 and 1864. See Jonathan D. Spence, *The Search for Modern China* (New York: Norton, 1990), 170–78.

25. Barbara A. Gannon, *The Won Cause: Black and White Comradeship in the Grand Army of the Republic* (Chapel Hill: University of North Carolina Press, 2011); Edward Longacre, *A Regiment of Slaves: The 4th United States Colored Infantry, 1863–1866* (Mechanicsburg, Penn.: 2003), 178.

26. Ferrer, *Insurgent Cuba*, 68.

27. W. E. B. Du Bois, *Black Reconstruction in America, 1860–1880* (New York: Atheneum, 1935).

28. Foner, *Reconstruction*, 317.

29. Ibid., 318.

30. Kenneth M. Stampp, *The Era of Reconstruction, 1865–1877* (New York: Vintage, 1965), 167.

31. Dubois, *Avengers of the New World*, 7.

32. Robin Blackburn, *The American Crucible: Slavery, Emancipation, and Human Rights* (London: Verso, 2011), pt. 3.

33. Philippe R. Girard, *The Slaves Who Defeated Napoleon: Toussaint Louverture and the Haitian War of Independence, 1801–1804* (Tuscaloosa: University of Alabama Press, 2011), 9–10.

34. Du Bois, *Black Reconstruction,* 728.

35. Demetrius L. Eudell, *The Political Languages of Emancipation in the British Caribbean and the U.S. South* (Chapel Hill: University of North Carolina Press, 2002).

36. Ibid., 180.

37. Ibid., 12.

38. Ibid., 100.

39. *International History Review* 25, no. 2 (June 2003): 422–23; *American Historical Review* 108, no. 1 (February 2003): 160–61; *South Carolina Historical Magazine* 104, no. 2 (April 2003): 126–27; *Journal of American History* 90, no. 1 (June 2003): 239–40.

40. Eudell, *Political Languages of Emancipation,* 14–15.

41. Ibid., 53.

42. Steven Hahn, *The Roots of Southern Populism: Yeoman Framers and the Transformation of the Georgia Upcountry, 1850–1890* (New York: Oxford University Press, 1983). Hahn's bibliography acknowledges the influence of British Marxist historians Eric Hobsbawn and Edward Thompson on his interpretation of the postbellum American South.

43. Steven Hahn, "Class and State in Postemancipation Societies: Southern Planters in Comparative Perspective," *American Historical Review* 95 (February 1990), 98.

44. C. Vann Woodward, *Origins of the New South, 1877–1913* (Baton Rouge: Louisiana State University Press, 1951).

45. Steven Hahn, *A Nation under our Feet: Black Political Struggles in the Rural South from Slavery to the Great Migration* (Cambridge, Mass.: Harvard University Press, 2003); Jeffrey R. Kerr-Ritchie, review of *Nation Under Our Feet* by Hahn, in *Virginia Magazine of History and Biography* 113, no. 4 (2005): 429–31.

46. Hahn, *Nation under our Feet,* 218, 115.

47. W. Fitzhugh Brundage, *Lynching in the New South: Georgia and Virginia, 1880–1930* (Urbana: University of Illinois Press, 1993).

48. Michael Craton, *Testing the Chains: Resistance to Slavery in the British West Indies* (Ithaca, N.Y.: Cornell University Press, 1982), 323–34.

49. Aline Helg, *Our Rightful Share: The Afro-Cuban Struggle for Equality, 1886–1912* (Chapel Hill: University of North Carolina Press, 1997), 222–26.

50. Jeremy Popkin, *You Are All Free: The Haitian Revolution and the Abolition of Slavery* (New York: Cambridge University Press, 2010), 41.

51. C. L. R. James, *The Black Jacobins: Toussaint L'Ouverture and the San Domingo Revolution* (New York: Vintage, 1963), 310.

52. James, *Black Jacobins,* 370–75; Dupuy, *Haiti in the World Economy,* 75–76.

53. Thomas C. Holt, "'An Empire over the Mind': Emancipation, Race, and Ideology in the British West Indies and the American South," in *Region, Race, and Reconstruction: Essays in Honor of C. Van Woodward,* ed. J. Morgan Kousser and James McPherson (New York: Oxford University Press, 1982), 283–313; Edward Rugemer, *The Problem of Emancipation: The Caribbean Roots of the American Civil War* (Baton Rouge: Louisiana State University Press, 2008).

54. Foner's *Nothing But Freedom* drew from his 1982 Fleming Lectures.

55. Stanley L. Engerman, *Slavery, Emancipation and Freedom: Comparative Perspectives* (Baton Rouge: Louisiana State University Press, 2007).

56. Ibid., 16.

57. Ibid., 33–36.

58. Ibid., 51.

59. Ibid., 62.

60. Ibid., 65.

61. Ibid., 91.

62. Ibid., x.

63. Verene Shepherd, Bridget Brereton, Barbara Bailey, eds., *Engendering History: Caribbean Women in Historical Perspective* (New York: St. Martin's Press, 1995); Madhavi Kale, *Fragments of Empire: Capital, Slavery, and Indian Indentured Labor in the British Caribbean* (Philadelphia: University of Pennsylvania Press, 1998); Rosemarijn Hoefte, *In Place of Slavery: A Social History of British Indian and Javanese Laborers in Suriname* (Gainesville: University Press of Florida 1998); Verene Shepherd, *Maharani's Misery: Narratives of a Passage of from India* (Mona, Jamaica: University of West Indies Press, 2002); Patricia Mohammed, *Gender Negotiations among Indians in Trinidad, 1917–1947* (Basingstoke, U.K.: Palgrave, 2002); Andrew Wilson, ed., *The Chinese in the Caribbean* (Princeton, N.J.: Marcus Wiener, 2004).

64. Paul Lovejoy, Book Review, *Journal of Interdisciplinary History* 39, no. 2 (Autumn 2008): 283. Engerman's sole reference to racism concerns the importation of sugar-plantation indentured workers to late nineteenth-century Australia (*Slavery, Emancipation*, 58).

65. Engerman, *Slavery, Emancipation*, 55.

66. For instance, we have not engaged the pioneering documentary work of the Freedmen and Southern Society Project at the University of Maryland. Although it seeks to place U.S. emancipation within a global framework of capitalist social relations, new property rights, and slave abolition, it is not explicitly comparative. See the published volumes listed on their website: www.history.umd.edu/Freedmen/ Similarly, influential comparative emancipation studies by Dylan Penningroth on post-abolition Georgia and the Gold Coast (now Ghana), Thomas Holt on post-abolition Jamaica and nineteenth-century Ireland, Rebecca Scott on post-emancipation Cuba and Louisiana, Fredrick Cooper on twentieth-century Francophone Africa, and Kim Butler on post-abolition urban Brazil are not critically examined because these works are less concerned with comparing U.S. emancipation. See bibliography for full references.

67. See chapter 3, below.

68. Jeffrey R. Kerr-Ritchie, *Rites of August First: Emancipation Day in the Black Atlantic World* (Baton Rouge: Louisiana State University Press, 2007).

69. For an interesting study of the cross-border wanderings of southern elites throughout the slave and free Americas, see Guterl, *American Mediterranean*.

CHAPTER ONE

Epigraph One: Antarah (530–608 CE) was the son of an enslaved Ethiopian woman called Zabiba. He became a famous warrior in western Arabia. See Ibrahim Mumayiz, ed., *Arabesques: Selections of Biography and Poetry from Classical Arabic Literature* (New York: Garant, 2006), 126.

Epigraph Two: Henry Bibb, Editorial, *Voice of the Fugitive*, July 30, 1851.

Epigraph Three: Graham Greene, *The Human Factor* (New York: Random House, 1992), x.

1. John Hope Franklin and Loren Schweninger, *Runaway Slaves: Rebels on the Plantation* (New York: Oxford University Press, 2000); Fergus M. Bordewich, *Bound for Canaan: The Epic Story of the Underground Railroad, America's First Civil Rights Movement* (New York: Amistad, 2005).

2. The concept of self-emancipators, of course, draws from a rich scholarly tradition in U.S. history and slave studies traceable through W. E. B. Du Bois, Charles Wesley, Herbert Aptheker, Benjamin Quarles, Lerone Bennett, Kenneth Porter, Vincent Harding, Robert Engs, the Freedmen and Southern Society Project at the University of Maryland, Steven Hahn, Margaret Washington, and others. This chapter's difference is that it pursues self-liberators *across* national borders.

3. For fugitive slaves and maroons in the Americas over four centuries, see Alvin O. Thompson, *Flight To Freedom: African Runaways and Maroons in the Americas* (Kingston, Jamaica; University of West Indies Press, 2006). For fugitive slaves and magnet communities in the pre-colonial Senegambia region of West Africa, see Boubacar Barry, *Senegambia and the Atlantic Slave Trade* (Cambridge, U.K.: Cambridge University Press, 1998). For frontier freedoms as opportunities for fugitives from Islamic slavery, see William Gervase Clarence-Smith, *Islam and the Abolition of Slavery* (New York: Oxford University Press, 2006), 36–42.

4. Rosalie Schwartz, *Across the Rio to Freedom: U.S. Negroes in Mexico* (El Paso: Texas Western Press, 1975), 3.

5. Peter H. Wood, *Black Majority: Negroes in Colonial South Carolina from 1670 through the Stono Rebellion* (New York: W. W. Norton, 1975), 304–5.

6. Schwartz, *Across the Rio*, 3–4; Kenneth Wiggins Porter, "Negroes and the Seminole War, 1817–1818," *Journal of Negro History* 36, no. 3 (July 1951): 250–51. The bias of some historical literature can be seen in the designation of fugitive slaves as being a "problem." For slaves, the problem was obtaining and retaining freedom within and beyond slave societies. The following comment is instructive: "[William] Green conceives the 'problem of the free society' [in the British Caribbean] as a problem of colonial administration whereas, for the colonized former slaves, the problem was that their liberty was not yet a reality. In other words, the problem should be defined not in terms of the survival of the plantations and the prosperity of the planters, but in terms of the survival and improved living standards of the former slaves" (O. Nigel Bolland, "Systems of Domination after Slavery: The Control of Land and Labor in the British West Indies after 1838," *Comparative Study of Society and History* 23, no. 4 [October 1981]: 592).

7. Schwartz, *Across the Rio*, 6; Bordewich, *Bound for Canaan*, 111–12; Porter, "Negroes and the Seminole War," 278.

8. Colin Palmer, *Slaves of the White God: Blacks in Mexico, 1570–1650* (New York: Cambridge University Press, 1976).

9. John Lynch, *The Spanish American Revolutions, 1808–1826* (London: W. W. Norton 1973), 332; Junius Rodriguez, ed., *Encyclopedia of Emancipation and Abolition in the Transatlantic World* (Armonk, N.Y.: Sharpe, 2007), vol. 3: 689.

10. Sean Kelley, "'Mexico in His Head': Slavery and the Texas-Mexico Border, 1810–1860," *Journal of Social History* 37, no. 3 (Spring 2004): 709.

11. Walter Johnson, *Soul by Soul: Life Inside the Antebellum Slave Market* (Cambridge, Mass.: Harvard University Press, 1999).

12. Schwartz, *Across the Rio*, 8–9 (original spelling).

13. Kelley, "'Mexico in his Head,'" 712; Randolph B. Campbell, *An Empire for Slavery: The Peculiar Institution in Texas, 1821–1865* (Baton Rouge: Louisiana State University Press, 1989), 62.

14. Campbell, *Empire for Slavery*, 44.

15. Ibid., 182.

16. Schwartz, *Across the Rio*, 31.

17. Schwartz, *Across the Rio*, 60n114; Campbell, *Empire for Slavery*, 63, 180; Kelley, "'Mexico in His Head,'" 722.

18. Frederick Law Olmsted, *A Journey Through Texas* (1857; Lincoln: University of Nebraska Press, 2004), 323–25.

19. Schwartz, *Across the Rio*, 33.

20. Campbell, *Empire of Slavery*, 63–64.

21. William A. Dobak, *Freedom by the Sword: The U.S. Colored Troops 1862–1867* (Washington, D.C.: Center of Military History, 2011), 425–28.

22. Jacob Branch, *The American Slave: A Composite Autobiography*, in *Texas Narratives*, ed. George P. Rawick (Westport, Conn.: Greenwood, 1972), vol. 4, pt. 1: 141 (original spelling).

23. Campbell, *Empire of Slavery*, 63.

24. Kelley, "'Mexico in His Head,'" 719.

25. Ibid.

26. Mary Rourke and Valerie J. Nelson, "Elizabeth Catlett Dies at 96; among 20th Century's Top Black Artists," *Los Angeles Times*, April 4, 2012, latimesblogs.latimes.com/world_now/2012/04/artistelizabeth-catlett-mexico-africanamerican.html

27. Robin W. Winks, *The Blacks in Canada: A History* (New Haven, Conn.: Yale University Press, 1971), 168–77.

28. Samuel Ringgold Ward, *Autobiography of a Fugitive Negro* (London: John Snow, 1855), 126–27 (original italics), available electronically at docsouth.unc.edu/neh/wards/ward.html. It was also reissued by Arno Press in 1968. All subsequent references are to the 1968 edition. For Ward's transnational peregrinations, and their political significance, see chapter 4 below.

29. Kerr-Ritchie, *Rites of August First*, 144.

30. Robin Law, *Ouidah: The Social History of a West African Slaving 'Port' 1727–1892* (Athens: Ohio University Press, 2004), 244.

31. Martin A. Klein, "Servitude among the Wolof and Sereer of Senegambia," in *Slavery in Africa: Historical and Anthropological Perspectives*, ed. Suzanne Miers and Igor Kopytoff (Madison: University of Wisconsin Press, 1977), 347.

32. Lovejoy, *Transformations in Slavery*, chap. 11.

33. Schwartz, *Across the Rio*, 8–9 (original spelling).

34. Ibid., 9–18.

35. Kerr-Ritchie, *Rites of August First*, 124–25; Karolyn Smardz Frost, *I've Got a Home in Glory Land: A Lost Tale of the Underground Railroad* (Toronto: Thomas Allen, 2007).

36. Kerr-Ritchie, *Rites of August First,* 125–26; Jane H. Pease and William H. Pease, *Black Utopia: Negro Communal Experiments in America* (Madison: State Historical Society of Wisconsin, 1963), 46. Jason H. Silverman's *Unwelcome Guests: Canada West's Response to American Fugitive Slaves, 1800–1865* (Greenwood, Conn.: Associated Faculty, 1985) provides the most persuasive case for racism toward fugitive slaves in Canada.

37. The major exception was British India, where abolition was legislated in 1842 because the colony fell under the jurisdiction of the East India Company, not the British Parliament.

38. Silverman, *Unwelcome Guests,* 37; Winks, *Blacks in Canada,* 169–70; Ward, *Autobiography,* 123.

39. "Fugitive Slave Act (1850)," in *Slavery in the United States: A Social, Political, and Historical Encyclopedia,* ed. Junius Rodriguez (Santa Barbara, Calif.: ABC-CLIO, 2007), vol. 2: 636–39; Kerr-Ritchie, *Rites of August First,* 169.

40. Christopher Hill, *Liberty Against the Law: Some Seventeenth-Century Controversies* (London: Penguin, 1996).

41. Schwartz, *Across the Rio,* 32, 50–51.

42. Ashraf Rushdy, November 16, 2011, personal communication.

43. This point was raised by Jim Barrett and Nelson Lichtenstein at this chapter's original presentation at the Newberry Conference, Chicago, in 2008.

44. For a succinct account, see James Brewer Stewart, *Holy Warriors: The Abolitionists and American Slavery* (New York: Hill and Wang, 1976), 157–58.

45. Kerr-Ritchie, *Rites of August First,* 135–36, 139–40.

46. Henry Bibb, *Narrative of the Life and Adventures of Henry Bibb: An American Slave, Written by Himself* (1849); reproduced online: docsouth.unc.edu/neh/bibb/menu.html; Kerr-Ritchie, *Rites of August First,* 146.

47. *Voice of the Fugitive,* January–December, July 30, 1851; Kerr-Ritchie, *Rites of August First,* 147.

48. *Voice of the Fugitive,* July 30, 1851; Kerr-Ritchie, *Rites of August First,* 148–49.

49. The classic study of the era is Eric Hobsbawn, *The Age of Capital 1848–1875* (New York: Vintage, 1975).

50. Kerr-Ritchie, *Rites of August First,* 151.

51. *Voice of the Fugitive,* October 22, 1851; Kerr-Ritchie, *Rites of August First,* 152–53.

52. Kerr-Ritchie, *Rites of August First,* 230–32.

53. Porter, "Negroes and the Seminole War," 253.

54. Ibid., 260–61.

55. Ibid., 263–75 (quote on 254); Alan Brinkley, *The Unfinished Nation: A Concise History of the American People,* vol. 1: *To 1877* (New York: McGraw Hill, 1993), 213–15. Kenneth Wiggins Porter, *The Negro on the American Frontier* (New York: Arno, 1971). For Porter's interesting journey from midwestern populism to graduate history at Harvard, see August Meier and Elliott Rudwick, *Black History and the Historical Profession 1915–1980* (Urbana: University of Illinois Press, 1986), 106.

56. Kerr-Ritchie, *Rites of August First,* 159–60; Harvey Amani Whitfield, *Blacks on the Border: The Black Refugees in British North America, 1815–1860* (Burlington: University of Vermont Press, 2006), 45.

57. Benjamin Drew, *A North-Side View of Slavery* (Boston: J. P. Jewett, 1856), 291–308; repro-

duced online: docsouth.unc.edu/neh/drew/drew.html; Samuel R. Howe, *Refugees from Slavery in Canada West* (1864), 70–71, in Fred Landon, "The Buxton Settlement in Canada," *Journal of Negro History* 3, no. 4 (October 1918): 366. Landon taught at the University of Western Ontario where he pioneered studies of borderland slavery, abolition, and politics, much of which was published in the *Journal of Negro History* during the 1920s.

58. Kerr-Ritchie, *Rites of August First,* 153.

59. Franklin Chase to John Appleton, October 13, 1857, U.S. Dept. of State, Dispatches from the U.S. Consuls in Tampico, 1824–1906, Dispatch Number 27, Microcopy Number T241, Record Group 59, National Archives.

60. Schwartz, *Across the Rio,* 40–44.

61. Brent Morris, "'Running Servants and All Others': The Diverse an[d] Elusive Maroons of the Great Dismal Swamp," in *Voices from within the Veil: African Americans and the Experience of Democracy,* ed. William H. Alexander et al. (Newcastle, U.K.: Cambridge Scholars, 2008), 85–112, quote on 85.

62. Schwartz, *Across the Rio,* 32–33.

63. Bordewich, *Bound for Canaan,* 284.

64. Ward, *Autobiography,* 104.

CHAPTER TWO

Epigraph One: Antarah in *Arabesques,* ed. Mumayiz, 127.

Epigraph Two: C. L. R. James, "Black Studies and the Contemporary Student," in *At the Rendezvous of Victory* (London: Allison & Busby, 1984), 193.

Epigraph Three: George Orwell, "Marrakech," in *George Orwell: A Collection of Essays* (New York: Harcourt Brace & Co., 1981), 187.

1. Exceptions include Peter M. Voelz, *Slave and Soldier: The Military Impact of Blacks in the Colonial Americas* (New York: Garland Publishing, 1993); Blanchard, *Under the Flags of Freedom.*

2. *Arming Slaves: From Classical Times to the Modern Age,* ed. Christopher Leslie Brown and Philip D. Morgan (New Haven, Conn.: Yale University Press, 2006); Jeffrey R. Kerr-Ritchie, book review, *William and Mary Quarterly* (October 2009): 1011–13.

3. Douglas R. Egerton, *Death or Liberty: African Americans and Revolutionary America* (New York: Oxford University Press, 2009), 6, 64, 75–77.

4. Ibid., 71.

5. Porter, "Negroes and the Seminole War"; John Hope Franklin and Evelyn Brooks Higginbotham, *From Slavery to Freedom: A History of African Americans,* 9th ed. (New York: McGraw Hill, 2011), 121–24.

6. Dubois, *Avengers of the New World,* 97, 262; Madison Smartt Bell, *Toussaint Louverture: A Biography* (New York: Vintage Books, 2007), 90, 157, 177, 220, 227.

7. Andrews, *Afro-Latin America,* 46.

8. Ted Vincent, "The Blacks Who Freed Mexico," *Journal of Negro History* 79, no. 3 (Summer 1994): 267.

9. Andrews, *Afro-Latin America,* 62.

10. Peter Blanchard, *Slavery and Abolition in Early Republican Peru* (Wilmington, Del.: Scholarly Resources, 1992), 11.

11. Rebecca J. Scott, *Slave Emancipation in Cuba: The Transition to Free Labor, 1860–1899* (Princeton, N.J.: Princeton University Press, 1985), 58–9, 112; Andrews, *Afro-Latin America*, 78; Ferrer, *Insurgent Cuba*, 25–37.

12. Blanchard, *Slavery and Abolition*, 192–97.

13. Ira Berlin, Joseph P. Reidy, Leslie S. Rowland, eds., *Freedom's Soldiers: The Black Military Experience in the Civil War* (New York: Cambridge University Press, 1998), 20.

14. Robert Francis Engs, *Freedom's First Generation: Black Hampton, Virginia, 1861–1890* (Philadelphia: University of Pennsylvania Press, 1979), 27.

15. Stampp, *The Era of Reconstruction*, 45 (150,000); Hahn, *A Nation under Our Feet*, 14 (165,000). *Glory* remains an important film because it was the first full-length movie treatment of the role of black soldiers during the American Civil War.

16. David Patrick Geggus, *Slavery, War, and Revolution: The British Occupation of Saint Domingue, 1793–1798* (Oxford, U.K.: Clarendon Press, 1982), 315.

17. Roger N. Buckley, "Slave or Freedman: The Question of the Legal Status of the British West India Soldiers, 1795–1807," *Caribbean Studies* 17, nos. 3–4 (1977–78): 107–9; Voelz, *Slave and Soldier*, 255. See also Roger N. Buckley, *Slaves in Redcoats: The British West India Regiments, 1795–1815* (New Haven, Conn.: Yale University Press, 1979).

18. Hendrik Kraay, "Arming Slaves in Brazil from the Seventeenth Century to the Nineteenth Century," in *Arming Slaves*, ed. Brown and Morgan, 169.

19. Dale Torston Graden, *From Slavery to Freedom in Brazil, Bahia, 1835–1900* (Albuquerque: University of New Mexico Press, 2006), 56.

20. The exception is the massive documentary collection concerning slaves during the American Civil War put together by the Freedmen and Southern Society Project.

21. Blanchard, *Under the Flags of Freedom*, 37.

22. Ibid., 1.

23. Quoted in Richard M. Reid, *Freedom for Themselves: North Carolina's Black Soldiers in the Civil War Era* (Chapel Hill: University of North Carolina Press, 2008), 297.

24. Fifty-fifth Massachusetts Infantry's petition to President Lincoln, July 16, 1864, in *Freedom's Soldiers*, ed. Berlin et al., 125 (spelling in the original).

25. Kraay, "Arming Slaves in Brazil," 169.

26. Ferrer, *Insurgent Cuba*, 25.

27. Geggus, *Slavery, War, and Revolution*, 317.

28. Lynda J. Morgan, *Emancipation in Virginia's Tobacco Belt, 1850–1870* (Athens: University of Georgia Press, 1992); W. Jeffrey Bolster, *Black Jacks: African American Seamen in the Age of Sail* (Cambridge, Mass.: Harvard University Press, 1997); Ira Berlin and Philip D. Morgan, eds., *Cultivation and Culture: Labor and the Shaping of Slave Life in the Americas* (Charlottesville: University of Virginia Press, 1993).

29. Blanchard, *Under the Flags of Freedom*, 64.

30. Ibid., 118.

31. Buckley, "Slave or Freedman," 89.

32. Berlin et al., *Freedom's Solders*, 114, 124–25.

33. Craton, *Testing the Chains*, 169.

34. Ferrer, *Insurgent Cuba*, 31.

35. Blanchard, *Under the Flags of Freedom*, 116; Scott, *Slave Emancipation in Cuba*, 58; Ferrer, *Insurgent Cuba*, 32.

36. Reid, *Freedom for Themselves*, chaps. 2–5.

37. Egerton, *Death or Liberty*, 71.

38. Dupuy, *Haiti in the World Economy*, 54; Dubois, *Avengers of the New World*, 302.

39. Blanchard, *Under the Flags of Freedom*, 90.

40. Colonel James S. Brisbin, October 20, 1864, in *Freedom's Soldiers*, ed. Berlin et al., 135.

41. Berlin et al., *Freedom's Solders*, 126.

42. Tim Hashaw, *The Birth of Black America: The First African Americans and the Pursuit of Freedom at Jamestown* (New York: Carrol & Graf, 2007), 160.

43. Philip D. Morgan and Andrew Jackson O'Shaughnessy, "Arming Slaves in the American Revolution," in *Arming Slaves*, ed. Brown and Morgan, 181.

44. Robert J. Allison, ed., *The Interesting Narrative of the Life of Olaudah Equiano, Written by Himself* (Boston: Bedford Books, 1995), 40.

45. John Thorton, "African Dimensions of the Stono Rebellion," *American Historical Review* 96, no. 4 (October 1991): 1102; Matt D. Childs, *The 1812 Aponte Rebellion in Cuba and the Struggle Against Atlantic Slavery* (Chapel Hill: University of North Carolina Press, 2006), 32–33.

46. Popkin, *You Are All Free*, 48.

47. Geggus, *Slavery, War, and Revolution*, 321; Geggus, "The Arming of Slaves in the Haitian Revolution," in *Arming Slaves*, ed. Brown and Morgan, 219–20.

48. Popkin, *You Are All Free*, 134.

49. Ibid., 316.

50. Buckley, "Slave or Freedman," 92.

51. João José Reis, *Slave Rebellion in Brazil: The Muslim Uprising of 1835 in Bahia* (Baltimore: John Hopkins University Press, 1993), 95, 141. See also Paul E. Lovejoy, "Backlog to Rebellion: The Origins of Muslim Slavery in Bahia," *Slavery & Abolition: A Journal of Slave and Post-Slave Societies* 15, no. 2 (1994): 151–80. According to Andrews, *Afro-Latin America*, 38–39, slave rebelliousness and flight to *quilombos* (runaway settlements) in colonial and independent Brazil was led by "veterans of African wars."

52. According to Frank A. Rollin, *Life and Public Services of Martin A. Delany* (Boston: Lee and Shepard, 1868), "original [French] Zouave tactics [were] introduced years ago by native Africans" (143). For a recent claim that Haitian soldiers influenced the fighting tactics of black soldiers during the American Civil War, see Mathew J. Clavin, "American Toussaints: Symbol, Subversion, and the Black Atlantic Tradition in the American Civil War," *Slavery & Abolition* 28, no. 1 (April 2007): 96.

53. David Eltis and David Richardson, *Atlas of the Transatlantic Slave Trade* (New Haven, Conn.: Yale University Press, 2010), 274.

54. Kerr-Ritchie, *Rites of August First*, 129.

55. Samuel Ward to Benjamin Coates, October 1852, rpt. in *Frederick Douglass' Paper*, Nov. 19, 1852, in *Black Abolitionist Papers* ed. Ripley (Chapel Hill: University of North Carolina, 1985), vol. 2: 240.

56. Quoted in David Herbert Donald, *Lincoln* (New York: Simon & Schuster, 1995), 429–30.

57. *Frederick Douglass' Paper*, August 10, 1855; Kerr-Ritchie, *Rites of August First*, chap. 6.

58. Hannah Geffert, personal communication, February 12, 2010.

59. Clavin, "American Toussaints," 92.

60. Budge Weidman, "Teaching With Documents: The Fight for Equal Rights: Black Soldiers in the Civil War," www.archives.gov/education/lessons/blacks-civil-war/article.html

61. Frederick Douglass, "Men of Color, to Arms!" *Douglass' Monthly*, March 1863.

62. Blanchard, *Under the Flags of Freedom*, 130.

63. Andrews, *Afro-Latin America*, 62.

64. Reid, *Freedom for Themselves*, 108.

65. Berlin et al., eds., *Freedom's Soldiers*, 126.

66. Quoted in James, "Black Studies," 193.

67. Lynch, *Spanish-American Revolutions*, 86.

68. Rosalyn Howard, *Black Seminoles in the Bahamas* (Gainesville: Florida University Press, 2002), 114.

69. Sean Purdy, "Luis Pacheco," in *Encyclopedia of Emancipation and Abolition*, ed. Rodriguez, vol. 2: 412.

70. Deborah Chotner, *Augustus Saint-Gaudens' Memorial to Robert Gould Shaw and the Massachusetts Fifty-fourth Regiment* (Washington, D.C.: National Gallery of Art, n.d.)

71. Berlin et al., eds., *Freedom's Soldiers*, 135.

72. "Flag Raising at Camp William Penn," *Christian Recorder*, August 1, 1863. This date was not accidental. It marked the thirtieth anniversary of the legal ending of British colonial slavery.

73. Laurent Dubois, *A Colony of Citizens: Revolution and Slave Emancipation in the French Caribbean, 1787–1804* (Chapel Hill: University of North Carolina Press, 2004), chap. 15.

74. Kenneth Wiggins Porter, *The Black Seminoles* (Gainesville: Florida University Press, 1996), chap. 1.

75. Blanchard, *Under the Flags of Freedom*, 133.

76. Kerr-Ritchie, *Rites of August First*, 128–29.

77. Cabble's military service record quoted in Weidman, "Teaching With Documents."

78. Recent research has been conducted on whether black troops were slaughtered at Fort Pillow. John Cimprich, "The Fort Pillow Massacre: Assessing the Evidence," in *Black Soldiers in Blue: African American Troops in the Civil War Era*, ed. John David Smith (Chapel Hill: University of North Carolina Press, 2002), 150–68, concludes "nearly all historians publishing on the subject today hold that a massacre took place, that some Confederates tried to cover it up, and that some Northerners tried to exploit the event to aid the war effort." On the other hand, black soldiers on the battlefield did not doubt white rebels murdered their comrades in cold blood.

79. Commissioner Sonthonax had a different view of slave soldiers in St. Domingue. Most, he argued, were little more than the "[un]thinking agents of the fury of a bloody cause." The "unfortunate Negroes fight only for their religion and for their king. . . . Liberty is not in their minds" (Popkin, *You Are All Free*, 135). Much of the recent historical literature on slave soldiers seeks to refute this traditional view of slave combatants as furies and unthinking tools.

80. Popkin, *You Are All Free*, 47.

81. Jean Fouchard, *Les Marrons de la Liberté* (Paris, 1972), 550. My thanks to Iyelli M. Hanks

for this reference. Popkin's *You Are All Free* is the most recent study of events at Le Cap in 1793 but does not mention these women fighters.

82. Girard, *The Slaves Who Defeated Napoleon*.

83. John Lynch, *Simón Bolívar: A Life* (New Haven, Conn.: Yale University Press, 2006), 74–75.

84. Blanchard, *Under the Flags of Freedom*, 145.

85. Berlin et al., eds., *Freedom's Soldiers*, 20.

86. Spence, *Search for Modern China*, 173.

87. Harriet Tubman's Pension Claim reproduced in Franklin and Higginbotham, *From Slavery to Freedom*, 223.

88. Ira Berlin, Barbara Fields, Steven F. Miller, Joseph P. Reidy, and Leslie S. Rowland, "The Wartime Genesis of Free Labor," in *Slaves No More: Three Essays on Emancipation and the Civil War* (New York: Cambridge University Press, 1992), 77–186.

89. Blanchard, "The Personal War of Slave Women," in *Under the Flags of Freedom*, 141–59.

90. Ferrer, *Insurgent Cuba*, 32–33.

91. Most studies of the Haitian Revolution pay lip service to the role of slave women and gender.

92. Scott, *Slave Emancipation in Cuba*, 114–15; Ferrer, *Insurgent Cuba*, 16, 68. For slave rebels as the last holdouts and the reason why, see my "'Their Much Hoped for Liberty': Slaves and Bacon's 1676 Revolt in Virginia," in *Voices from within the Veil*, ed. Alexander, 75–84.

93. Joseph P. Reidy, "Armed Slaves and the Struggles for Republican Liberty in the U.S. Civil War," in *Arming Slaves*, ed. Brown and Morgan, 295.

94. The Spanish colony of Cuba and monarchical Brazil were the sole slaveholding societies in the Americas after slavery was legally abolished in the United States in 1865. Slavery was abolished in just over two decades in both societies, abolitions traceable primarily to internal factors but also to the political decline of the most powerful slave society in the hemisphere.

95. There is a debate about the role of the Paraguayan war in general, and that of wartime slave recruitment especially, in destabilizing slavery in Brazil. For its limited impact, see Kraay, "Arming Slaves in Brazil," 169. For its contribution to abolition, see Graden, *From Slavery to Freedom*, chap. 3.

96. Thompson, *Flight To Freedom*, 148–50. However, the author also points out that some slave soldiers were reported to have absconded to Maroon encampments during these expeditions.

97. Craton, *Testing the Chains*, chap. 13.

98. Andrews, *Afro-Latin America*, 57, 64.

99. This "gift" of freedom was the dominant motif in the iconography of emancipation. For a critical analysis of this iconography and its liberties with historical accuracy, see my "Slaves' Supplicant and Slaves' Triumphant: The Middle Passage of an Abolitionist Icon" in *Paths of the Atlantic Slave Trade: Interactions, Identities, and Images*, ed. Ana Lucia Araujo (New York: Cambria Press), 327–58.

100. Mimi Scheller, "Acting as Free Men: Subaltern Masculinities and Citizenship in Post-slavery Jamaica," in *Gender and Slave Emancipation in the Atlantic World*, ed. Pamela Scully and Diana Paton (Durham, N.C.: Duke University Press, 2005), 80.

101. Sue Peabody, "Negresse, Mulatresse, Citoyenne: Gender and Emancipation in the French Caribbean, 1650–1848," in *Gender and Slave Emancipation*, ed. Scully and Paton, 57.

102. Scully and Paton, eds., *Gender and Slave Emancipation*, 21.

103. This latter point is examined in greater depth in chapter 5, below.

104. Scheller, "Acting as Free Men," 79–98.

105. James Shaw, *Our Last Campaign and Subsequent Service in Texas* (Providence, R.I.: Society, 1905); Luis F. Emilio, *A Brave Black Regiment: The History of the 54th Massachusetts, 1863–1865* (Boston, 1891). For a similar view from a free colored veteran, see Christian A. Fleetwood, *The Negro as a Soldier* (Washington D.C.: Howard University, 1895). Many of these memoirs are available on microfilm at the Library of Congress.

106. Ferrer, *Insurgent Cuba*, 76–80, 63.

107. Reidy, "Armed Slaves," 297.

108. Reid, *Freedom for Themselves*, 299.

109. Robin Blackburn, *Banking on Death: Or, Investing in Life: The History and Future of Pensions* (London: Verso, 2002), 43.

110. Lorenzo J. Greene, "Some Observations on the Black Regiment of Rhode Island in the American Revolution," *Journal of Negro History* 37, no. 2 (April 1952): 171.

111. Buckley, "Slave or Freedmen," 95. A "bitt" equaled six pence sterling.

112. Richard B. Sheridan, "From Jamaican Slavery to Haitian Freedom: The Case of the Black Crew of the Pilot Boat, Deep Nine," *Journal of Negro History* 67, no. 4 (Winter 1982): 330.

113. Kerr-Ritchie, *Rites of August First*, 129.

114. Reid, *Freedom for Themselves*, 322; Reidy, "Armed Slaves," 297.

115. The issue of ex-slaves and the importance of land in comparative terms is examined more extensively in chapter 6, below.

116. Jeffrey R. Kerr-Ritchie, "Forty Acres, or, An Act of Bad Faith," in *Redress for Historical Injustices in the United States: On Reparations for Slavery, Jim Crow, and Their Legacies*, ed. Michael T. Martin and Marilyn Yaquinto (Durham, N.C.: Duke University Press, 2007), 222–37.

117. Ferrer, *Insurgent Cuba*, 101.

118. Robert K. Lacerte, "The Evolution of Land and Labor in the Haitian Revolution, 1791–1820," *The Americas* 34, no. 4 (April 1978): 457–58. One *carreaux* equals 3.3 acres.

119. Lorna McDaniel, "Memory Spirituals of the Ex-Slave American Soldiers in Trinidad's 'Company Villages,'" *Black Music Research Journal* 14, no. 2 (Autumn 1994): 123. My thanks to Godfrey Vincent for sending me this article.

120. Ferrer, *Insurgent Cuba*, 77.

121. According to Clavin, "American Toussaints," 107, black soldiers in the American Civil War "surpassed" the accomplishments of black soldiers in the Haitian Revolution because they "avoided partaking in the excesses" of the latter event. The comparison is dubious because it ignores the actions of Haiti's political elite in fomenting racial attacks, flattens complicated narratives of revolutionary violence, and misses U.S. Colored Troops' killing of Confederate prisoners. Second Lieutenant Walter Chapman of the Fifty-first U.S. Colored Infantry described his men's action in southern Louisiana in 1863: "As soon as our niggers caught sight of the retreating . . . rebs the very devil could not hold them. . . . The rebs were panic struck[,] . . . threw down their arms and run for their lives over to the white troops on our left to give themselves up, to save

being butchered by our niggers. The niggers did not take a prisoner, they killed all they took to a man" (Dobak, *Freedom by the Sword*, 152, 351–52).

122. Richard Paul Fuke, *Imperfect Equality: African Americans and the Confines of White Racial Attitudes in Post-Emancipation Maryland* (New York: Fordham University Press, 1999), 185–86.

123. Reid, *Freedom for Themselves*, 310; David S. Cecelski, "Abraham H. Galloway: Wilmington's Lost Prophet and the Rise of Black Radicalism in the American South," in *Time Longer Than Rope: A Century of African-American Activism, 1850–1950* (New York: New York University Press, 2003), 55; Otis A. Singletary, *Negro Militias and Reconstruction* (Austin: University of Texas Press, 1957).

124. *Herald and Georgian*, August 19, 1875, in Greg Mixon, "Black Militias in 1870s Georgia," unpublished manuscript, Association for the Study of Afro-American Life and History, Atlanta, September 2006.

125. Eric Foner's *Freedom's Lawmakers: A Directory of Black Officeholders During Reconstruction* (Baton Rouge: Louisiana State University Press, 1993), 292–93, lists 130 black officials who saw military service during the Civil War.

CHAPTER THREE

Epigraph One: Alexander Pétion to James M'Kewan, January 30, 1817, in Sheridan, "From Jamaican Slavery to Haitian Freedom," 333.

Epigraph Two: Madison Washington quote in James O. and Lois E. Horton, *In Hope of Liberty: Culture, Community and Protest Among Northern Free Blacks, 1700–1860* (New York: Oxford University Press, 1997), 245.

Epigraph Three: P. O. Esebede, *Pan-Africanism: The Idea and Movement, 1776–1991* (Washington D.C.: Howard University Press, 1994), 8.

1. James Silk Buckingham, *The Slave States in America* (London: Fisher & Son, 1842), vol. 2: 433 (italics in original).

2. Ibid., 422.

3. James Sherrard Scott, "The Common Wind: Currents of Afro-American Communication in the Era of the Haitian Revolution," PhD diss., Duke University, 1986.

4. The example of emancipation in Mexico and its cross-border impact has already been examined in chapter 1, above.

5. Scott, "Common Wind"; James Sherrard Scott, "Crisscrossing Empires: Ships, Sailors, and Resistance in the Lesser Antilles in the Eighteenth Century," in *The Lesser Antilles in the Age of European Expansion*, ed. Robert L. Paquette and Stanley L. Engerman (Gainesville: University of Florida Press, 1996), 128–43; Alfred N. Hunt, *Haiti's Influence on Antebellum America: Slumbering Volcano in the Caribbean* (Baton Rouge: Louisiana State University Press, 1988); Bolster, *Black Jacks*; David Barry Gaspar and David Patrick Geggus, eds., *A Turbulent Time: The French Revolution and the Greater Caribbean* (Bloomington: Indiana University Press, 1997); Peter Linebaugh and Marcus Rediker, *Many-Headed Hydra: Sailors, Slaves, Commoners, and the Hidden History of the Revolutionary Atlantic* (Boston: Beacon Press, 2000); David Geggus, "The Influence of the

Haitian Revolution on Blacks in Latin America and the Caribbean," in *Blacks, Coloureds and National Identity in Nineteenth-Century Latin America,* ed. Nancy Priscilla Naro (London: University of London, 2003), 38–59; Childs, *1812 Aponte Rebellion.*

6. James Sidbury, "Saint Domingue in Virginia: Ideology, Local Meanings, and Resistance to Slavery, 1790–1800," *Journal of Southern History* 63, no. 3 (August 1997): 531–32. 541 (original italics).

7. Gwendolyn Midlo Hall, *Africans in Colonial Louisiana: The Development of Afro-Creole Culture in the Eighteenth Century* (Baton Rouge: Louisiana State University Press, 1992), 343–74.

8. Johannes Postma, *Slave Revolts* (Westport, Conn.: Greenwood Press, 2008), 60.

9. Childs, *1812 Aponte Rebellion,* 127.

10. Reis, *Slave Rebellion in Brazil,* 48; Geggus, "Influence of the Haitian Revolution," 41.

11. Craton, *Testing the Chains,* 233–38; quote on 236.

12. Herbert Aptheker, *American Negro Slave Revolts* (New York: International Publishers, 1963), 98, 249; Eugene D. Genovese, *From Rebellion to Revolution: Afro-American Slave Revolts in the Making of the Modern World* (Baton Rouge: Louisiana State University Press, 1979), 43; Robert L. Paquette, "Revolutionary Saint Domingue in the Making of Territorial Louisiana," in *Turbulent Time,* ed. Gaspar and Geggus, 219; Daniel Rasmussen, *American Uprising: The Untold Story of America's Largest Slave Revolt* (New York: Harper, 2011), 74.

13. Paquette, "Revolutionary Saint Domingue," 218; Rasmussen, *American Uprising.* The largest slave rebellion in U.S. history occurred during the American Civil War through slaves' self-emancipation en masse, laboring for federal armies, and fighting and dying for the Union. It also succeeded in destroying U.S. slavery.

14. Andrews, *Afro-Latin America,* 68.

15. Karina Williamson, ed., *Contrary Voices: Representations of West Indian Slavery, 1657–1834* (Mona, Jamaica: University of West Indies Press, 2008), 339.

16. Monroe Fordham, "Nineteenth-Century Black Thought in the United States: Some Influences of the Santo Domingo Revolution," *Journal of Black Studies* 6, no. 2 (December 1975): 118.

17. Ibid., 119.

18. Johnson, *Soul by Soul.*

19. John Lofton, *Denmark Vesey's Revolt: The Slave Plot that Lit a Fuse to Fort Sumter* (Kent, Ohio: Kent State University Press, 1964); Fordham, "Nineteenth-Century Black Thought"; Douglas R. Egerton, *He Shall Go Out Free: The Lives of Denmark Vesey* (Lanham, Md.: Rowman & Littlefield, 2004); Robert L. Pacquette and Douglas R. Egerton, "Of Facts and Fables: New Light on the Denmark Vesey Affair," *South Carolina Historical Magazine* 105 (January 2004): 7–47.

20. Eric Robert Taylor, *If We Must Die: Shipboard Insurrections in the Era of the Atlantic Slave Trade* (Baton Rouge: Louisiana State University Press, 2006), 147–50.

21. Ibid., 150–51.

22. Reis, *Slave Rebellion in Brazil,* 40–72.

23. Peter P. Hinks, ed., *David Walker's Appeal to the Colored Citizens of the World* (University Park: Pennsylvania State University Press, 2000), 22.

24. Ibid., 23.

25. James McCune Smith, "Abolition," in *Negro Orators and Their Orations,* ed. Carter G. Woodson (Washington, D.C.: Associated Publishers, 1925), 120.

26. James McCune Smith, *A Lecture on the Haytien Revolutions with a Sketch of the Character of Toussaint L'Ouverture* (New York: Daniel Fanshaw, 1841).

27. Martin R. Delany, " The Redemption of Cuba," in *Martin Delany: A Documentary Reader,* ed. Robert S. Levine (Chapel Hill: University of North Carolina Press, 2003), 167.

28. Clavin, "American Toussaints," 87–113.

29. Guterl, *American Mediterranean,* 41.

30. Thomas C. Holt, *The Problem of Freedom: Race, Labor, and Politics in Jamaica and Britain, 1832–1938* (Baltimore: John Hopkins University Press, 1992), 263–309; Gad J. Heuman, *The Killing Time: The Morant Bay Rebellion in Jamaica* (Knoxville: University of Tennessee Press, 1994. See chapter 4, below, for further comment.

31. William Law Mathieson, *British Slavery and Emancipation, 1838–1849* (London: Longmans, 1932), 195–96.

32. William A. Green, *British Slave Emancipation: The Sugar Colonies and the Great Experiment, 1830–1865* (Oxford: Clarendon Press, 1976), 390.

33. C. Van Woodward, *The Old World's New World* (New York: Oxford University Press, 1991), 17.

34. Benedict Anderson, *Imagined Communities: Reflections on the Origin and Spread of Nationalism* (London: Verso, 1991), xiii, 47–66.

35. David Nicholls, *From Dessalines to Duvalier: Race, Color and National Independence in Haiti* (New Brunswick, N.J.: Rutgers University Press, 1991), 33–66; Dupuy, *Haiti in the World Economy,* 85–113.

36. Lynch, *Simón Bolívar,* 97.

37. T. G. Steward, *The Haitian Revolution, 1791 to 1804* (New York: Thomas Crowell, 1914), 261; Nicholls, *From Dessalines to Duvalier,* 46.

38. Steward, *Haitian Revolution,* 261.

39. Lynch, *Simón Bolívar,* 109.

40. Andrews, *Afro-Latin America,* 57.

41. Sheridan, "Jamaican Slavery to Haitian Freedom," 337.

42. Nicholls, *From Dessalines to Duvalier,* 62.

43. Sheridan, "Jamaican Slavery to Haitian Freedom," 332.

44. Ibid., 333.

45. Sheridan, "Jamaican Slavery to Haitian Freedom," 339; Nicholls, *From Dessalines to Duvalier,* 47; Dupuy, *Haiti in the World Economy,* 78; Ada Ferrer, "Haiti, Free Soil, and Antislavery in the Revolutionary Atlantic," *American Historical Review* 117, no. 1 (February 2012): 43.

46. Sheridan, "From Jamaican Slavery to Haitian Freedom," 335.

47. Christopher Leslie Brown, *Moral Capital: Foundations of British Abolitionism* (Chapel Hill: University of North Carolina Press), 96–98.

48. Nicholls, *From Dessalines to Duvalier,* 35.

49. Frank Moya Pons, *History of the Caribbean: Plantations, Trade, and War in the Atlantic World* (Princeton, N.J.: Markus Wiener Publishers, 2007), 175–77.

50. Dupuy, *Haiti in World Economy,* 85–114.

51. Mahommah Gardo Baquaqua, *Biography of Mahommah G. Baquaqua* (Detroit: George E. Pomeroy, 1854, 55–57.

52. Bolster, *Black Jacks,* 144–53; quote on 153.

53. Rebecca Scott and Jean M. Hebrard, *Freedom Papers: An Atlantic Odyssey in the Age of Emancipation* (Cambridge, Mass.: Harvard University Press, 2012), 261.

54. Nicholls, *From Dessalines to Duvalier,* 61.

55. Chris Dixon, *African America and Haiti: Emigration and Black Nationalism in the Nineteenth Century* (Westport, Conn.: Greenwood Press, 2000).

56. Susan Eva O'Donovan, *Becoming Free in the Cotton South* (Cambridge, Mass.: Harvard University Press, 2007), 55.

57. James D. Lockett, "Abraham Lincoln and Colonization: An Episode That Ends in Tragedy at L'Ile a Vache, Haiti, 1863–1864," *Journal of Black Studies* 21, no. 4 (June 1991): 428–44; Michael Vorenberg, "Abraham Lincoln and the Politics of Black Colonization," *Journal of the Abraham Lincoln Association* 14, no. 2 (Summer 1993): 1–45.

58. Dixon, *Africa America and Haiti.*

59. Nicholls, *From Dessalines to Duvalier,* 37.

60. Ibid.

61. Dubois, *Avengers of the New World,* 7; Blackburn, *American Crucible,* pt. 3; Ferrer, "Haiti, Free Soil."

62. Kerr-Ritchie, *Rites of August First,* 13–48.

63. Alexis de Tocqueville, "The Emancipation of Slaves" (1843), in *Alexis de Tocqueville: Writings on Empire and Slavery,* ed. Jennifer Pitts (Baltimore: John Hopkins University Press, 2001), 202.

64. Ibid., 258.

65. Karen F. Olwig, *Adaption and Resistance on St. John: Three Centuries of Afro-Caribbean Life* (Gainesville: University of Florida Press, 1986), 41.

66. *The Liberator,* April 1, 1842.

67. Olwig, *Adaption and Resistance,* 42, 50. These escapes via canoe exemplify how slave work facilitated freedom.

68. Neville A. T. Hall, *Slave Society in the Danish West Indies: St. Thomas, St. John and St. Croix,* ed. B. W. Higman (Mona, Jamaica: University of West Indies Press, 1992), 31.

69. Ibid., 208–27.

70. Aptheker, *American Negro Slave Revolts,* 338–39.

71. Edward D. Jervey and C. Harold Huber, "The Creole Affair," *Journal of Negro History* 65, no. 3 (Summer 1980): 203.

72. Philine Georgette Vega, "Creole Case (1841)," in *Encyclopedia of Emancipation and Abolition,* ed. Rodriguez, vol. 1: 148–49; Horton and Horton, *In Hope of Liberty,* 245; Taylor, *If We Must Die,* 156–59; Jervey and Huber, "Creole Affair," 200; George and Willene Hendrick, *The Creole Mutiny: A Tale of Revolt Aboard a Slave Ship* (Chicago: Dee, 2003).

73. Kerr-Ritchie, *Rites of August First.*

74. Frederick Douglass, "Canandaigua, New York, 3 August 1857," in *The Frederick Douglass Papers,* ed., John W. Blassingame (New Haven, Conn.: Yale University Press, 1985), vol. 3: 200, 199, 207.

75. Ibid., 207.

76. Ibid. 207–8.

77. Henry Bleby, *Missionary From Barbados, On The Results of Emancipation in the British West Indies Colonies, Delivered At The Celebration of Massachusetts Anti-Slavery Society, Held at Island Grove, Abington, July 31, 1858* (Boston: R. F. Wallcut, 1858), 3.

78. Ibid., 4.

79. Ibid., 6.

80. Ibid., 7–8.

81. Ibid., 8.

82. Ibid., 9.

83. Ibid., 10.

84. Ibid., 4.

85. Genovese, *From Rebellion to Revolution*, 25.

86. These scholars were often published in the *Journal of Negro History* because flagship journals like the *American Historical Review*, the *Journal of American History*, and the *Journal of Southern History* considered their work too radical. In other words, they were ahead of their time.

87. Bell Irvin Wiley, *Southern Negroes, 1861–1865* (New Haven, Conn.: Yale University Press, 1938). 67.

88. *Herald of Freedom*, August 13, 1841.

89. Aptheker, *American Negro Slave Revolts*, 50.

90. Davidson Burns McKibben, "Negro Slave Insurrections in Mississippi, 1800–1865," *Journal of Negro History* 34, no. 1 (January 1949): 79.

91. Aptheker, *American Negro Slave Revolts*, 366.

92. Dobak, *Freedom by the Sword*, 89–154.

93. Rasmussen, *American Uprising*.

94. Hall, *Africans in Colonial Louisiana*, 344–74.

95. Charles L. Perdue, Thomas E. Barden, and Robert K. Phillips, eds., *Weevils in the Wheat: Interviews with Virginia Ex-Slaves* (Charlottesville: University of Virginia Press, 1976); E. P. Thompson, *Customs in Common: Studies in Traditional Popular Culture* (New York: New Press, 1993).

96. *DeBow's Review* (New Orleans), quod.lib.umich.edu/m/moajrnl/browse.journals/debo.1846.html

97. McKibben, "Negro Slave Insurrections," 83; Lawrence Dunbar, *The Negro in the New Orleans Press, 1850–1860: A Study in Attitudes and Propaganda* (Chicago: University of Chicago, 1941).

98. Winthrop D. Jordan, *Tumult and Silence at Second Creek: An Inquiry into a Civil War Slave Conspiracy* (Baton Rouge: Louisiana State University Press, 1993).

99. Benjamin Garstad, "'Death to the Masters!' The Role of Slave Revolt in the Fiction of Robert E. Howard," *Slavery & Abolition* 31, no. 2 (June 2010): 245–46.

100. Jordan, *Tumult and Silence*, 95.

101. Postma, *Slave Revolts*, xv–xix; Craton, *Testing the Chains*, 335–40.

102. Kerr-Ritchie, *Rites of August First*, 49–117.

103. William W. Freehling, *The Road to Secession: Secessionists at Bay, 1776–1854* (New York: Oxford University Press, 1990), 388–94; Rugemer, *Problem of Emancipation*, 204–21.

104. Charles M. Wiltse, *John C. Calhoun*, vol. 3: *Sectionalist, 1840–1850* (Indianapolis: Bobbs-Merrill, 1951), 154.

105. Robert L. Pacquette, *Sugar Is Made with Blood: The Conspiracy of La Escalera and the Conflict between Empires over Slavery in Cuba* (Middletown, Conn.: Wesleyan University Press, 1988), 131–82; Jonathan Curry-Machado, "Catalysts in the Crucible: Kidnapped Caribbeans, Free Black British Subjects and Migrant British Machinists in the Failed Cuban Revolution of 1843," in *Blacks, Coloureds*, ed. Naro, 123–25.

106. W. E. B. DuBois, *The Suppression of the African Slave-Trade to the United States of America, 1638–1870* (New York: Longmans, Green, and Co., 1896).

107. Leon F. Litwack, *North of Slavery: The Negro in the Free States 1790–1860* (Chicago: University of Chicago Press, 1961), chap. 1; Ira Berlin, *Many Thousands Gone: The First Two Centuries of Slavery in North America* (Cambridge, Mass.: Harvard University Press, 1998), pt. 3.

108. Horton and Horton, *In Hope of Liberty*, 71.

109. Berlin, *Many Thousands Gone*, 369.

110. Litwack, *North of Slavery*, 3.

111. Bordewich, *Bound for Canaan*, 136.

112. Horton and Horton, *In Hope of Liberty*, 229–30; Stewart, *Holy Warriors*, 109.

113. Stewart, *Holy Warriors*, 50–51; Bordewich, *Bound for Canaan*, 143–45; Horton and Horton, *In Hope of Liberty*, 224–25.

114. Kerr-Ritchie, *Rites of August First*, 59–81; Rugemer, *Problem of Emancipation*, 222–57.

115. Horton and Horton, *In Hope of Liberty*, 257; Kerr-Ritchie, *Rites of August First*, 170–71.

116. Bordewich, *Bound for Canaan*, 107.

117. Ibid., 112.

118. Richard S. Newman, "'Lucky to Be Born in Pennsylvania': Free Soil, Fugitive Slaves and the Making of Pennsylvania's Anti-Slavery Borderland," *Slavery & Abolition* 32, no. 3 (September 2011): 415, 417, 421.

119. Clement Eaton, *The Freedom of Thought Struggle in the Old South* (New York: Harper & Row, 1964), 117–25; Hinks, ed., *David Walker's Appeal*, xxxviii–xli, 125.

120. Bordewich, *Bound for Canaan*, 105, 120, 127.

121. Graham Russell Gao Hodges, *David Ruggles: A Radical Black Abolitionist and the Underground Railroad in New York City* (Chapel Hill: University of North Carolina Press, 2010), 156.

122. Bordewich, *Bound for Canaan*, 408.

123. Newman, "'Lucky to Be Born in Pennsylvania,'" 418.

124. Dubois, *Avengers of the New World*; David Geggus, "Slavery, War, and Revolution in the Greater Caribbean, 1789–1815," in *Turbulent Time*, ed. Gaspar and Geggus, 1–50; Geggus, "Influence of the Haitian Revolution," 38–59; Ferrer, "Haiti, Free Soil"; Postma, *Slave Revolts*, 55–67.

125. Van Gosse, "'As a Nation, the English Are Our Friends': The Emergence of African American Politics in the British Atlantic World, 1772–1861," *American Historical Review* 113, no. 4 (October 2008): 1003–28.

126. Paul Gilroy, *The Black Atlantic: Modernity and Double Consciousness* (Cambridge, Mass.: Harvard University Press, 1993); Franklin Knight, "Blacks and the Forging of National Identity in the Caribbean," in *Blacks, Coloureds*, ed. Naro, 94.

127. Rasmussen, *American Uprising*.

128. Manuel Barcia, *The Great African Slave Revolt of 1825: Cuba and the Fight for Freedom in Matanzas* (Baton Rouge: Louisiana State University Press, 2012).

CHAPTER FOUR

Epigraph One: Ward to Henry Bibb, Oct. 16, 1851, in *Black Abolitionist Papers,* ed., Ripley, vol. 2: 179.

Epigraph Two: Ward, *Autobiography,* 322.

Epigraph Three: Editorial, "West India Emancipation," *The Colored American,* August 5, 1837.

1. For these three views respectively, see C. Peter Ripley, ed., *Witness for Freedom: African American Voices on Race, Slavery, and Emancipation* (Chapel Hill: University of North Carolina Press, 1993), 277; Ronald K. Burke, *Samuel Ringgold Ward: Christian Abolitionist* (New York: Garland, 1995); R. J. M. Blackett, *Building an Antislavery Wall: Black Americans in the Atlantic Abolitionist Movement 1830–1860* (Baton Rouge: Louisiana State University Press, 1983).

2. For an authoritative statement on the production, mediation, and reception of the antebellum slave narrative, see Ashraf H. A. Rushdy, *Neo-Slave Narratives: Studies in the Social Logic of a Literary Form* (New York: Oxford University Press, 1999), 118–19.

3. For a "black American" framework of the slave narrative, see Audrey A. Fisch, ed., *The Cambridge Companion to the African American Slave Narrative* (New York: Cambridge, 2007).

4. For recent studies of British imperial liberties in which slaves are largely depicted as grateful subjects, see Adam Hochschild, *Bury the Chains: Prophets and Rebels in the Fight to Free an Empire's Slaves* (New York: Houghton Mifflin, 2005); Brown, *Moral Capital*; Simon Schama, *Rough Crossings: The Slaves, the British, and the American Revolution* (New York: Harper, 2006).

5. Fiona Spiers, "Black Americans in Britain and the Struggle for Black Freedom in the United States, 1820–70," in *Essays on the History of Blacks in Britain,* ed. Jagdish S. Gundara and Ian Duffield (Aldershot, U.K.: Avebury, 1992), 85.

6. Ward, *Autobiography,* iv, 236.

7. Elisa Tamarkin, *Anglophilia: Deference, Devotion, and Antebellum America* (Chicago: University of Chicago Press, 2008), 190, 178–246.

8. Jeffrey R. Kerr-Ritchie, "Samuel Ringgold Ward," in *Encyclopedia of Emancipation and Abolition,* ed. Rodriguez, vol. 2: 559–60.

9. Ward to Gerrit Smith, April 18, 1842, in *Black Abolitionist Papers,* ed. Ripley, vol. 3: 384.

10. For insights into this activist milieu, see Hodges, *David Ruggles.*

11. *Colored American,* August 11, 1838.

12. Samuel R. Ward to Nathaniel P. Rogers, June 27, 1840, in *Black Abolitionist Papers,* ed., Ripley, vol. 3, no. 46.

13. Samuel Ward, speech, March 25, 1850, in *Black Abolitionist Papers,* ed. Ripley, vol. 4: 48.

14. Ibid., 49.

15. Ibid., 51; Ward, *Autobiography,* 107–10.

16. McHenry self-emancipated from slavery in Missouri and worked as a cooper in Syracuse, after which his owner sent an agent to arrest him under the Fugitive Slave Act. Once arrested, a crowd of blacks and whites freed McHenry and helped him escape to Kingston, Canada West. Twenty-six men were indicted, including Ward, who along with eight other blacks crossed the border. See *Black Abolitionist Papers,* ed. Ripley, vol. 2: 180.

17. Ward, *Autobiography*, 127.

18. Ibid., 157; Kerr-Ritchie, *Rites of August First*, 125.

19. Ward, *Autobiography*, 154.

20. Ibid., 176. It is difficult to authenticate this story. The parallels with President Andrew Jackson, known as "Old Hickory," however, imply poetic license by Ward.

21. Ibid., 177–79.

22. Ibid., 227.

23. Ibid., 8.

24. Ibid., 236.

25. *British Banner*, August 20, 1853, rpt. in *Pennsylvania Freeman*, August 25, 1853, 135.

26. Ward, *Autobiography*, 253. For accounts of Ward's activities in the United Kingdom, see *National Anti-Slavery Standard*, August 19, 1854; *Liberator*, August 25, 1854.

27. Ward, *Autobiography*, 147, 28.

28. Ibid., 149.

29. Ibid., 236. It is Ward's self-assured tone throughout his *Autobiography* that makes it hard to view him as a sycophant.

30. *A Narrative of the Adventures and Escape of Moses Roper from American Slavery* (Philadelphia, 1838), in *North Carolina Slave Narratives: The Lives of Moses Roper, Lunsford Lane, Moses Grandy, and Thomas H. Jones*, ed. William L. Andrews (Chapel Hill: University of North Carolina Press, 2003), 71.

31. Ward, *Autobiography*, 149–50.

32. Ibid., 227.

33. Ibid., 322.

34. Mary Daly, "Revisionism and Irish History: The Great Famine," in *The Making of Modern Irish History*, ed. D. George Boyce and Alan O'Day (London: Routledge, 1996), 73–76.

35. Fionnghuala Sweeney, *Frederick Douglass and the Atlantic World* (Liverpool: Liverpool University Press, 2007), chap. 4 (quotes from page 71).

36. For the Morant Bay rebellion, see Heuman, *Killing Time*.

37. Samuel R. Ward, "Reflections Upon the Gordon Rebellion" (n.p., 1866). Thanks to the staff in the Special Collections Library at the University of Michigan for providing a photocopy at short notice.

38. Ward, "Reflections," 1.

39. Ibid.

40. Ibid., 4.

41. Ibid., 6.

42. Ibid., 7.

43. Ibid., 8.

44. There is some evidence to suggest that intra-racial difference helped fuel deep animosity between Marcus Garvey and W. E. B Du Bois. See Du Bois's "A Lunatic or a Traitor," *The Crisis* (May 1924): 200.

45. But see Ward, *Autobiography*, 261.

46. Peter Fryer, *Staying Power: The History of Black People in Britain* (London: Pluto, 1984), chap. 8.

47. Gundara and Duffield, eds., *Essays on the History of Blacks*; Dorothy Thompson, "Ireland and the Irish in English Radicalism before 1850," in *Outsiders: Class, Gender, Nation* (London: Verso, 1993), 103–33.

48. Paul Gilroy, *"There Ain't No Black in the Union Jack": The Cultural Politics of Race and Nation* (Chicago: University of Chicago Press, 1991), chap. 3.

49. Ward to Henry Bibb, October 16, 1851, in *Black Abolitionist Papers*, ed. Ripley, vol. 2: 182.

50. Ward, *Autobiography*, 135.

51. Bibb, *Narrative*; *Voice of the Fugitive*, January 1851.

52. Mary Ann Shadd, *A Plea for the Emigration or, Notes of Canada West* (1851).

53. *Provincial Freeman*, September 23, 1854.

54. Blackett, *Building an Antislavery Wall*, 174.

55. *The Falmouth Post and Jamaica General Advertiser*, May 4, 1858, in Burke, *Samuel Ringgold Ward*, 59.

56. Ward, *Autobiography*, 117.

57. Ibid., 155–56.

58. Ibid., 193–99.

59. Ibid., 197.

60. Holt, *Problem of Freedom*, 144.

61. Kerr-Ritchie, *Rites of August First*, 199.

62. Ward, *Autobiography*, 27.

63. This makes Ward's silence on the role of poor soil and the difficulties of farming in provoking the uprising in Morant Bay all the more puzzling.

64. Whitfield, *Blacks on the Border*, chap. 3.

65. Jane Rhodes, *Mary Ann Shadd Cary: The Black Press and Protest in the Nineteenth Century* (Bloomington: Indiana University Press, 1998), 35, 43–44.

66. Ward, *Autobiography*, 139.

67. Ibid., 31–33.

68. Ibid., 80–81 (italics in original). The parallels with the outcome of the first African American presidency in the United States and history's verdict on the first working-class presidency of Lula de Silva in Brazil are striking.

69. Sylvia R. Frey and Betty Wood, *Come Shouting To Zion: African American Protestantism in the American South and British Caribbean to 1830* (Chapel Hill: University of North Carolina Press, 1998).

70. James Mursell Phillippo, *Jamaica: Its Past and Present State* (Philadelphia: J. M. Campbell, 1843); Kerr-Ritchie, *Rites of August First*, 42. Myalism is a Jamaican folk religion drawing upon ancestral spirituality and mediated through drums, dance, possession, sacrifice, and herbalism.

71. Wilson Jeremiah Moses, *Alexander Crummell: A Study of Civilization and Discontent* (Oxford, U.K.: Oxford University Press, 1989).

72. Kerr-Ritchie, *Rites of August First*, 199.

73. Ibid., 211–17.

74. For eloquent statements of this self-serving view of Africans' fitness for slavery, see *The Ideology of Slavery: Proslavery Thought in the Antebellum South, 1830–1860*, ed. Drew Gilpin Faust (Baton Rouge: Louisiana State University Press, 1981).

75. C. H. A. Dall, "West India Emancipation," *Liberator*, August 20, 1852. For the Afro-Asiatic roots of world civilization, see Ward, *Autobiography*, 274–75.

76. *Provincial Freeman*, July 15, 1854.

77. Ward, *Autobiography*, 411 (italics in original).

78. Chinua Achebe, *Things Fall Apart* (London: Heinemann, 1959).

79. For black loyalists during the American Revolution, see Egerton, *Death or Liberty*. For black loyalists during the American Civil War, see Berlin et al., eds., *Freedom's Soldiers*.

CHAPTER FIVE

Epigraph One: Keith Thomas, *Religion and the Decline of Magic* (New York: Oxford University Press, 1971), x.

Epigraph Two: Frank McGlynn and Seymour Drescher, eds., *The Meaning of Freedom: Economics, Politics, and Culture after Slavery* (Pittsburgh: University of Pittsburgh Press, 1992), 278.

Epigraph Three: Bridget Brereton, "Family Strategies, Gender, and the Shift to Wage Labor in the British Caribbean," in *Gender and Slave Emancipation*, ed. Scully and Paton, 156.

Epigraph Four: Joan Wallach Scott, *Gender and the Politics of History* (1988; New York: Columbia University Press, 1999), 17.

1. The historical literature is extensive. Many sources are listed in this chapter's endnotes. For some major contributions from the 1990s and early 2000s, see Diana Paton's "Bibliographic Essay," in *Gender and Slave Emancipation*, ed. Scully and Paton, 328–56. The best single source for materials published over the last decade may be located in the annual bibliographical supplement published in the December editions of *Slavery & Abolition: A Journal of Slave and Post-Slave Societies*.

2. Brian L. Moore, B. W. Higman, Carl Campbell, and Patrick Bryan, eds., *Slavery, Freedom, Gender: The Dynamics of Caribbean Society* (Mona, Jamaica: University of West Indies, 2003); Shepherd, Brereton, and Bailey, eds., *Engendering History*.

3. David Barry Gaspar and Darlene Clark Hine, eds., *Beyond Bondage: Free Women of Color in the Americas* (Urbana: University of Illinois Press, 2004); Jane Landers, ed., *Against the Odds: Free Blacks in the Slave Societies of the Americas* (London: Frank Cass, 1996).

4. Scully and Paton, eds., *Gender and Slave Emancipation*, 1.

5. Camillia Cowling, Book Review, "David Barry Gaspar and Darlene Clark Hine, eds., *Beyond Bondage: Free Women of Color in the Americas* (Urbana: University of Illinois Press, 2004)," *Caribbean Studies* 34, no. 1 (Summer 2006): 353.

6. "Introduction: Gender and Slave Emancipation in Comparative Perspective," *Gender and Slave Emancipation*, ed. Scully and Paton, 1–34.

7. On page 20 of *Engendering History*, ed., Shepherd, Brereton, and Bailey, Patricia Mohammed insists, "To write gender into history, the historical construction of masculinity and femininity or the construction of gender identities must itself be posed as the problem." I agree, but this is quite difficult with comparative analysis.

8. Pamela Scully, "Masculinity, Citizenship, and the Production of Knowledge in the Postemancipation Cape Colony, 1834–1844," in *Gender and Slave Emancipation,* ed. Scully and Paton, 52; Kale, *Fragments of Empire,* 3.

9. I should emphasize that the documentary record on U.S. emancipation is far greater than for other abolition societies.

10. Robert Edgar Conrad, ed., *Children's of God's Fire: A Documentary History of Black Slavery in Brazil* (University Park: Pennsylvania State University Press, 1994), 317.

11. Mary C. Karasch, "Free Women of Color in Central Brazil, 1779–1832," in *Beyond Bondage,* ed. Gaspar and Hine, 237, chap. 12.

12. R. J. Barickman and Martha Few, "Ana Paulinha de Queiros, Joaquina da Costa, and Their Neighbors: Free Women of Color as Household Heads in Rural Bahia (Brazil), 1835," in *Beyond Bondage,* ed. Gaspar and Hine, 172.

13. Robert Walsh, *Notices of Brazil in 1828 and 1829* (London, 1830), reproduced in Conrad, *Children of God's Fire,* 218.

14. Bernard Moitt, "In the Shadow of the Plantation: Women of Color and the *Libres de fait* of Martinique and Guadeloupe, 1685–1848," in *Beyond Bondage,* ed. Gaspar and Hine, 56, chap. 3.

15. Popkin, *You Are All Free,* 147.

16. Melanie J. Newton, *The Children of Africa in the Colonies: Free People of Color in Barbados in the Age of Emancipation* (Baton Rouge: Louisiana State University Press, 2008), 38.

17. Scott, *Slave Emancipation in Cuba,* 14.

18. Richard B. Allen, "Free Women of Color and Socioeconomic Marginality in Mauritius," in *Women and Slavery,* ed. Gwyn Campbell, Suzanne Miers, and Joseph C. Miller (Athens: Ohio University Press, 2007), 362–63; Loren Schweninger, "The Fragile Nature of Freedom: Free Women of Color in the U.S. South," in *Beyond Bondage,* ed. Gaspar and Hine, 107, chap. 6; Ira Berlin, *Slaves Without Masters: The Free Negro in the Antebellum South* (New York: Vintage, 1976), 177.

19. Schweninger, "Fragile Nature of Freedom," 107.

20. Newton, *Children of Africa,* 38.

21. Popkin, *You Are All Free,* 225. It is possible that the children were also Isnard's.

22. Andrews, *Afro-Latin America,* 42–43; Allen, "Free Women of Color," 363.

23. "Emancipation Bill," reproduced in Wirt J. Carrington, *A History of Halifax County, Virginia* (Baltimore: Regional Publishers, 1924), 50–51.

24. Berlin, *Generations of Captivity,* table 3; Population of the United States (1860), www.civilwarhome.com/population1860.htm

25. Knight, *Slave Society in Cuba,* 86.

26. Conrad, *Destruction of Slavery in Brazil,* table 2, 210. Conrad includes a table for the 1874 slave and free populations, but the latter category does not distinguish between whites and free coloreds.

27. Andrews, *Afro-Latin America,* 57.

28. Jane Landers, "Maroon Women in Colonial Spanish America: Case Studies in the Circum-Caribbean from the Sixteenth through the Eighteenth Centuries," in *Beyond Bondage,* ed. Gaspar and Hine, 11.

29. Dubois, *Avengers of the New World*, 51–59; Carolyn E. Fick, *The Making of Haiti: The Saint Domingue Revolution from Below* (Knoxville: University of Tennessee Press, 1990), 51–55.

30. Eltis and Richardson, *Atlas of the Transatlantic Slave Trade*, 162.

31. Thompson, *Flight To Freedom*.

32. Gerald W. Mullin, *Flight and Rebellion: Slave Resistance in Eighteenth-Century Virginia* (New York: Oxford University Press, 1972), 40.

33. Wood, *Black Majority*, 241.

34. Michael Mullin, *Africa in America: Slave Acculturation and Resistance in the American South and the British Caribbean 1736–1831* (Urbana: University of Illinois Press, 1992), 28, 289.

35. Franklin and Schweninger, *Runaway Slaves*, 211–12.

36. Leon F. Litwack, *Been in the Storm So Long: The Aftermath of Slavery* (New York: Vintage, 1979), 236.

37. Elizabeth Fox-Genovese, *Within the Plantation Household: Black and White Women of the Old South* (Chapel Hill: University of North Carolina Press, 1988), 320.

38. Geggus, *Slavery, War, and Revolution*, 308–9; Fick, *Making of Haiti*, chap. 7.

39. Deposition of Octave Johnson, February? 1864, in *Free At Last: A Documentary History of Slavery, Freedom, and the Civil War*, ed. Ira Berlin, Barbara J. Fields, Steven F. Miller, Joseph P. Reidy, and Leslie S. Rowland (New York: New Press, 1992), 51.

40. Butler to Scott, May 27, 1861, in *Free At Last*, ed. Berlin et al.

41. A. E. Burnside to E. M. Stanton, March 21, 1862, U.S. War Department, *The War of the Rebellion: A Compilation of the Official Records of the Union and Confederate Armies* (Washington D.C.: Government Printing Office, 1880–1901), ser. 1, vol. 9: 199–201; Cecelski, "Abraham H. Galloway," 44.

42. Clarence L. Mohr, *On the Threshold of Freedom: Masters and Slaves in Civil War Georgia* (Athens: University of Georgia Press, 1986), 73–74.

43. R. Q. Mallard, T. W. Fleming, E. Stacy, to General Mercer, Aug. 1, 1862, in *Free At Last*, ed. Berlin et al., 62.

44. Leslie A. Schwalm, *Emancipation's Diaspora: Race and Reconstruction in the Upper Midwest* (Chapel Hill: University of North Carolina Press, 2009), 43–44, 59.

45. Carol Faulkner, "A Nation's Sin: White Women and U.S. Policy toward Freedpeople," in *Gender and Slave Emancipation*, ed. Scully and Paton, 129. The victim status—meant to attract relief funds for the migrants—should not detract from the initiative of these women during wartime.

46. Litwack, *Been in the Storm*, 135–39; Berlin et al., *Slaves No More*, 178.

47. Egerton, *Death or Liberty*, 69–70.

48. Philip Morgan, *Slave Counterpoint: Black Culture in the Eighteenth-Century Chesapeake and Lowcountry* (Chapel Hill: University of North Carolina Press, 1998), 81–83.

49. Blanchard, *Under the Flags of Freedom*, 144–6.

50. Scott, *Slave Emancipation in Cuba*, 49; Ferrer, *Insurgent Cuba*, 32–33, 174.

51. Mohr, *On the Threshold of Freedom*, 94–6; Tera W. Hunter, *To 'Joy My Freedom: Southern Black Women's Lives and Labors After the Civil War* (Cambridge, Mass.: Harvard University Press, 1997), 20.

52. Popkin, *You Are All Free*, 40–47.

53. Gus Askew, "The American Slave: A Composite Autobiography," in *Alabama Narratives,* ed. George P. Rawick (Westport, Conn.: Greenwood, 1972), vol. 6, pt. 1: 15 (original spelling); Jim Gillard, "The American Slave: A Composite Autobiography," in *Alabama Narratives,* ed. Rawick, vol. 6, pt. 1: 156 (original spelling).

54. James Bolton, "The American Slave: A Composite Autobiography," in *Georgia Narratives,* ed. George P. Rawick (Westport, Conn.: Greenwood, 1972), vol. 12, pt. 1: 102 (original spelling).

55. Ferrer, *Insurgent Cuba,* 208.

56. Waring to General Halleck, Dec. 19, 1861, in *Free At Last,* ed. Berlin et al., 27–28.

57. Mohr, *On the Threshold of Freedom,* 94–96; Hunter, *To 'Joy My Freedom,* 20.

58. Blanchard, *Under the Flags of Freedom,* 144–46.

59. Popkin, *You Are All Free,* 49, 128.

60. Schwalm, *Emancipation's Diaspora,* 64. For a powerful statement on the psychological costs of slavery from African American women narratives that is not always persuasive, see Elizabeth Fox-Genovese, "Unspeakable Things Unspoken: Ghosts and Memories in the Narratives of African American Women," in *Slavery, Freedom and Gender,* ed. Moore et al., 254–75.

61. Fox-Genovese, *Within the Plantation Household,* 294, 325, 379; Scott, *Slave Emancipation in Cuba,* 64–66; Knight, *Slave Society in Cuba,* 172–77.

62. According to one scholar of the region, Caribbean historians "see interracial unions more positively." See Trevor Burnard, "'Do Thou in Gentle Phibia Smile': Scenes from an Interracial Marriage, Jamaica, 1754–68," in *Beyond Bondage,* ed. Gaspar and Hine, 85.

63. Eddie Donoghue, *Black Women, White Men: The Sexual Exploitation of Female Slaves in the Danish West Indies* (Trenton, N.J.: Africa World Press, 2002), xv.

64. Mary Prince, *The History of Mary Prince, a West Indian Slave* (London: F. Westley and A. H. Davis, 1831), 67–68. For the electronic version, see docsouth.unc.edu/neh/prince/prince.html

65. Linda Brent, *Incidents in the Life of a Slave Girl. Written by Herself* (1861; New York: Harvest, 1973), 53–58. The electronic version is at docsouth.unc.edu/fpn/jacobs/menu.html

66. Conrad, *Children of God's Fire,* 273–81.

67. Blanchard, *Under the Flags of Freedom,* 147.

68. Personal communication from Edna Medford, April 2012.

69. Jeffrey R. Kerr-Ritchie, *Freedpeople in the Tobacco South, Virginia 1860–1900* (Chapel Hill: University of North Carolina Press, 1999), 87.

70. Berlin et al., eds., *Freedom's Soldiers,* 173.

71. David V. Trotman, "Women and Crime in Late Nineteenth Century Trinidad," in *Caribbean Freedom: Economy and Society from Emancipation to the Present,* ed. Hilary Beckles and Verene Shepherd (Princeton, N.J.: Markus Wiener, 1996), 254.

72. Pamela Scully, *Liberating the Family? Gender and British Slave Emancipation in the Rural Western Cape, South Africa, 1823–1853* (Portsmouth, N.H.: Heinemann, 1997), 81.

73. Digna Castaneda, "The Female Slave in Cuba During the First Half of the Nineteenth Century," in *Engendering History,* ed. Shepherd, Brereton, Bailey, 145–47.

74. Not all slave societies in the nineteenth-century Americas experienced domestic slave trading. According to Bergad, *Comparative Histories,* 177: "there was no interregional slave trade of any major significance in Cuba that could have had the same kind of devastating impact on families."

190 NOTES TO PAGES 114–117

75. Conrad, *Children of God's Fire*, 351–52.

76. Johnson, *Soul by Soul*, 18.

77. Perdue, Barden, and Phillips, eds., *Weevils in the Wheat*, 71. Virtually all of the 157 ex-slaves interviewed in this collection recalled the horrors of the interregional slave trade.

78. Conrad, *Children of God's Fire*, 432.

79. Dolores E. Janiewski, *Sisterhood Denied: Race, Gender, and Class in a New South Community* (Philadelphia: Temple University Press, 1985), 8, 63–64; Hunter, *To 'Joy My Freedom*, 28–29.

80. B. W. Higman, "Slave Populations of the British West Indies," in *Slavery in the South-West Indian Ocean*, ed. Bissoondoyal and Servansing, 241. The first gang traditionally consisted of the youngest, strongest, and most productive male workers.

81. Popkin, *You Are All Free*, 40.

82. Moore et al., eds., *Slavery, Freedom, Gender*, 184.

83. Holt, *Problem of Freedom*, 152.

84. Castaneda, "The Female Slave in Cuba," 144.

85. Newton, *Children of Africa*, 32; Popkin, *You Are All Free*, 40.

86. Kerr-Ritchie, *Freedpeople in the Tobacco South*, chap. 1.

87. Roger L. Ransom and Richard Sutch, *One Kind of Freedom: The Economic Consequences of Emancipation* (New York: Cambridge University Press, 1977), 233.

88. Stanley J. Stein, *Vassouras: A Brazilian Coffee County, 1850–1900: The Rise of Planter and Slave in a Plantation Society* (1958; Princeton, N.J.: Princeton University Press, 1985), 262.

89. Foner, *Reconstruction*, 85.

90. Leslie A. Schwalm, *A Hard Fight for We: Women's Transition from Slavery to Freedom in South Carolina* (Urbana: University of Illinois Press, 1997), 206–7.

91. Kerr-Ritchie, *Freedpeople in the Tobacco South*, 106.

92. Ibid., 60. Lt. Lyon's report epitomizes the problem of the male chronicler. Was he correct that freedmen directed the household and made familial decisions about work? According to Hoefte, *In Place of Slavery*, 112, a major source of indentured women's oppression in post-abolition Suriname "was the women's subordinated position in the family, where men exercised authority and power." On the other hand, were the likes of Lt. Lyon ignorant of personal household details and simply assumed a patriarchal family unit because it was normative and expected?

93. Pieter Emmer, *The Dutch in the Atlantic Economy, 1580–1880: Trade, Slavery and Emancipation* (Brookfield, Vt.: Ashgate, 1998), 235.

94. Brereton, "Family Strategies," in *Gender and Slave Emancipation*, ed. Scully and Paton, 148.

95. Moore et al., eds., *Slavery, Freedom, Gender*, 192; Pons, *History of the Caribbean*, 207; Holt, *Problem of Freedom*, 152.

96. Ransom and Sutch, *One Kind of Freedom*, 232–6.

97. This link is explored more fully in chapter 6, below. Male indentured workers were still preferred over female indentured workers in the sugar fields, even though enslaved women had predominated as the agricultural labor force in the decades leading up to abolition.

98. Pons, *History of the Caribbean*, 171–73.

99. Ibid., 180–81.

100. Olwig, *Adaption and Resistance*, 49–50.

101. Brereton, "Family Strategies," 151–54.

102. Jones, *Labor of Love*, 68.

103. Foner, *Reconstruction*, 85–8.

104. Kerr-Ritchie, *Freedpeople in the Tobacco South*, 57–8.

105. Sharon Holt, "Making Freedom Pay: Freedpeople Working for Themselves, North Carolina, 1865–1900, *Journal of Social History* 60, no. 2 (May 1994): 228–62; Laura Edwards, *Gendered Strife and Confusion: The Political Culture of Reconstruction* (Urbana: University of Illinois Press, 1997).

106. Schwalm, *A Hard Fight for We*, 177.

107. Julie Saville, *The Work of Reconstruction: From Slave to Wage Laborer in South Carolina, 1860–1870* (New York: Cambridge University Press, 1994), chap. 4; quote on 110.

108. Schwalm, *Emancipation's Diaspora*, 137–43.

109. Elizabeth A. Regosin and Donald R. Shaffer, *Voices of Emancipation: Understanding Slavery, the Civil War, and Reconstruction through the U.S. Pension Bureau Files* (New York: New York University Press, 2008), 95.

110. Even though slaveholders in the U.S. South referred to their slaves as "servants," and influential historians Eugene Genovese and Elizabeth Fox-Genovese have articulated familial relations between planters and slaves through conceptualizations of hegemonic power, the fact remains that former slaves quickly established independent household economies, especially in the plantation South. Their post-abolition decisions cast further doubt on the indubitable master-slave relationship favored by so many scholars of slavery.

111. Scott, *Slave Emancipation in Cuba*, 243–45.

112. Stein, *Vassouras*, 162, 272.

113. For slavery's reproduction through interregional slave trades in the U.S. South and Brazil, see Bergad, *Comparative Histories*, chap. 4.

114. Scully and Paton, eds., *Gender and Slave Emancipation*, 21.

115. I used to put it this way in classes on African American history, slavery and emancipation, history of empire: if we follow this normative definition, we are left with the conclusion that black Americans, former slaves, colonized peoples, and so forth, did not have politics until the extension of the vote, de-colonization, etc., a rather pedantic interpretation.

116. Kerr-Ritchie, *Freedpeople in the Tobacco South*, 75.

117. Saville, *Work of Reconstruction*, 99.

118. Fick, *Making of Haiti*, 170. She bases her comments on western/southern St. Domingue's commissioner Polverel's statement.

119. Kerr-Ritchie, *Rites of August First*, 27.

120. Holt, *Problem of Freedom*, 63–65.

121. When I first drafted this section, women and girls took to the streets of Cairo in what was reported to be the largest demonstration of its kind in order to end the abuse of women demonstrators in the Egyptian revolution. See Ayman Mohyeldin, "Egyptian Women March on Front Lines of Country's Revolution," December 20, 2011, NBC.com, accessed Dec. 22, 2011.

122. Taylor, *If We Must Die*, 89–90; for further examples of women and children as insurgents, see 85–103.

123. For a comparative treatment of women and resistance during slavery, see part 3 of David Barry Gaspar, Darlene Clark Hine, eds., *More Than Chattel: Black Women and Slavery in the Americas* (Bloomington: Indiana University Press, 1996), 193–314. Again, it is sketchy rather than methodical because none of the six chapters is explicitly comparative and five chapters cover the British and French Caribbean only.

124. Scully and Paton, eds., *Gender and Slave Emancipation*, 18.

125. Mimi Sheller, "Quasheba, Mother: Black Women's Public Leadership and Political Protest in Post-Emancipation Jamaica, 1834–65," *Slavery & Abolition* 19, no. 3 (1998): 90–117.

126. Swithin Wilmot, "'Females of Abandoned Character?' Women and Protest in Jamaica, 1838–65," in *Engendering History*, ed. Shepherd, Brereton, and Bailey, 287–89.

127. Newton, *Children of Africa*, 272.

128. Richard G. Lowe, *Republicans and Reconstruction in Virginia, 1856–70* (Charlottesville: University of Virginia Press, 1991), 119.

129. Hunter, *To 'Joy My Freedom*, 32–33.

130. Saville, *Work of Reconstruction*, 169; Thomas Holt, *Black over White: Negro Political Leadership in South Carolina during Reconstruction* (Urbana: University of Illinois Press, 1979), 34–35. For references to women's politicking in Louisiana and urban Virginia, see Scully and Paton, eds., *Gender and Slave Emancipation*, 18.

131. Barbara Jeanne Fields, *Slavery and Freedom on the Middle Ground: Maryland during the Nineteenth Century* (New Haven, Conn.: Yale University Press, 1985), chap. 6; Scully, *Liberating the Family?* 97–104; Scott, *Slave Emancipation in Cuba*, 166.

132. My attempt in *Rites of August First*, 200–201, is thin and restricted to the black Anglo-Atlantic.

CHAPTER SIX

Epigraph One: Benjamin W. Arnold, *History of the Tobacco Industry in Virginia from 1860 to 1894* (Baltimore: John Hopkins University Studies, 1897).

Epigraph Two: Olwig, *Adaption and Resistance*, 104.

Epigraph Three: Butler, *Freedoms Given, Freedom Won*, 6.

Epigraph Four: Sven Beckert, "Emancipation and Empire: Reconstructing the Worldwide Web of Cotton Production in the Age of the American Civil War," *American Historical Review* 109, no. 5 (December 2004): 44.

1. Engs, *Freedom's First Generation*.

2. Ibid., xii.

3. Kerr-Ritchie, *Freedpeople in the Tobacco South*, 101, 275; Steven Hahn, Book Review, "*Freedpeople in the Tobacco South, Virginia 1860–1900*, Jeffrey R. Kerr-Ritchie (Chapel Hill: University of North Carolina Press, 1999)," *Slavery & Abolition* (April 2000): 167.

4. John Bigelow, *Jamaica in 1850, or, The Effects of Sixteen Years of Freedom on a Slave Colony* (Champaign: University of Illinois Press, 2006).

5. Stein, *Vassouras*, 278; Butler, *Freedoms Given, Freedom Won*, 25–29; Green, *British Slave Emancipation*, table 13, 246.

6. According to Engerman, *Slavery, Emancipation*, 54: "The other cases of successful emancipation, at least as measured by increased sugar production in the long run (after about twenty to thirty years), were British Guiana and Trinidad." The question here is: success for *whom* in the British Caribbean and by extension other post-abolition societies?

7. Despite its somewhat worn historical materialism, the best overview of this process, replete with suggestive comparisons, is Robin Blackburn, *The Making of New World Slavery: From the Baroque to the Modern, 1492–1800* (London: Verso, 1997).   •

8. Pons, *History of the Caribbean*, 171; James G. Leyburn, *The Haitian People* (New Haven, Conn.: Yale University Press, 1966), 320.

9. Pons, *History of the Caribbean*, 199–201.

10. Green, *British Slave Emancipation*, table 13, 246.

11. A. B. Aderibigbe, "Slavery in South-West of Indian Ocean," in *Slavery in the South-West Indian Ocean*, ed. Bissoondoyal and Servansing, 24.

12. Ibid., 218.

13. Olwig, *Adaption and Resistance*, 90; Lori Lee, "Emancipation in the Danish West Indies," in *Encyclopedia of Emancipation and Abolition*, ed. Rodriguez, vol. 1: 162.

14. Emmer, "Between Slavery and Freedom," in *Dutch in Atlantic Economy*, 254. According to Rosemarin Hoefte, sugar and coffee production in post-abolition Surinam declined because of agricultural and financial mismanagement, lack of capital, preferential tariffs imposed from Europe, and competition from the new beet sugar industry. The author is mute on the possibility of the lack of cooperation by former slaves in plantation production. See Hoefte, *In Place of Slavery*, 15.

15. Luis A. Figueroa, *Sugar, Slavery, and Freedom in Nineteenth-Century Puerto Rico* (Chapel Hill: University of North Carolina Press, 2005), 71, 205.

16. Christopher Schmidt-Nowara, *Empire and Antislavery: Spain, Cuba, and Puerto Rico, 1833–1874* (Pittsburgh: University of Pittsburgh Press, 1999).

17. John Scott Strickland, "Traditional Culture and Moral Economy: Social and Economic Change in the South Carolina Low Country, 1865–1910," in *The Countryside in the Age of Capitalist Transformation: Essays in the Social History of Rural America*, ed. Steven Hahn and Jonathan Prude (Chapel Hill: University of North Carolina Press, 1985), 166.

18. Kerr-Ritchie, *Freedpeople in the Tobacco South*, 14, 128, 134.

19. Strickland, "Traditional Culture and Moral Economy," 167; John Hope Franklin, *Reconstruction After the Civil War* (Chicago: University of Chicago Press, 1961), 180.

20. Cotton and tobacco did eventually reach unprecedented production levels in the post-abolition U.S. South by 1890. This was primarily due to the entry of white tenant farmers and sharecroppers—not freedpeople—drawn into cash-crop production and eventually tied in through the crop-lien and debt-peonage systems. For the post-emancipation cotton South, see Hahn, *Roots of Southern Populism*; Gavin Wright, *Old South, New South: Revolutions in the Southern Economy Since the Civil War* (New York: Basic Books, 1986), 34–39; and Beckert, "Emancipation and Empire," 41–43. For the post-emancipation tobacco south, see Nannie M. Tilley, *The Bright Tobacco Industry, 1860–1900* (Chapel Hill: University of North Carolina Press, 1948); Kerr-Ritchie, *Freedpeople in the Tobacco South*, chaps. 5 and 6.

21. Kerr-Ritchie, *Freedpeople in the Tobacco South*, 97; Figueroa, *Sugar, Slavery, and Freedom*, 205.

22. Olwig, *Adaption and Resistance*, 90; James H. Tuten, *Lowcountry Time and Tide: The Fall of the South Carolina Kingdom* (Columbia: University of South Carolina Press, 2010), 50.

23. Popkin, *You Are All Free*, 171.

24. Georgia State Parks and Historic Sites, Hofwyl-Broadfield Plantation (n.d.).

25. Popkin, *You Are All Free*, 41, 47.

26. Kerr-Ritchie, *Freedpeople in the Tobacco South*, 96.

27. Based upon an examination of thirty-eight claims by ex-slaves in twelve tobacco counties of Virginia, Southern Claims Commission, Records of the Department of Treasury, Record Group 56, National Archives.

28. Georgia State Parks and Historic Sites, Hofwyl-Broadfield Plantation (n.d.).

29. Popkin, *You Are All Free*, 128.

30. Pons, *History of the Caribbean*, 171–72, 218.

31. Ibid.

32. Pons, *History of the Caribbean*, 217–19.

33. Olwig, *Adaption and Resistance*, 54; Lee, "Emancipation in the Danish West Indies," 162.

34. Pons, *History of the Caribbean*, 199–201.

35. Ibid., 268.

36. Strickland, "Traditional Culture and Moral Economy," 163.

37. Graden, *From Slavery to Freedom*, 214–15.

38. Stein, *Vassouras*, 280, 287–88.

39. Kerr-Ritchie, *Freedpeople in the Tobacco South*, chap. 8.

40. For the conceptualization of slaves' labor withdrawal during the American Civil War as a general strike, see Du Bois, *Black Reconstruction*, chap. 4.

41. Sidney Mintz, *Caribbean Transformations* (1974; Baltimore: John Hopkins University Press, 1984).

42. Stuart B. Schwartz, *Slaves, Peasants, and Rebels: Reconsidering Brazilian Slavery* (Urbana: University of Illinois Press, 1992); Reis, *Slave Rebellion in Brazil*; Mullin, *Africa in America*; Berlin and Morgan, eds., *Cultivation and Culture*.

43. For accounts that rely on the land-labor ratio, see Green, *British Slave Emancipation*, 13, 190–92; Foner, *Nothing But Freedom*, 14; Engerman, *Slavery, Emancipation*, 52. For a dated but still instructive debate, see Bolland, "Systems of Domination," 591–619; William A. Green, "The Perils of Comparative History: Belize and the British Sugar Colonies after Slavery," *Comparative Studies in Society and History* 26, no. 1 (1984): 112–19; O. Nigel Bolland, "Reply to William A. Green's 'The Perils of Comparative History,'" *Comparative Studies in Society and History* 26, no. 1 (1984), 120–25.

44. Debt peonage was a complicated socioeconomic relationship, but essentially consisted of tying former slaves' labor to the land through credit arrangements that favored merchants and landlords in post-abolition societies.

45. Pons, *History of the Caribbean*, 303.

46. Andres Ramos Mattei quoted in Figueroa, *Sugar, Slavery, and Freedom*, 126.

47. Scott, *Slave Emancipation in Cuba*, 261–62.

48. Blanchard, *Slavery and Abolition*, 274; Stein, *Vassouras*, 260.

49. For this legal process in the cotton plantation South, see Harold D. Woodman, *New South–New Law: The Legal Foundations of Credit and Labor Relations in the Postbellum Agricultural South* (Baton Rouge: Louisiana State University Press, 1995); for the tobacco South, see Kerr-Ritchie, *Freedpeople in the Tobacco South*, chap. 6.

50. John Grace, "Slavery and Emancipation among the Mende in Sierra Leone, 1896–1928," in *Slavery in Africa*, ed. Miers and Kopytoff, 429.

51. This is the problem with Kim Butler's statement that "[Brazilian abolition] was part of a general program of economic modernization that entailed coercing freedmen into specific sectors of employment" (*Freedoms Given, Freedom Won*, 6), especially its comparative claim for the coercive economic modernization of post-abolition societies.

52. Geggus, *Slavery, War, and Revolution*, 301.

53. Pons, *History of the Caribbean*, 171.

54. Lacerte, "Evolution of Land and Labor in the Haitian Revolution," 457–58. In addition, Article 12 of the May 20, 1805, Constitution of Haiti stipulated: "No whiteman [*sic*] of whatever nation he may be, shall put his foot on this territory with the title of master or proprietor, neither shall he in future acquire any property therein." See www.webster.edu/~corbetre/haiti/history/earlyhaiti/1805-const.htm

55. Pons, *History of the Caribbean*, 218.

56. Ibid., 209, 266; Holt, *Problem of Freedom*, 144. These ex-slaves' land acquisitions in the post-abolition Caribbean provided a useful negative comparison for those opposed to ex-slaves' landholding in the U.S. South. Of land sales in Beaufort, South Carolina, North Carolina politician Zebulon Vance reported: "It is said by some that Beaufort is destined to become a second Jamaica" (Vance to David L. Swain, January 2, 1864, in *North Carolina Civil War Documentary*, ed. W. Buck Yearns and John G. Barrett [Chapel Hill: University of North Carolina Press, 2002], 304).

57. Figueroa, *Sugar, Slavery, Freedom*, 153–54.

58. Scott, *Slave Emancipation in Cuba*, 247, 255–78. It is unclear whether these landholdings were obtained either pre- or post-abolition.

59. Sadasivam Reddi, "Aspects of Slavery During the British Administration," in *Slavery in the South-West Indian Ocean*, ed. Bissoondoyal and Servansing, 120–21.

60. Dr. Edna Medford, personal communication, May 2012; Daryl Cumber Dance, *The Lineage of Abraham, The Biography of a Free Black Family in Charles City, VA* (n.p., 1998).

61. Engs, *Freedom's First Generation*, 177.

62. Kerr-Ritchie, *Freedpeople in the Tobacco South*, 212–14.

63. Edward Atkinson, *The Future Supply of Cotton* (Boston: Crosby & Nichols, 1864), 14.

64. Akiko Ochiai, *Harvesting Freedom: African American Agrarianism in Civil War Era South Carolina* (Westport, Conn.: Praeger, 2004), 217.

65. Carol K. Rothwick Bleser, *The Promised Land: The History of the South Carolina Land Commission, 1869–1890* (Columbia: University of South Carolina Press, 1969), 83–84, 144, 157.

66. Karen Bell, "Full and Fair Compensation: Free Labor Ideology and the Liminal Spaces of Freedom in Low Country Georgia, 1865–1868," 13–14, Annual Meeting, Organization of American Historians, Washington, D.C., April 2010.

67. Wright, *Old South, New South*, 106.

68. Ted Ownby, *American Dreams in Mississippi: Consumers, Poverty, and Culture, 1830–1998* (Chapel Hill: University of North Carolina Press, 1999), 77.

69. Hahn, *A Nation under Our Feet,* 457; Regosin and Shaffer, *Voices of Emancipation,* 79; Wright, *Old South, New South,* 119–20; Edward L. Ayers, *The Promise of the New South: Life After Reconstruction* (New York: Oxford University Press, 1992), 208.

70. Carol Bleser interviewed Derquis Moragne Hawes, granddaughter of Calvin Moragne, an original settler on the promised land community in South Carolina, during the early 1960s. She still lived on the original site. She and her husband worked a garden and raised turkeys and quails. Moreover, nineteen families still lived on land belonging to their ancestors. See Bleser, *Promised Land,* 151–53.

71. Fick, *Making of Haiti,* 180, 207, 250.

72. Zora Neale Hurston, "Cudjo's Own Story," *Journal of Negro History* 12 (1927), 648–63; Sylviana Anna Diouf, *Dreams of Africa in Alabama: The Slave Ship Clotilda and the Story of the Last Africans Brought to America* (New York: Oxford University Press, 2007).

73. Figueroa, *Sugar, Slavery, and Freedom,* 11. This is an important revisionist point because Sidney Mintz's pioneering research on the Caribbean proto-peasantry began in Puerto Rico.

74. Olwig, *Adaption and Resistance,* 42.

75. Mullin, *Africa in America,* 127, chap. 6.

76. Strickland, "Traditional Culture and Moral Economy."

77. Roderick A. McDonald, "Independent Economic Production by Slaves on Antebellum Louisiana Sugar Plantations," in *Cultivation and Culture,* ed. Berlin and Morgan, 299, passim.

78. Dylan C. Penningroth, *The Claims of Kinfolk: African American Property and Community in the Nineteenth-Century South* (Chapel Hill: University of North Carolina Press, 2003), 9.

79. Foner, *Reconstruction,* 105.

80. Ochiai, *Harvesting Freedom,* 123.

81. Kerr-Ritchie, "Forty Acres," 222–37.

82. For the ubiquity of the notion of "progress" shared by capitalists and communists in mid-nineteenth-century Europe, see Hobsbawn, *The Age of Capital.* For a powerful critique of scholarly approaches toward progress that masks imperialism in U.S. historiography, see Gregg, *Inside Out, Outside In.*

83. Tom Lansford, "Abolition in the British West Indies," in *Encyclopedia of Emancipation and Abolition,* ed. Rodriguez, vol. 1: 89.

84. Ronald E. Young, "Abolition in Cuba," in *Encyclopedia of Emancipation and Abolition,* ed. Rodriguez, vol. 1: 151.

85. Bergard, *Comparative Histories,* chap. 4.

86. Michael Zuckerman, "The Power of Blackness: Thomas Jefferson and the Revolution in St. Domingue," in *Almost Chosen People: Oblique Biographies in the American Grain* (Berkeley: University of California Press, 1993): 175–218; Robert Gregg, personal communication, Aug. 29, Aug. 31, 2011.

87. Sheridan, "From Jamaican Slavery to Haitian Freedom," 330.

88. Thomas Fiehrer, "Saint-Domingue/Haiti: Louisiana's Caribbean Connection," *Louisiana History* 30, no. 4 (Fall 1989): 430.

89. For a microscopic treatment of the shifting borders of freedom and slavery, see Scott and Hebrard, *Freedom Papers.*

90. Christopher Schmidt-Nowara, *Empire and Antislavery.*

91. Knight, *Slave Society in Cuba,* 28.

92. Kale, *Fragments of Empire,* 1, 112, 144.

93. Hugh Tinker, *A New System of Slavery: The Export of Indian Labour Overseas, 1830–1920* (London: Oxford University Press, 1974); Hoefte, *In Place of Slavery,* 106–7.

94. The similar transoceanic death rate of around one-fifth, however, should not hide the greater body count in New World slavery. One scholar estimates 5 million dead in Africa, on the ships, and during the first year of plantation labor. See Marcus Rediker, *The Slave Ship: A Human History* (New York: Viking, 2007), 347.

95. Tinker, *New System of Slavery,* 177–235.

96. Mimi Sheller, "Acting as Free Men: Subaltern Masculinities and Citizenship in Postslavery Jamaica," in *Gender and Slave Emancipation,* ed. Scully and Paton, 87–88.

97. Green, *British Slave Emancipation,* table 13, 246.

98. Rosamunde Renard, "Immigration and Indentureship in the French West Indies, 1848–1870," in *Caribbean Freedom,* ed. Beckles and Shepherd, 161.

99. Celine Flory, "New Africans in the Postslavery French West Indies and Guiana, 1854–1889," in *Paths of the Atlantic Slave Trade,* ed. Araujo, 117. The parallel with landing slaves is striking and probably intentional.

100. Ibid., 109–30.

101. Hoefte, *In Place of Slavery,* 106–13.

102. Aderibigbe, "Slavery in South-West of Indian Ocean," 324; Pons, *History of the Caribbean,* 199; Tinker, *New System of Slavery,* chap. 6.

103. Frenise A. Logan, "India—Britain's Substitute for American Cotton, 1861–1865," *Journal of Southern History* 24, no. 4 (November 1958): 472–80.

104. Beckert, "Emancipation and Empire," 15. According to John A. Todd, *The World's Cotton Crops* (London A. & C. Black, 1915), 421, Egypt's cotton production increased from 596,000 kantars (1 kantar = 100 pounds) to 2,140,000 kantars during the same years.

105. Todd, *World's Cotton Crops,* 431.

106. Clarence-Smith, *Islam and the Abolition of Slavery,* 10.

107. Beckert, "Emancipation and Empire," 15–16; E. J. Owen, *Cotton and the Egyptian Economy, 1820–1914: A Study in Trade and Development* (Oxford: Clarendon Press, 1969), chap. 4; David S. Landes, *Bankers and Pashas: International Finance and Economic Imperialism in Egypt* (1958; New York: Harper Torchbook, 1969), chap. 3.

108. For the domination of cash-crop over food-crop production in the slave sugar and cotton regional economies respectively, see Bigelow, *Jamaica in 1850,* and Wright, *Old South, New South,* 34–39.

109. Stanley J. Stein, *The Brazilian Cotton Manufacture; Textile Enterprise in an Underdeveloped Area, 1850–1950* (Cambridge, Mass.: Harvard University Press, 1957), chap. 4; Beckert, "Emancipation and Empire," 7–16.

110. Beckert's essay persuasively links U.S. emancipation and global imperialism in the cotton economy although it skirts the vital decision-making of former slaves not to work old crops and the consequences.

111. Willie Lee Rose, *Rehearsal for Reconstruction: The Port Royal Experiment* (New York:

Oxford University Press, 1964); 37–38, 204, 226; Kerr-Ritchie, "Forty Acres"; Atkinson, *Future Supply of Cotton,* 13.

112. Frenise A. Logan, "India's Loss of the British Cotton Market after 1865," *Journal of Southern History* 31, no. 1 (February 1965): 40–50; Beckert, "Emancipation and Empire," 40–41.

113. Owen, *Cotton and the Egyptian Economy,* 147–49.

114. Landes, *Bankers and Pashas,* chap. 3; Beckert, "Emancipation and Empire," 40–41.

115. Beckert, "Emancipation and Empire," 42.

116. Ibid., 44. The British officially colonized Egypt in 1882. The major reason was to protect access to the new Suez Canal serving as a vital link to British-controlled India. This imperial aggrandizement should be linked to the protection of a new vital source of cotton production for the British textile industry.

117. Penningroth, *Claims of Kinfolk,* 20; Lovejoy, *Transformations in Slavery,* chap. 7.

118. Clarence-Smith, *Islam and the Abolition of Slavery,* 10.

119. Robin Blackburn, "Emancipation and Empire, from Cromwell to Karl Rove," *Daedalus* 134, no. 2 (Spring, 2005): 73–74.

120. Lovejoy, *Transformations in Slavery,* chap. 10.

121. For insights into transatlantic colonialism and antislavery, see John Hope Franklin, *George Washington Williams: A Biography* (Chicago: University of Chicago Press, 1985), and Adam Hochschild, *King Leopold's Ghost: A Story of Greed, Terror, and Heroism in Colonial Africa* (New York: Houghton Mifflin, 1998).

EPILOGUE

Epigraph: April 6 Youth News, posted on Marko, January 15, 2011, in Jean-Pierre Filiu, *The Arab Revolution: Ten Lessons from the Democratic Uprising* (New York: Oxford University Press, 2011), 157.

1. Ellen Meiksins Wood and John Bellamy Foster, eds., *In Defense of History: Marxism and the Postmodern Agenda* (New York: Monthly Review Press, 1997); Arjun Appadurai, *Modernity at Large: Cultural Dimensions of Globalization* (Minneapolis: University of Minnesota Press, 1996); Arif Dirlik, *Global Modernity: Modernity in the Age of Global Capitalism* (Boulder, Colo.; Paradigm Publishers, 2007).

2. CIA—The World Factbook—www.cia.gov/library/publications/the-world-factbook/

3. Official website, Government of the Republic of South Sudan, www.goss.org/

4. Eric Hobsbawn, *The Age of Empire, 1875–1914* (New York: Vintage, 1989), 59.

5. Blackburn, *Making of New World Slavery.*

6. Kevin Bales, *Disposable People: New Slavery in the Global Economy* (Berkeley: University of California Press, 1999), 8–11.

7. Adam Blenford, "U.S. Trafficking Report reveals 'modern slavery' toll," BBC News, June 19, 2012, www.bbc.co.uk/news/world-us-canada-18514626

8. Anti-Slavery International, *Reporter* (Winter 2012): 4.

9. Gulnara Shahinian, "Report of the Special Rapporteur on Contemporary Forms of Slavery, Including Its Causes and Consequences," *Human Rights Council,* Fifteenth Session, Agenda Item 3 (June 18, 2010): 21–22.

10. Bales, *Disposable People,* chap. 2.

11. Anti-Slavery International, *Reporter* (Winter 2008): 4.

12. Bales, *Disposable People*, 111, 159.

13. Ibid., 83–84.

14. Anti-Slavery International, *Reporter* (Winter 2012): 9.

15. I recall a conversation with a retired senior New York police officer in the bar of the Washington Hilton on March 30, 2012, who told me that the major problem facing the United States was illegal immigrants taking jobs and using medical services. His argument, already unpersuasive, was not helped by his inebriation.

16. Yasmin Ryan, "French Right focuses on Radical Muslims," April 6, 2012, *Al Jazeera*, www.aljazeera.com/indepth/features/2012/04/201244102955800772.html. The United Kingdom Independent Party (Ukip) represents a new political party with an anti-immigration policy. In local council elections in April 2013, Ukip won around 25 percent of the seats it contested. This was the biggest surge by a fourth party in Britain since the Second World War (Nicholas Watt, "Ukip Will Change the Face of British Politics Like SDP, says Nigel Farage," May 3, 2013, www.guardian.co.uk/politics/2013/may/03/nigel-farage-ukip-change-british-politics; Patrick Wintour, "Ukip Confirms Immigration Policy Is Under Review," May 3, 2013, www.guardian.co.uk/politics/2013/may/03/ukip-immigration-policy-under-review").

17. Nigel Morris, "Keep Your Arab Spring Migrants, May tells France," *The Independent*, June 7, 2011, www.independent.co.uk/news/uk/politics/keep-your-arab-spring-migrants-may-tells-france-2293852.html

18. See Enoch Powel's infamous 1969 "Rivers of Blood Speech" decrying black immigration to England at www.youtube.com/watch?v=HP7fETsKYkA

19. Jeffrey R. Kerr-Ritchie, "9/11 and the United Kingdom," *Radical History Review* 111 (Fall 2011): 203–9.

20. Of course, this inspiration was international and hardly surprising given the atrocious record of his predecessor.

21. A somber comparison further reveals the horror of Haiti's recent earthquake. In one day, 316,000 people were to lose their lives, whereas thirteen years of slave revolt, colonial invasion, and national liberation struggles between 1791 and 1804 claimed between 100,000 and 200,000 lives. See "Haiti Raises Death toll on Anniversary," Canadian Broadcasting News, January 12, 2011, www.cbc.ca/news/world/story/2011/01/12/haiti-anniversary-memorials.html

22. William Gumede, "African Unity Must be More Selective: A Blueprint for Change," July 14, 2011, no. 539, pambazuka.org/en/category/features/74902

23. National Public Radio, March 6, 2013.

24. As I write this, the modern Bolívarian revolution is at a crossroads because of the death of Chavez on March 5, 2013.

25. This is not to underestimate existing challenges to the democratic voting process. See John Lewis, "Why We Still Need the Voting Rights Acts," February 24, 2013, *Washington Post*, mail.google.com/mail/?shva=1#label/US-Vote/13d148592bc8855d

26. "Minority Report: The Trouble with Integration," in "The Art of the Impossible: A Survey of France," *Economist* (October 25, 2006): 11.

27. "Thousands of Lives Lost to Flames of Revolution," *Financial Times* (December 17–18, 2011): 6.

BIBLIOGRAPHY

Achebe, Chinua. *Things Fall Apart*. London: Heinemann, 1959.

Aderibigbe, A. B. "Slavery in South-West of Indian Ocean." In *Slavery in the South-West Indian Ocean*, ed. Bissoondoyal and Servansing, 320–29.

Allison, Robert J., ed. *The Interesting Narrative of the Life of Olaudah Equiano, Written by Himself*. Boston: Bedford Books, 1995.

Anderson, Benedict. *Imagined Communities: Reflections on the Origin and Spread of Nationalism*. London: Verso, 1991.

Andrews, George Reid. *Afro-Latin America 1800–2000*. New York: Oxford University Press, 2004.

Andrews, William L., ed. *North Carolina Slave Narratives: The Lives of Moses Roper, Lunsford Lane, Moses Grandy, & Thomas H. Jones*. Chapel Hill: University of North Carolina Press, 2003.

Anna, Timothy A. *The Fall of the Royal Government in Peru*. Lincoln: University of Nebraska, 1979.

Anonymous. "Cuba—Its Position, Dimensions and Population," *Debow's Review* 2, no. 4 (April 1850): 314.

———. "Flag Raising at Camp William Penn." *Christian Recorder*, August 1, 1863.

Anti-Slavery Bugle (Salem, Ohio). August 7, 1858.

Anti-Slavery International. *Reporter*. 2006–12.

"Appendix to Report From a Select Committee of the House of Assembly, Appointed to Inquire into the Origin, Causes, and Progress of the Late Insurrection (1818)." In *Contrary Voices: Representations of West Indian Slavery, 1657–1834*, ed. Karina Williamson. Mona, Jamaica: University of West Indies Press, 2008, 335–45.

Aptheker, Herbert. *American Negro Slave Revolts*. New York: International Publishers, 1963.

———. *Nat Turner's Slave Rebellion*. New York: Grove Press, 1966.

Arnold, Benjamin W. *History of the Tobacco Industry in Virginia from 1860 to 1894*. Baltimore: John Hopkins University Studies, 1897.

Askew, Gus. "The American Slave: A Composite Autobiography." In *Alabama Narratives*, ed. George P. Rawick. Westport, Conn.: Greenwood, 1972. Vol. 6, pt. 1.

Atkinson, Edward. *The Future Supply of Cotton*. Boston: Crosby & Nichols, 1864.

Ayers, Edward L. *The Promise of the New South: Life After Reconstruction*. New York: Oxford University Press, 1992.

Bales, Kevin. *Disposable People: New Slavery in the Global Economy*. Berkeley: University of California Press, 1999.

Baquaqua, Mahommah Gardo. *Biography of Mahommah G. Baquaqua.* Detroit: George
E. Pomeroy, 1854. docsouth.unc.edu/neh/baquaqua/baquaqua.html

Barcia, Manuel. *The Great African Slave Revolt of 1825: Cuba and the Fight for Freedom in
Matanzas.* Baton Rouge: Louisiana State University Press, 2012.

Barker, Eugene C. "The Influence of Slavery in the Colonization of Texas," *Southwest-
ern Historical Quarterly,* 28, no. 1 (July 1924): 1–33.

Barry, Boubacar. *Senegambia and the Atlantic Slave Trade.* Cambridge, U.K.: Cambridge
University Press, 1998.

Beckert, Sven. "Emancipation and Empire: Reconstructing the Worldwide Web of Cotton Production in the Age of the American Civil War." *American Historical Review*
109, no. 5 (December 2004): 1–64.

Beckles, Hilary, and Verene Shepherd, eds. *Caribbean Freedom: Economy and Society
from Emancipation to the Present.* Princeton, N.J.: Markus Wiener, 1996.

Bell, Karen. "Full and Fair Compensation: Free Labor Ideology and the Liminal Spaces
of Freedom in Low Country Georgia, 1865–1868." Paper, Annual Meeting of Organization of American Historians. Washington D.C., 2010.

Bell, Madison Smartt. *Toussaint Louverture: A Biography.* New York: Vintage Books, 2007.

Bergad, Laird W. *The Comparative Histories of Slavery in Brazil, Cuba, and the United
States.* New York: Cambridge University Press, 2007.

Berlin, Ira. *Generations of Captivity: A History of African-American Slaves.* Cambridge,
Mass.: Harvard University Press, 2004.

———. *Many Thousands Gone: The First Two Centuries of Slavery in North America.* Cambridge, Mass.: Harvard University Press, 1998.

———. *Slaves Without Masters: The Free Negro in the Antebellum South.* New York: Vintage, 1976.

Berlin, Ira, Barbara Fields, Steven F. Miller, Joseph P. Reidy, and Leslie S. Rowland.
Slaves No More: Three Essays on Emancipation and the Civil War. New York: Cambridge University Press, 1992.

———, eds. *Free At Last: A Documentary History of Slavery, Freedom, and the Civil War.*
New York: New Press, 1992.

Berlin, Ira, and Philip D. Morgan, eds. *Cultivation and Culture: Labor and the Shaping of
Slave Life in the Americas.* Charlottesville: University of Virginia Press, 1993.

Berlin, Ira, Joseph P. Reidy, and Leslie S. Rowland, eds. *Freedom's Soldiers: The Black
Military Experience in the Civil War.* New York: Cambridge University Press, 1998.

Bibb, Henry. Editorial. *Voice of the Fugitive,* July 30, 1851.

———. *Narrative of the Life and Adventures of Henry Bibb: An American Slave, Written by
Himself.* New York: Self-published, 1849.

Bigelow, John. *Jamaica in 1850, or, The Effects of Sixteen Years of Freedom on a Slave
Colony.* Champaign: University of Illinois Press, 2006.

Bissoondoyal, U., and S. B. C. Servansing, eds. *Slavery in the South-West Indian Ocean.* Moka, Mauritius: Mahatma Gandhi Institute, 1989.

Blackburn, Robin. *The American Crucible: Slavery, Emancipation, and Human Rights.* London: Verso, 2011.

———. *Banking on Death: Or, Investing in Life: The History and Future of Pensions.* London: Verso, 2002.

———. "Emancipation and Empire, from Cromwell to Karl Rove." *Daedalus* 134, no. 2 (Spring 2005): 72–87.

———. "Haiti, Slavery, and the Age of Democratic Revolution." *William and Mary Quarterly* 63, no. 4 (2006): 1–21, www://historycooperative.org.

———. *The Making of New World Slavery: From the Baroque to the Modern, 1492–1800.* London: Verso, 1997.

Blackett, R. J. M. *Building an Antislavery Wall: Black Americans in the Atlantic Abolitionist Movement 1830–1860.* Baton Rouge: Louisiana State University Press, 1983.

Blanchard, Peter. *Slavery and Abolition in Early Republican Peru.* Wilmington, Del.: Scholarly Resources, 1992.

———. *Under the Flags of Freedom: Slave Soldiers and the Wars of Independence in Spanish South America.* Pittsburgh: University of Pittsburgh Press, 2008.

Bleby, Henry. *Missionary From Barbados, On The Results of Emancipation in the British West Indies Colonies, Delivered At The Celebration of Massachusetts Anti-Slavery Society, Held at Island Grove, Abington, July 31, 1858.* Boston: R. F. Wallcut, 1858.

Bleser, Carol K. R. *The Promised Land: The History of the South Carolina Land Commission, 1869–1890.* Columbia: University of South Carolina Press, 1969.

Bolland, O. Nigel. "Reply to William A. Green's 'The Perils of Comparative History.'" *Comparative Study of Society and History* 26, no. 1 (1984): 120–25.

———. "Systems of Domination after Slavery: The Control of Land and Labor in the British West Indies after 1838." *Comparative Study of Society and History* 23, no. 4 (October 1981): 591–619.

Bolster, W. Jeffrey. *Black Jacks: African American Seamen in the Age of Sail.* Cambridge, Mass.: Harvard University Press, 1997.

Bolton, James. "The American Slave: A Composite Autobiography." In *Georgia Narratives,* ed. George P. Rawick. Westport, Conn.: Greenwood, 1972. Vol. 12, pt. 1.

Bordewich, Fergus M. *Bound for Canaan: The Epic Story of the Underground Railroad, America's First Civil Rights Movement.* New York: Amistad, 2005.

Bose, Sugata. *A Hundred Horizons: The Indian Ocean in the Age of Global Empire.* Cambridge, Mass.: Harvard University Press, 2006.

Branch, Jacob. "The American Slave: A Composite Autobiography." In *Texas Narratives,* ed. George P. Rawick. Westport, Conn.: Greenwood Press, 1972. Vol. 4, pt. 1.

Brent, Linda. *Incidents in the Life of a Slave Girl.* 1861. New York: Harvest, 1973.

Brinkley, Alan. *The Unfinished Nation: A Concise History of the American People.* Vol. 1: *To 1877.* New York: McGraw Hill, 1993.

British Parliamentary Papers. *Report of the Select Committee on the Extinction of Slavery Throughout the British Dominions, 1831–1832.* Shannon: Irish University Press, 1968. Vol. 2.

Brown, Christopher Leslie. *Moral Capital: Foundations of British Abolitionism.* Chapel Hill: University of North Carolina Press, 2006.

———, and Philip D. Morgan, eds. *Arming Slaves: From Classical Times to the Modern Age.* New Haven: Yale University Press, 2006.

Brundage, W. Fitzhugh. *Lynching in the New South: Georgia and Virginia, 1880–1930.* Urbana: University of Illinois Press, 1993.

Buckingham, James Silk. *The Slave States in America.* London: Fisher & Son, 1842.

Buckley, Roger N. "Slave or Freedman: The Question of the Legal Status of the British West India Soldiers, 1795–1807." *Caribbean Studies* 17, nos. 3–4 (1977–78): 83–113.

———. *Slaves in Redcoats: The British West India Regiments, 1795–1815.* New Haven: Yale University Press, 1979.

Burke, Ronald K. *Samuel Ringgold Ward: Christian Abolitionist.* New York: Garland, 1995.

Butler, Kim D. "Abolition and the Politics of Identity in the Afro-Atlantic Diaspora: Toward a Comparative Approach." In *Crossing Boundaries: Comparative History of Black People in Diaspora,* ed. Darlene C. Hine and Jacqueline A. McCleod. Bloomington: Indiana University Press, 1999), 121–33.

———. *Freedoms Given, Freedom Won: Afro-Brazilians in Post-Abolition Sao Paulo and Salvador.* New Brunswick, N.J.: Rutgers University Press, 1998.

Campbell, Gwyn, Suzanne Miers, and Joseph C. Miller, eds. *Women and Slavery.* Athens: Ohio University Press, 2007.

Campbell, Randolph B. *An Empire for Slavery: The Peculiar Institution in Texas, 1821–1865.* Baton Rouge: Louisiana State University Press, 1989.

Campbell, Stanley W. *The Slave Catchers: Enforcement of the Fugitive Slave Law, 1850–1860.* Chapel Hill: University of North Carolina Press, 1968.

Caroll, Joseph Cephas. *Slave Insurrections in the United States, 1800–1865.* 1938; Mineola, NY.: Dover Publications, 2004.

Carrington, Wirt J. *A History of Halifax County, Virginia.* Baltimore: Regional Publishers, 1924.

Cecelski, David S. "Abraham H. Galloway: Wilmington's Lost Prophet and the Rise of Black Radicalism in the American South." In *Time Longer Than Rope: A Century of African-American Activism, 1850–1950,* ed. Charles M. Payne and Adam Green. New York: New York University Press, 2003, 37–67.

———. *The Waterman's Song: Slavery and Freedom in Maritime North Carolina.* Chapel Hill: University of North Carolina Press, 2001.

Chase, Franklin, to John Appleton. October 13, 1857. U.S. Department of State, Dispatches from the U.S. Consuls in Tampico, 1824–1906. Dispatch Number 27, Microcopy Number T241, Record Group 59, National Archives.

Chernow, Ron. *Alexander Hamilton*. London: Penguin, 2004.

Childs, Matt D. *The 1812 Aponte Rebellion in Cuba and the Struggle Against Atlantic Slavery*. Chapel Hill: University of North Carolina Press, 2006.

Chotner, Deborah. *Augustus Saint-Gaudens' Memorial to Robert Gould Shaw and the Massachusetts Fifty-fourth Regiment*. Washington, D.C.: National Gallery of Art, n.d.

Cimprich, John. "The Fort Pillow Massacre: Assessing the Evidence." In *Black Soldiers in Blue: African American Troops in the Civil War Era*, ed. John David Smith. Chapel Hill: University of North Carolina Press, 2002, 150–68.

Clarence-Smith, William Gervase. *Islam and the Abolition of Slavery*. New York: Oxford University Press, 2006.

Clavin, Mathew J. "American Toussaints: Symbol, Subversion, and the Black Atlantic Tradition in the American Civil War," *Slavery & Abolition* 28, no. 1 (April 2007): 87–113.

The Colored American (New York). August 5, 1837; August 11, 1838.

Conrad, Robert. *The Destruction of Slavery in Brazil, 1850–1888*. Malabar, Fla.: Krieger Publishing Co., 1993.

———, ed. *Children's of God's Fire: A Documentary History of Black Slavery in Brazil*. University Park: Pennsylvania State University Press, 1994.

Cooper, Frederick, and Thomas S. Holt, and Rebecca J. Scott. *Beyond Slavery: Explorations of Race, Labor, and Citizenship in Postemancipation Societies*. Chapel Hill: University of North Carolina, 2000.

Cowling, Camillia. Book Review. "David Barry Gaspar and Darlene Clark Hine, eds., *Beyond Bondage: Free Women of Color in the Americas* (Urbana: University of Illinois Press, 2004)." *Caribbean Studies* 34, no. 1 (Summer 2006): 348–56.

Craton, Michael. *Testing the Chains: Resistance to Slavery in the British West Indies*. Ithaca, N.Y.: Cornell University Press, 1982.

Curry-Machado, Jonathan. "Catalysts in the Crucible: Kidnapped Caribbeans, Free Black British Subjects and Migrant British Machinists in the Failed Cuban Revolution of 1843." In *Blacks, Coloureds*, ed. Naro, 123–42.

Dall, C. H. A. "West India Emancipation." *The Liberator* (Boston), August 20, 1852.

Daly, Mary. "Revisionism and Irish History: The Great Famine." In *The Making of Modern Irish History*, ed. D. George Boyce and Alan O'Day. London: Routledge, 1996, 71–89.

Davidson, Basil. *The Black Man's Burden: Africa and the Curse of the Nation-State*. New York: Random House, 1992.

DeBow's Review (New Orleans). quod.lib.umich.edu/m/moajrnl/browse.journals/debo.1846.html

DeCaro, Louis A., Jr. *"Fire from the Midst of You": A Religious Life of John Brown.* New York: New York University Press, 2002.

Delany, Martin R. "The Redemption of Cuba." In *Martin Delany: A Documentary Reader,* ed. Robert S. Levine. Chapel Hill: University of North Carolina Press, 2003, 167–69.

Diouf, Sylviana Anna. *Dreams of Africa in Alabama: The Slave Ship Clotilda and the Story of the Last Africans Brought to America.* New York: Oxford University Press, 2007.

Dixon, Chris. *African America and Haiti: Emigration and Black Nationalism in the Nineteenth Century.* Westport, Conn.: Greenwood Press, 2000.

Dobak, William A. *Freedom by the Sword: The U.S. Colored Troops 1862–1867.* Washington, D.C.: Center of Military History, 2011.

Documenting the American South. "North American Slave Narratives." University Library, University of North Carolina at Chapel Hill, docsouth.unc.edu/neh/

Donald, David Herbert. *Lincoln.* New York: Simon & Schuster, 1995.

Donoghue, Eddie. *Black Women, White Men: The Sexual Exploitation of Female Slaves in the Danish West Indies.* Trenton, N.J.: Africa World Press, 2002.

Douglass, Frederick. "Canandaigua, New York, 3 August 1857." In *The Frederick Douglass Papers,* ed. John W. Blassingame (New Haven: Yale University Press, 1985). Vol. 3: 184–208.

Drew, Benjamin. *A North-Side View of Slavery.* Boston: J. P. Jewett, 1856.

Dubois, Laurent. *Avengers of the New World: The Story of the Haitian Revolution.* Cambridge, Mass.: Harvard University Press, 2004.

———. *A Colony of Citizens: Revolution and Slave Emancipation in the French Caribbean, 1787–1804.* Chapel Hill: University of North Carolina Press, 2004.

Du Bois, William E. B. *Black Reconstruction in America, 1860–1880.* 1935. New York: Atheneum, 1992.

———. "A Lunatic or a Traitor." *The Crisis* (May 1924): 200.

———. *The Suppression of the African Slave-Trade to the United States of America, 1638–1870.* New York: Longmans, Green, and Co., 1896. Kindle version.

Dunbar, Lawrence. *The Negro in the New Orleans Press, 1850–1860: A Study in Attitudes and Propaganda.* Chicago: University of Chicago, 1941.

Dupuy, Alex. *Haiti in the World Economy: Class, Race, and Underdevelopment Since 1700.* Boulder, Colo.: Westview Press, 1989.

Eaton, Clement. *The Freedom of Thought Struggle in the Old South.* New York: Harper & Row, 1964.

Edwards, Laura. *Gendered Strife and Confusion: The Political Culture of Reconstruction.* Urbana: University of Illinois Press, 1997.

Egerton, Douglas R. *Death or Liberty: African Americans and Revolutionary America.* New York: Oxford University Press, 2009.

Elkins, Stanley. *Slavery: A Problem in American Institutional and Intellectual Life.* Chicago: University of Chicago Press, 1959.

Eltis, David, and David Richardson. *Atlas of the Transatlantic Slave Trade*. New Haven, Conn.: Yale University Press, 2010.

Emilio, Luis F. *A Brave Black Regiment: The History of the 54th Massachusetts, 1863–1865*. Boston, 1891.

Emmer, Pieter. *The Dutch in the Atlantic Economy, 1580–1880: Trade, Slavery and Emancipation*. Brookfield, Vt.: Ashgate, 1998.

Engerman, Stanley L. *Slavery, Emancipation, and Freedom: Comparative Perspectives*. Baton Rouge: Louisiana State University Press, 2007.

Engs, Robert Francis. *Freedom's First Generation: Black Hampton, Virginia, 1861–1890*. 1979. New York: Fordham University Press, 2004.

En Vogue. *Free Your Mind*. www.youtube.com/watch?v=9tIYpvlQPs

Ernest, John. *Liberation Historiography: African American Writers and the Challenge of History, 1794–1861*. Chapel Hill: University of North Carolina Press, 2004.

Esebede, P. O. *Pan-Africanism: The Idea and Movement, 1776–1991*. Washington D.C.: Howard University Press, 1994.

Eudell, Demetrius L. *The Political Languages of Emancipation in the British Caribbean and the U.S. South*. Chapel Hill: University of North Carolina Press, 2002.

Evans, Richard J. *In Defense of History*. New York: Norton, 1999.

Faragher, John Mack, Mari Jo Buhle, Daniel Czitrom, and Susan H. Armitage. *Out of Many: A History of the American People*. 4th ed. Upper Saddle River, N.J.: Prentice Hall, 2005. Vol. 1.

Faust, Drew Gilpin, ed. *The Ideology of Slavery: Proslavery Thought in the Antebellum South, 1830–1860*. Baton Rouge: Louisiana State University Press, 1981.

Ferrer, Ada. "Haiti, Free Soil, and Antislavery in the Revolutionary Atlantic." *American Historical Review* 117, no. 1 (February 2012): 40–66.

———. *Insurgent Cuba: Race, Nation, and Revolution, 1868–1898*. Chapel Hill: University of North Carolina Press, 1999.

Fick, Carolyn E. *The Making of Haiti: The Saint Domingue Revolution from Below*. Knoxville: University of Tennessee Press, 1990.

Fiehrer, Thomas. "Saint-Domingue/Haiti: Louisiana's Caribbean Connection." *Louisiana History* 30, no. 4 (Fall 1989): 419–37.

Fields, Barbara Jeanne. *Slavery and Freedom on the Middle Ground: Maryland during the Nineteenth Century*. New Haven: Yale University Press, 1985.

Figueroa, Luis A. *Sugar, Slavery, and Freedom in Nineteenth-Century Puerto Rico*. Chapel Hill: University of North Carolina Press, 2005.

Filiu, Jean-Pierre. *The Arab Revolution: Ten Lessons from the Democratic Uprising*. New York: Oxford University Press, 2011.

Fink, Leon, ed. *Workers Across the Americas: The Transnational Turn in Labor History*. New York: Oxford University Press, 2011.

Finley, Moses I. *Ancient Slavery and Modern Ideology*. Princeton, N.J.: Markus Wiener, 1998.

Fisch, Audrey A., ed. *The Cambridge Companion to the African American Slave Narrative.* New York: Cambridge University Press, 2007.

Fleetwood, Christian A. *The Negro as a Soldier.* Washington D.C.: Howard University, 1895.

Flory, Celine. "New Africans in the Postslavery French West Indies and Guiana, 1854–1889." In *Paths of the Atlantic Slave Trade: Interactions, Identities, and Images,* ed. Ana Lucia Araujo. Amherst, N.Y.: Cambria Press, 2011, 109–30.

Foner, Eric. *Freedom's Lawmakers: A Directory of Black Officeholders During Reconstruction.* Baton Rouge: Louisiana State University Press, 1993.

———. *Nothing But Freedom: Emancipation and Its Legacy.* Baton Rouge: Louisiana State University Press, 1983.

———. *Reconstruction: America's Unfinished Revolution.* New York: Harper and Row, 1988.

Fordham, Monroe. "Nineteenth-Century Black Thought in the United States: Some Influences of the Santo Domingo Revolution," *Journal of Black Studies* 6, no. 2 (December 1975): 115–26.

Fouchard, Jean. *Les Marrons de la Liberté.* Paris: Deschamps, 1972.

Fox-Genovese, Elizabeth. "Unspeakable Things Unspoken: Ghosts and Memories in the Narratives of African American Women." In *Slavery, Freedom and Gender,* ed. Moore et al., 254–75.

———. *Within the Plantation Household: Black and White Women of the Old South.* Chapel Hill: University of North Carolina Press, 1988.

Frank Leslie's Illustrated Newspaper (New York City). June 27, 1863.

Franklin, John Hope. *George Washington Williams: A Biography.* Chicago: University of Chicago Press, 1985.

———. *Reconstruction After the Civil War.* Chicago: University of Chicago Press, 1961.

———, and Evelyn Brooks Higginbotham. *From Slavery to Freedom: A History of African Americans.* 9th ed. New York: McGraw Hill, 2011.

———, and Loren Schweninger. *Runaway Slaves: Rebels on the Plantation.* New York: Oxford University Press, 2000.

Frederick Douglass' Paper (Rochester, N.Y.). August 10, 1855.

Fredrickson, George. "After Emancipation: A Comparative Study of The White Responses to the New Order of Race Relations in the American South, Jamaica, and the Cape Colony of South Africa." In *What Was Freedom's Price?* ed. Sansing, 71–92.

———. "From Exceptionalism to Viability: Recent Developments in Cross-National Comparative History." *Journal of American History* (September 1995): 587–604.

———. "White Responses to Emancipation: The American South, Jamaica, and the Cape of Good Hope." In George Fredrickson, *The Arrogance of Race: Historical Perspectives on Slavery, Racism, and Social Inequality.* Middletown, Conn.: Wesleyan University Press, 1988, 236–53.

Freedmen and Southern Society Project. University of Maryland. www.history.umd. edu/Freedmen/

Freehling, William W. *The Road to Secession: Secessionists at Bay, 1776–1854*. New York: Oxford University Press, 1990.

Frey, Sylvia R., and Betty Wood. *Come Shouting To Zion: African American Protestantism in the American South and British Caribbean to 1830*. Chapel Hill: University of North Carolina Press, 1998.

Frost, Karolyn Smardz. *I've Got a Home in Glory Land: A Lost Tale of the Underground Railroad*. Toronto: Thomas Allen, 2007.

Fryer, Peter. *Staying Power: The History of Black People in Britain*. London: Pluto, 1984.

Fuke, Richard Paul. *Imperfect Equality: African Americans and the Confines of White Racial Attitudes in Post-Emancipation Maryland*. New York: Fordham University Press, 1999.

Gannon, Barbara A. *The Won Cause: Black and White Comradeship in the Grand Army of the Republic*. Chapel Hill: University of North Carolina Press, 2011.

Garstad, Benjamin. "'Death to the Masters!' The Role of Slave Revolt in the Fiction of Robert E. Howard." *Slavery & Abolition* 31, no. 2 (June 2010): 233–56.

Gaspar, David Barry, and David Patrick Geggus, eds. *A Turbulent Time: The French Revolution and the Greater Caribbean*. Bloomington: Indiana University Press, 1997.

———, and Darlene Clark Hine, eds. *Beyond Bondage: Free Women of Color in the Americas*. Urbana: University of Illinois Press, 2004.

Geggus, David Patrick. "The Influence of the Haitian Revolution on Blacks in Latin America and the Caribbean." In *Blacks, Coloureds*, ed. Naro, 38–59.

———. "Slavery, War, and Revolution in the Greater Caribbean, 1789–1815." In *Turbulent Time*, ed. Gaspar and Geggus, 1–50.

———. *Slavery, War, and Revolution: The British Occupation of Saint Domingue, 1793–1798*. Oxford, U.K.: Clarendon Press, 1982.

Genovese, Eugene D. *From Rebellion to Revolution: Afro-American Slave Revolts in the Making of the Modern World*. Baton Rouge: Louisiana State University Press, 1979.

———, ed. *The Slave Economies: Historical and Theoretical Perspectives*. New York: John Wiley, 1973. Vol. 1.

Gillard, Jim. "The American Slave: A Composite Autobiography." In *Alabama Narratives*, ed. George P. Rawick. Westport, Conn.: Greenwood, 1972. Vol. 6, pt. 1.

Gilroy, Paul. *The Black Atlantic: Modernity and Double Consciousness*. Cambridge, Mass.: Harvard University Press, 1993.

———. *"There Ain't No Black in the Union Jack": The Cultural Politics of Race and Nation*. Chicago: University of Chicago Press, 1991.

Girard, Philippe R. *The Slaves Who Defeated Napoleon: Toussaint Louverture and the Haitian War of Independence, 1801–1804*. Tuscaloosa: University of Alabama Press, 2011.

Gosse, Van. "'As a Nation, the English Are Our Friends': The Emergence of African American Politics in the British Atlantic World, 1772–1861." *American Historical Review* 113, no. 4 (October 2008): 1003–28.

Grace, John. "Slavery and Emancipation among the Mende in Sierra Leone, 1896–1928." In *Slavery in Africa*, ed. Miers and Kopytoff, 415–31.

Graden, Dale Torston. *From Slavery to Freedom in Brazil, Bahia, 1835–1900*. Albuquerque: University of New Mexico Press, 2006.

Green, William A. *British Slave Emancipation: The Sugar Colonies and the Great Experiment, 1830–1865*. Oxford: Clarendon Press, 1976.

———. "The Perils of Comparative History: Belize and the British Sugar Colonies after Slavery." *Comparative Study of Society and History* 26, no. 1 (1984): 112–19.

Greenberg, Kenneth S., ed., *The Confessions of Nat Turner and Related Documents*. New York: Bedford St. Martins, 1996.

Greene, Graham. *The Human Factor*. 1978. New York: Random House, 1992.

Greene, Lorenzo J. "Some Observations on the Black Regiment of Rhode Island in the American Revolution." *Journal of Negro History* 37, no. 2 (April 1952): 142–72.

Gregg, Robert. *Inside Out, Outside In: Essays in Comparative History*. New York: St. Martin's Press, 2000.

Gundara, Jagdish S., and Ian Duffield, eds. *Essays on the History of Blacks in Britain*. Aldershot, U.K.: Avebury, 1992.

Guterl, Matthew Pratt. *American Mediterranean: Southern Slaveholders in the Age of Emancipation*. Cambridge, Mass.: Harvard University Press, 2008.

Hahn, Steven. Book Review. "*Freedpeople in the Tobacco South, Virginia 1860–1900*, Jeffrey R. Kerr-Ritchie (Chapel Hill: University of North Carolina Press, 1999)." *Slavery & Abolition* (April 2000): 167–68.

———. "Class and State in Postemancipation Societies: Southern Planters in Comparative Perspective." *American Historical Review* 95 (February 1990): 75–98.

———. *A Nation under Our Feet: Black Political Struggles in the Rural South from Slavery to the Great Migration*. Cambridge, Mass.: Harvard University Press, 2003.

———. *The Roots of Southern Populism: Yeoman Farmers and the Transformation of the Georgia Upcountry, 1850–1890*. New York: Oxford University Press, 1983.

Hall, Gwendolyn Midlo. *Africans in Colonial Louisiana: The Development of Afro-Creole Culture in the Eighteenth Century*. Baton Rouge: Louisiana State University Press, 1992.

Hall, Neville A. T. *Slave Society in the Danish West Indies: St. Thomas, St. John & St. Croix*, ed. B. W. Higman. Mona, Jamaica: University of West Indies Press, 1992.

Hart, Richard. *Slaves Who Abolished Slavery: Blacks in Rebellion*. Mona, Jamaica: University of West Indies Press, 1985.

Hashaw, Tim. *The Birth of Black America: The First African Americans and the Pursuit of Freedom at Jamestown*. New York: Carrol & Graf, 2007.

Helg, Aline. *Our Rightful Share: The Afro-Cuban Struggle for Equality, 1886–1912.* Chapel Hill: University of North Carolina Press, 1997.

Hendrick, George and Willene. *The Creole Mutiny: A Tale of Revolt Aboard a Slave Ship.* Chicago: Dee, 2003.

Herald of Freedom (Concord, Mass.). August 13, 1841.

Heuman, Gad J. *The Killing Time: The Morant Bay Rebellion in Jamaica.* Knoxville: University of Tennessee Press, 1994.

Higman, B. W. "Slave Populations of the British West Indies." In *Slavery in the South-West Indian Ocean*, ed. Bissoondoyal and Servansing, 233–46.

Hill, Christopher. *Liberty Against the Law: Some Seventeenth-Century Controversies.* London: Penguin, 1996.

Hinks, Peter P., ed. *David Walker's Appeal to the Colored Citizens of the World.* University Park: Pennsylvania State University Press, 2000.

Hobsbawn, Eric. *The Age of Capital, 1848–1875.* New York: Vintage, 1975.

———. *The Age of Extremes: A History of the World, 1914–1991.* New York: Pantheon Books, 1994.

Hochschild, Adam. *Bury the Chains: Prophets and Rebels in the Fight to Free an Empire's Slaves.* New York: Houghton Mifflin, 2005.

———. *King Leopold's Ghost: A Story of Greed, Terror, and Heroism in Colonial Africa.* New York: Houghton Mifflin, 1998.

Hodges, Graham Russell Gao. *David Ruggles: A Radical Black Abolitionist and the Underground Railroad in New York City.* Chapel Hill: University of North Carolina Press, 2010.

Hoefte, Rosemarijn. *In Place of Slavery: A Social History of British Indian and Javanese Laborers in Suriname.* Gainesville: University Press of Florida, 1998.

Holt, Sharon. "Making Freedom Pay: Freedpeople Working for Themselves, North Carolina, 1865–1900." *Journal of Social History* 60, no. 2 (May 1994): 228–62.

Holt, Thomas C. *Black over White: Negro Political Leadership in South Carolina during Reconstruction.* Urbana: University of Illinois Press, 1979.

———. "'An Empire over the Mind': Emancipation, Race, and Ideology in the British West Indies and the American South." In *Region, Race, and Reconstruction: Essays in Honor of C. Van Woodward*, ed. J. Morgan Kousser and James McPherson. New York: Oxford University Press, 1982, 283–313.

———. *The Problem of Freedom: Race, Labor, and Politics in Jamaica and Britain, 1832–1938.* Baltimore: John Hopkins University Press, 1992.

———. "Slavery and Freedom in the Atlantic World: Reflections on the Diasporan Framework." In *Crossing Boundaries: Comparative History of Black People in Diaspora*, ed. Darlene C. Hine and Jacqueline A. McCleod. Bloomington: Indiana University Press, 1999), 33–44.

Horton, James O. and Lois E. *In Hope of Liberty: Culture, Community and Protest Among Northern Free Blacks, 1700–1860*. New York: Oxford University Press, 1997.

Howard, Rosalyn. *Black Seminoles in the Bahamas*. Gainesville: University Press of Florida, 2002.

Hunt, Alfred N. *Haiti's Influence on Antebellum America: Slumbering Volcano in the Caribbean*. Baton Rouge: Louisiana State University Press, 1988.

Hunter, Tera W. *To 'Joy My Freedom: Southern Black Women's Lives and Labors After the Civil War*. Cambridge, Mass.: Harvard University Press, 1997.

Hurston, Zora Neale. "Cudjo's Own Story" *Journal of Negro History* 12 (1927): 648–63.

James, C. L. R. *The Black Jacobins: Toussaint L'Ouverture and the San Domingo Revolution*. 1938. New York: Vintage, 1963.

———. "Black Studies and the Contemporary Student." In *At the Rendezvous of Victory*. London: Allison & Busby, 1984, 186–201.

Janiewski, Dolores E. *Sisterhood Denied: Race, Gender, and Class in a New South Community*. Philadelphia: Temple University Press, 1985.

Jervey, Edward D., and C. Harold Huber. "The Creole Affair." *Journal of Negro History* 65, no. 3 (Summer 1980): 196–211.

Johnson, Michael P. "Denmark Vesey and his Co-Conspirators." *William and Mary Quarterly* 58 (October 2001): 915–76.

Johnson, Walter. *Soul by Soul: Life Inside the Antebellum Slave Market*. Cambridge, Mass.: Harvard University Press, 1999.

Jones, Jacqueline. *Labor of Love, Labor of Sorrow: Black Women, Work, and the Family from Slavery to the Present*. New York: Vintage Books, 1986.

Jones, Thomas H. *The Experience of Rev. Thomas H. Jones, Who Was a Slave for Forty-Three Years. Written by a Friend, as Related to Him by Brother Jones*. New Bedford, Mass.: E. Anthony & Sons, 1885.

Jordan, Winthrop D. *Tumult and Silence at Second Creek: An Inquiry into a Civil War Slave Conspiracy*. Baton Rouge: Louisiana State University Press, 1993.

Judd, Denis. *Empire: The British Imperial Experience, From 1865 to the Present*. London: Fontana, 1996.

Kale, Madhavi. *Fragments of Empire: Capital, Slavery, and Indian Indentured Labor in the British Caribbean*. Philadelphia: University of Pennsylvania Press, 1998.

Kelley, Sean. "'Mexico in His Head': Slavery and the Texas-Mexico Border, 1810–1860." *Journal of Social History* 37, no. 3 (Spring 2004): 709–23.

Kerr-Ritchie, Jeffrey R. "Forty Acres, or, An Act of Bad Faith." In *Redress for Historical Injustices in the United States: On Reparations for Slavery, Jim Crow, and Their Legacies*, ed. Michael Martin and Marilyn Yaquinto. Durham, N.C.: Duke University Press, 2007, 222–37.

———. *Freedpeople in the Tobacco South, Virginia 1860–1900*. Chapel Hill: University of North Carolina Press, 1999.

———. "9/11 and the United Kingdom." *Radical History Review* 111 (Fall 2011): 203–9.

———. *Rites of August First: Emancipation Day in the Black Atlantic World*. Baton Rouge: Louisiana State University Press, 2007.

———. "Samuel Ringgold Ward." In *Encyclopedia of Emancipation and Abolition in the Transatlantic World*, ed. Rodriguez, vol. 2: 559–60.

———. "Slave Revolt Across Borders." *Journal of African Diaspora Archaeology and Heritage* 2, no. 1 (May 2013): 65–92.

———. "Slaves' Supplicant and Slaves' Triumphant: The Middle Passage of an Abolitionist Icon." In *Paths of the Atlantic Slave Trade: Interactions, Identities, and Images*, ed Ana Lucia Araujo. New York: Cambria Press, 327–58.

———. "'Their Much Hoped for Liberty': Slaves and Bacon's 1676 Revolt in Virginia." In *Voices from within the Veil: America's 400th Anniversary*, ed. William H. Alexander. Cambridge, U.K.: Cambridge Scholars Publishing, 2008, 75–84.

Knight, Franklin W. "Blacks and the Forging of National Identity in the Caribbean," in *Blacks, Coloureds*, ed. Naro, 81–94.

———. *Slave Society in Cuba During the Nineteenth Century*. Madison: University of Wisconsin Press, 1970.

Kolchin, Peter. *American Slavery, 1619–1877*. New York: Hill & Wang, 1993.

Lacerte, Robert K. "The Evolution of Land and Labor in the Haitian Revolution, 1791–1820." *The Americas* 34, no. 4 (April 1978): 449–59.

Landers, Jane, ed. *Against the Odds: Free Blacks in the Slave Societies of the Americas*. London: Frank Cass, 1996.

Landes, David S. *Bankers and Pashas: International Finance and Economic Imperialism in Egypt*. 1958. New York: Harper Torchbook, 1969.

Landon, Fred. "The Buxton Settlement in Canada." *Journal of Negro History* 3, no. 4 (October 1918): 360–67.

Law, Robin. *Ouidah: The Social History of a West African Slaving 'Port' 1727–1892*. Athens: Ohio University Press, 2004.

Lee, Lori. "Emancipation in the Danish West Indies." In *Encyclopedia of Emancipation and Abolition in the Transatlantic World*, ed. Rodriguez, vol. 1: 160–62.

Leyburn, James, G. *The Haitian People*. New Haven: Yale University Press, 1966.

The Liberator (Boston). July 31, 1840; April 1, 1842; August 25, 1854; July 29, 1859.

Linebaugh, Peter, and Marcus Rediker. *Many-Headed Hydra: Sailors, Slaves, Commoners, and the Hidden History of the Revolutionary Atlantic*. Boston: Beacon Press, 2000.

Litwack, Leon F. *Been in the Storm So Long: The Aftermath of Slavery*. New York: Vintage, 1979.

———. *North of Slavery: The Negro in the Free States 1790–1860*. Chicago: University of Chicago Press, 1961.

Lockett, James D. "Abraham Lincoln and Colonization: An Episode That Ends in Tragedy at L'Ile a Vache, Haiti, 1863–1864." *Journal of Black Studies* 21, no. 4 (June 1991): 428–44.

Lofton, John. *Denmark Vesey's Revolt: The Slave Plot that Lit a Fuse to Fort Sumter.* Kent, Ohio: Kent State University Press, 1964.

Logan, Frenise A. "India—Britain's Substitute for American Cotton, 1861–1865." *Journal of Southern History* 24, no. 4 (November 1958): 472–80.

———. "India's Loss of the British Cotton Market after 1865." *Journal of Southern History* 31, no. 1 (February 1965): 40–50.

Longacre, Edward. *A Regiment of Slaves: The 4th United States Colored Infantry, 1863–1866.* Mechanicsburg, Pa.: 2003.

Lovejoy, Paul E. "Backlog to Rebellion: The Origins of Muslim Slavery in Bahia." *Slavery & Abolition* 15, no. 2 (1994): 151–80.

———. *Transformations in Slavery: A History of Slavery in Africa.* 1983. New York, Cambridge University Press, 2012.

Lowe, Richard G. *Republicans and Reconstruction in Virginia, 1856–70.* Charlottesville: University of Virginia Press, 1991.

Lynch, John. *Simón Bolívar: A Life.* New Haven: Yale University Press, 2006.

———. *The Spanish-American Revolutions, 1808–1826.* New York: W. W. Norton, 1973.

Mandela, Nelson. *Long Walk to Freedom: The Autobiography of Nelson Mandela.* New York: Little, Brown, and Co., 1994.

Manning, Patrick. *The African Diaspora: A History through Culture.* New York: Columbia University Press, 2009.

Mathieson, William Law. *British Slavery and Emancipation, 1838–1849.* London: Longmans, 1932.

McDaniel, Lorna. "Memory Spirituals of the Ex-Slave American Soldiers in Trinidad's Company Villages." *Black Music Research Journal* 14, no. 2 (Autumn 1994): 119–43.

McGlynn, Frank, and Seymour Drescher, eds. *The Meaning of Freedom: Economics, Politics, and Culture After Slavery.* Pittsburgh: University of Pittsburgh Press, 1992.

McKibben, Davidson Burns. "Negro Slave Insurrections in Mississippi, 1800–1865," *The Journal of Negro History* 34, no. 1 (January 1949): 73–91.

Meier, August, and Elliott Rudwick. *Black History and the Historical Profession 1915–1980.* Urbana: University of Illinois Press, 1986.

Meillassoux, Claude. *The Anthropology of Slavery: The Womb of Iron and Gold.* 1986. Chicago: University of Chicago Press, 1991.

Miers, Suzanne, and Igor Kopytoff, eds. *Slavery in Africa: Historical and Anthropological Perspectives.* Madison: University of Wisconsin Press, 1977.

Mintz, Sidney. *Caribbean Transformations.* 1974. Baltimore: John Hopkins University Press, 1984.

Missionary Record of the United Presbyterian Church (Edinburgh, Scotland). February 1853.

Mixon, Greg. "Black Militias in 1870s Georgia." Unpublished manuscript. Association for the Study of Afro-American Life and History, Atlanta.

Mohr, Clarence L. *On the Threshold of Freedom: Masters and Slaves in Civil War Georgia.* Athens: University of Georgia Press, 1986.

Moore, Brian L., B. W. Higman, Carl Campbell, and Patrick Bryan, eds. *Slavery, Freedom and Gender: The Dynamics of Caribbean Society.* Kingston, Jamaica: University of West Indies, 2001.

Morgan, Lynda J. *Emancipation in Virginia's Tobacco Belt, 1850–1870.* Athens: University of Georgia Press, 1992.

Morgan, Philip D. *Slave Counterpoint: Black Culture in the Eighteenth-Century Chesapeake and Lowcountry.* Chapel Hill: University of North Carolina Press, 1998.

Morris, Brent. "'Running Servants and All Others': The Diverse and Elusive Maroons of the Great Dismal Swamp." In *Voices from within the Veil: African Americans and the Experience of Democracy,* ed. William H. Alexander. Newcastle, U.K.: Cambridge Scholars, 2008, 85–112.

Morris, Nigel. "Keep Your Arab Spring Migrants, May tells France." *The Independent,* June 7, 2011, www.independent.co.uk/news/uk/politics/keep-your-arab-spring-migrants-may-tells-france-2293852.html

Moses, Wilson Jeremiah. *Alexander Crummell: A Study of Civilization and Discontent.* Oxford: Oxford University Press, 1989.

Mullin, Gerald W. *Flight and Rebellion: Slave Resistance in Eighteenth-Century Virginia.* New York: Oxford University Press, 1972.

Mullin, Michael. *Africa in America: Slave Acculturation and Resistance in the American South and the British Caribbean 1736–1831.* Urbana: University of Illinois Press, 1992.

Mumayiz, Ibrahim, ed. *Arabesques: Selections of Biography and Poetry from Classical Arabic Literature.* New York: Garant, 2006.

Naro, Nancy Priscilla, ed. *Blacks, Coloureds and National Identity in Nineteenth-Century Latin America.* London: University of London, 2003.

National Anti-Slavery Standard (New York City). August 19, 1854; August 14, 1858.

Newman, Richard S., "'Lucky to Be Born in Pennsylvania': Free Soil, Fugitive Slaves and the Making of Pennsylvania's Anti-Slavery Borderland," *Slavery & Abolition* vol. 32, no. 3 (September 2011): 413–30.

Newton, Melanie J. *The Children of Africa in the Colonies: Free People of Color in Barbados in the Age of Emancipation.* Baton Rouge: Louisiana State University Press, 2008.

Nicholls, David. *From Dessalines to Duvalier: Race, Color and National Independence in Haiti.* New Brunswick, N.J.: Rutgers University Press, 1991.

Oates, Stephen B. *The Fires of Jubilee: Nat Turner's Fierce Rebellion.* New York: Harper Perennial, 1975.

Ochiai, Akiko. *Harvesting Freedom: African American Agrarianism in Civil War Era South Carolina.* Westport, Conn.: Praeger, 2004.

O'Donovan, Susan Eva. *Becoming Free in the Cotton South.* Cambridge, Mass.: Harvard University Press, 2007.

Olmsted, Frederick Law. *A Journey Through Texas.* 1857. Lincoln: University of Nebraska, 2004.

Olwig, Karen F. *Adaption and Resistance on St. John: Three Centuries of Afro-Caribbean Life.* Gainesville: University of Florida Press, 1986.

Orwell, George. *George Orwell: A Collection of Essays.* New York: Harcourt Brace & Co., 1981.

Ott, Thomas O. *The Haitian Revolution, 1789–1804.* Knoxville: University of Tennessee Press, 1972.

Owen, E. J. *Cotton and the Egyptian Economy, 1820–1914: A Study in Trade and Development.* Oxford: Clarendon Press, 1969.

Ownby, Ted. *American Dreams in Mississippi: Consumers, Poverty, and Culture, 1830–1998.* Chapel Hill: University of North Carolina Press, 1999.

Pacquette, Robert L. "Revolutionary Saint Domingue in the Making of Territorial Louisiana." In *Turbulent Time,* ed. Gaspar and Geggus, 204–25.

———. *Sugar Is Made with Blood: The Conspiracy of La Escalera and the Conflict between Empires over Slavery in Cuba.* Middletown, Conn.: Wesleyan University Press, 1988.

———, and Douglas R. Egerton. "Of Facts and Fables: New Light on the Denmark Vesey Affair." *South Carolina Historical Magazine* 105 (January 2004): 7–47.

Palmer, Colin. *Slaves of the White God: Blacks in Mexico, 1570–1650.* New York: Cambridge University Press, 1976.

Pease, Jane H. and William H. *Black Utopia: Negro Communal Experiments in America.* Madison: State Historical Society of Wisconsin, 1963.

Penningroth, Dylan C. *The Claims of Kinfolk: African American Property and Community in the Nineteenth-Century South.* Chapel Hill: University of North Carolina Press, 2003.

Pennsylvania Freeman. August 25, 1853.

Perdue, Charles L. Jr., Thomas E. Barden, and Robert K. Phillips, eds. *Weevils in the Wheat: Interviews with Virginia Ex-Slaves.* Charlottesville: University of Virginia Press, 1976.

Phillippo, James Mursell. *Jamaica: Its Past and Present State.* Philadelphia: J. M. Campbell, 1843.

Pons, Frank Moya. *History of the Caribbean: Plantations, Trade, and War in the Atlantic World.* Princeton, N.J.: Markus Wiener Publishers, 2007.

Pontecorvo, Gillo, dir. *Burn!* Film. United Artists, 1969.

Popkin, Jeremy. *You Are All Free: The Haitian Revolution and the Abolition of Slavery.* New York: Cambridge University Press, 2010.

Porter, Kenneth Wiggins. *The Black Seminoles.* Gainesville: Florida University Press, 1996.

———. "Negroes and the Seminole War, 1817–1818." *Journal of Negro History* 36, no. 3 (July 1951): 249–80.

Postma, Johannes. *Slave Revolts*. Westport, Conn.: Greenwood Press, 2008.

Pratt, Fletcher. *Civil War in Pictures*. New York: Garden City Books, 1955.

Prince, Mary, *The History of Mary Prince, A West Indian Slave*. London: F. Westley and A. H. Davis, 1831.

Provincial Freeman (Toronto, Canada West). July 15, 1854; September 23, 1854.

Ransom, Roger L., and Richard Sutch. *One Kind of Freedom: The Economic Consequences of Emancipation*. New York: Cambridge University Press, 1977.

Rasmussen, Daniel. *American Uprising: The Untold Story of America's Largest Slave Revolt*. New York: Harper, 2011.

Reckord, Mary. "The Jamaica Slave Rebellion of 1831." *Past and Present* 40 (July 1968): 108–25.

Reddi, Sadasivam. "Aspects of Slavery During the British Administration." In *Slavery in the South-West Indian Ocean*, ed. Bissoondoyal and Servansing.

Reddick, Lawrence Dunbar. *The Negro in The New Orleans Press, 1850–1860: A Study in Attitudes and Propaganda*. Chicago: University of Chicago Libraries, 1941.

Rediker, Marcus. *The Slave Ship: A Human History*. New York: Viking, 2007.

Redlich, Fritz. "Toward Comparative Historiography." *Kyklos* 11 (1958).

Regosin, Elizabeth A., and Donald R. Shaffer. *Voices of Emancipation: Understanding Slavery, the Civil War, and Reconstruction through the U.S. Pension Bureau Files*. New York: New York University Press, 2008.

Reid, Richard M. *Freedom for Themselves: North Carolina's Black Soldiers in the Civil War Era*. Chapel Hill: University of North Carolina Press, 2008.

Reis, João José. *Slave Rebellion in Brazil: The Muslim Uprising of 1835 in Bahia*. Baltimore: John Hopkins University Press, 1993.

Rhodes, Jane. *Mary Ann Shadd Cary: The Black Press and Protest in the Nineteenth Century*. Bloomington: Indiana University Press, 1998.

Ripley, Peter C., ed. *The Black Abolitionist Papers*. Vol. 2: *Canada*. Chapel Hill: University of North Carolina, 1985.

———, ed. *Witness for Freedom: African American Voices on Race, Slavery, and Emancipation*. Chapel Hill: University of North Carolina Press, 1993.

Rodriguez, Junius P., ed. *Encyclopedia of Emancipation and Abolition in the Transatlantic World*. Armonk, N.Y.: M. E. Sharpe, 2007. Vols. 1–3.

———, ed. *Slavery in the United States: A Social, Political, and Historical Encyclopedia*. Santa Barbara, Calif.: ABC-CLIO, 2007. Vols. 1–2.

Rollin, Frank A. *Life and Public Services of Martin A. Delany*. Boston: Lee and Shepard, 1868.

Rose, Willie Lee. *Rehearsal for Reconstruction: The Port Royal Experiment*. New York: Oxford University Press, 1964.

Rourke, Mary, and Valerie J. Nelson. "Elizabeth Catlett Dies at 96; among 20th Century's Top Black Artists." *Los Angeles Times*. April 4, 2012, latimesblogs.latimes.com/worldnow/2012/04/artist-elizabeth-catlett-mexico-african-american.html

Rugemer, Edward. *The Problem of Emancipation: The Caribbean Roots of the American Civil War.* Baton Rouge: Louisiana State University Press, 2008.

Rushdy, Ashraf H. A. *Neo-Slave Narratives: Studies in the Social Logic of a Literary Form.* New York: Oxford University Press, 1999.

Sansing, David G., ed. *What Was Freedom's Price?* Jackson: University of Mississippi Press, 1978.

Saunders, Frederick, ed. *Our National Centennial Jubilee.* New York: E. B. Treat, 1877.

Saville, Julie. *The Work of Reconstruction: From Slave to Wage Laborer in South Carolina, 1860–1870.* New York: Cambridge University Press, 1994.

Schama, Simon. *Rough Crossings: The Slaves, the British, and the American Revolution.* New York: Harper, 2006.

Schmidt-Nowara, Christopher. *Empire and Antislavery: Spain, Cuba, and Puerto Rico, 1833–1874.* Pittsburgh: University of Pittsburgh Press, 1999.

Schwalm, Leslie A. *Emancipation's Diaspora: Race and Reconstruction in the Upper Midwest.* Chapel Hill: University of North Carolina Press, 2009.

———. *A Hard Fight for We: Women's Transition from Slavery to Freedom in South Carolina.* Urbana: University of Illinois Press, 1997.

Schwartz, Rosalie. *Across the Rio to Freedom: U.S. Negroes in Mexico.* El Paso: Texas Western Press, 1975.

Schwartz, Stuart B. *Slaves, Peasants, and Rebels: Reconsidering Brazilian Slavery.* Urbana: University of Illinois Press, 1992.

Scott, James Sherrard. "The Common Wind: Currents of Afro-American Communication in the Era of the Haitian Revolution." PhD diss., Duke University, 1986.

———. "Crisscrossing Empires: Ships. Sailors, and Resistance in the Lesser Antilles in the Eighteenth Century." In *The Lesser Antilles in the Age of European Expansion,* ed. Robert L. Paquette and Stanley L. Engerman. Gainesville: University of Florida Press, 1996, 128–43.

Scott, Joan Wallach. *Gender and the Politics of History.* 1988. New York: Columbia University Press, 1999.

Scott, Rebecca J. *Degrees of Freedom: Louisiana and Cuba After Slavery.* Cambridge, Mass.: Harvard University Press, 2005.

———. *Slave Emancipation in Cuba: The Transition to Free Labor, 1860–1899.* Princeton, N.J.: Princeton University Press, 1985.

———, and Jean M. Hebrard. *Freedom Papers: An Atlantic Odyssey in the Age of Emancipation.* Cambridge, Mass.: Harvard University Press, 2012.

Scully, Pamela. *Liberating the Family? Gender and British Slave Emancipation in the Rural Western Cape, South Africa, 1823–1853.* Portsmouth, N.H.: Heinemann, 1997.

———, and Diana Paton, eds. *Gender and Slave Emancipation in the Atlantic World.* Durham, N.C.: Duke University Press, 2005.

Shadd, Mary Ann. *A Plea for the Emigration or, Notes of Canada West.* 1851. Toronto, 1998.

Shahinian, Gulnara. "Report of the Special Rapporteur on Contemporary Forms of Slavery, Including its Causes and Consequences." *Human Rights Council*, Fifteenth Session, Agenda Item 3 (June 18, 2010): 21–22.

Sharp, Captain J. W., to Colonel Orlando Brown. February 28, 1866, Monthly Reports, Bureau of Refugees, Freedmen, and Abandoned Lands, Record Group 105, US National Archives.

Shaw, James. *Our Last Campaign and Subsequent Service in Texas*. Providence, R.I.: Society, 1905.

Shepherd, Verene, Bridget Brereton, and Barbara Bailey, eds. *Engendering History: Caribbean Women in Historical Perspective*. New York: St. Martin's Press, 1995.

Shepperson, George, and Thomas Price. *Independent African: John Chilembwe and the Origins, Setting and Significance of the Nysaland Native Rising of 1915*. Edinburgh: University Press, 1958.

Sheridan, Richard B. "From Jamaican Slavery to Haitian Freedom: The Case of the Black Crew of the Pilot Boat, Deep Nine." *Journal of Negro History* 67, no. 4 (Winter 1982): 328–39.

Sidbury, James. "Saint Domingue in Virginia: Ideology, Local Meanings, and Resistance to Slavery, 1790–1800." *Journal of Southern History* 63, no. 3 (August 1997): 531–52.

Silverman, Jason H. *Unwelcome Guests: Canada West's Response to American Fugitive Slaves, 1800–1865*. Greenwood, Conn.: Associated Faculty, 1985.

Singletary, Otis A. *Negro Militias and Reconstruction*. Austin: University of Texas Press, 1957.

Smith, James McCune. "Abolition." In *Negro Orators and Their Orations*, ed. Carter G. Woodson. Washington, D.C.: Associated Publishers, 1925.

———. *A Lecture on the Haytien Revolutions with a Sketch of the Character of Toussaint L'Ouverture*. New York: Daniel Fanshaw, 1841.

Spence, Jonathan D. *The Search for Modern China*. New York: Norton, 1990.

Spiers, Fiona. "Black Americans in Britain and the Struggle for Black Freedom in the United States, 1820–70." In *Essays on the History of Blacks in Britain*, ed. Jagdish S. Gundara and Ian Duffield. Aldershot, U.K.: Avebury, 1992.

Stampp, Kenneth M. *The Era of Reconstruction, 1865–1877*. New York: Vintage, 1965.

Stein, Stanley J. *The Brazilian Cotton Manufacture; Textile Enterprise in an Underdeveloped Area, 1850–1950*. Cambridge, Mass.: Harvard University Press, 1957.

———. *Vassouras: A Brazilian Coffee County, 1850–1900: The Rise of Planter and Slave in a Plantation Society*. 1958. Princeton, N.J.: Princeton University Press, 1985.

Steward, T. G. *The Haitian Revolution, 1791 to 1804*. New York: Thomas Crowell, 1914.

Stewart, James Brewer. *Holy Warriors: The Abolitionists and American Slavery*. New York: Hill and Wang, 1976.

Strickland, John Scott. "Traditional Culture and Moral Economy: Social and Economic

Change in the South Carolina Low Country, 1865–1910." In *The Countryside in the Age of Capitalist Transformation: Essays in the Social History of Rural America,* ed. Steven Hahn and Jonathan Prude. Chapel Hill: University of North Carolina Press, 1985, 141–78.

Svalesen, Leif. *The Slave Ship Fredensborg.* Bloomington: Indiana University Press, 2000.

Sweeney, Fionnghuala. *Frederick Douglass and the Atlantic World.* Liverpool: Liverpool University Press, 2007.

Tannenbaum, Frank. *Slave and Citizen: The Negro in the Americas.* New York: Vintage, 1946.

Tamarkin, Elisa. *Anglophilia: Deference, Devotion, and Antebellum America.* Chicago: University of Chicago Press, 2008.

Taylor, Eric Robert. *If We Must Die: Shipboard Insurrections in the Era of the Atlantic Slave Trade.* Baron Rouge: Louisiana State University Press, 2006.

Thomas, Keith. *Religion and the Decline of Magic.* New York: Oxford University Press, 1971.

Thompson, Alvin O. *Flight To Freedom: African Runaways and Maroons in the Americas.* Kingston, Jamaica; University of West Indies Press, 2006.

Thompson, Dorothy. "Ireland and the Irish in English Radicalism before 1850." In *Outsiders: Class, Gender, Nation.* London: Verso, 1993.

Thompson, E. P. *Customs in Common: Studies in Traditional Popular Culture.* New York: New Press, 1993.

Thorton, John. "African Dimensions of the Stono Rebellion." *American Historical Review* 96, no. 4 (October 1991): 1101–13.

Tilley, Nannie May. *The Bright Tobacco Industry, 1860–1900.* Chapel Hill: University of North Carolina Press, 1948.

Tinker, Hugh. *A New System of Slavery: The Export of Indian Labour Overseas, 1830–1920.* London: Oxford University Press, 1974.

Tocqueville, Alexis de. "The Emancipation of Slaves." 1843. In *Alexis de Tocqueville: Writings on Empire and Slavery,* ed. Jennifer Pitts. Baltimore: John Hopkins University Press, 2001), 199–226.

Todd, John A. *The World's Cotton Crops.* London: A. & C. Black, 1915.

Turner, Mary. *Slaves and Missionaries: The Disintegration of Jamaican Slave Society, 1787–1834.* Urbana: University of Illinois Press, 1982.

Tuten, James H. *Lowcountry Time and Tide: The Fall of the South Carolina Kingdom.* Columbia: University of South Carolina Press, 2010.

Tyrell, Ian. "American Exceptionalism in an Age of International History." *American Historical Review* 96 (October 1991): 1031–55.

———. "Making Nations/Making States: American Historians in the Context of Empire." *Journal of American History* (December 1999): 1015–44.

U.S. War Department. *The War of the Rebellion: A Compilation of the Official Records of the Union and Confederate Armies.* Washington D.C.: Government Printing Office, 1880–1901), ser. 1, vol. 9.

Vega, Philine Georgette. "Creole Case (1841)." In *Encyclopedia of Emancipation and Abolition in the Transatlantic World,* ed. Rodriguez, vol. 1: 148–49.

Vincent, Ted. "The Blacks Who Freed Mexico." *Journal of Negro History* 79, no. 3 (Summer 1994): 257–76.

Voelz, Peter M. *Slave and Soldier: The Military Impact of Blacks in the Colonial Americas.* New York: Garland Publishing, 1993.

Voice of the Fugitive (Sandwich, Canada West). 1851–54.

Vorenberg, Michael. "Abraham Lincoln and the Politics of Black Colonization." *Journal of the Abraham Lincoln Association* 14, no. 2 (Summer 1993): 1–45.

Walker, David. *David Walker's Appeal to the Colored Citizens of the World,* ed. Peter P. Hinks. University Park: Pennsylvania State University Press, 2000.

Ward, Samuel Ringgold, *Autobiography of a Fugitive Negro.* 1855. New York: Arno Press, 1968.

———. "Reflections Upon the Gordon Rebellion." N.p., 1866. Special Collections Library, University of Michigan.

Watt, Nicholas. "Ukip Will Change the Face of British Politics Like SDP, says Nigel Farage." May 3 2013, www.guardian.co.uk/politics/2013/may/03/nigel-farage-ukip-change-british-politics

Weidman, Budge. "Teaching With Documents: The Fight for Equal Rights: Black Soldiers in the Civil War," www.archives.gov/education/lessons/blacks-civil-war/article.html

Whitfield, Harvey Amani. *Blacks on the Border: The Black Refugees in British North America, 1815–1860.* Burlington: University of Vermont Press, 2006.

Wiener, Jonathan M. *Social Origins of the New South: Alabama, 1860–1885.* Baton Rouge: Louisiana State University Press, 1978.

Wiley, Bell Irvin. *Southern Negroes, 1861–1865.* New Haven, Conn.: Yale University Press, 1938.

Williams, Gwyn A. *Artisans and Sans-Culottes: Popular Movements in France and Britain During the French Revolution.* London: Edward Arnold, 1968.

Williamson, Karina, ed. *Contrary Voices: Representations of West Indian Slavery, 1657–1834.* Mona, Jamaica: University of West Indies Press, 2008.

Wilmot, Swithin. "'Females of Abandoned Character?' Women and Protest in Jamaica, 1838–65." In *Engendering History,* ed. Shepherd, Brereton, and Bailey, 279–93.

Wilson, Andrew, ed. *The Chinese in the Caribbean.* Princeton, N.J.: Marcus Wiener, 2004.

Wiltse, Charles M. *John C. Calhoun.* Vol. 3: *Sectionalist, 1840–1850.* Indianapolis: Bobbs-Merrill, 1951.

Winks, Robin W. *The Blacks in Canada: A History.* New Haven, Conn.: Yale University Press, 1971.

Wintour, Patrick. "Ukip Confirms Immigration Policy Is Under Review," May 3, 2013, www.guardian.co.uk/politics/2013/may/03/ukip-immigration-policy-under-review

Wood, Peter H. *Black Majority: Negroes in Colonial South Carolina from 1670 through the Stono Rebellion.* New York: W. W. Norton, 1975.

Woodman, Harold D. *New South–New Law: The Legal Foundations of Credit and Labor Relations in the Postbellum Agricultural South.* Baton Rouge: Louisiana State University Press, 1995.

Woodward, C. Vann. "Emancipations and Reconstructions: A Comparative Study." International Congress of Historical Sciences. Moscow: NAUKA Publishing House, 1970.

———. *The Old World's New World.* New York: Oxford University Press, 1991.

———. *Origins of the New South, 1877–1913.* Baton Rouge: Louisiana State University Press, 1951.

———. *The Strange Career of Jim Crow.* New York: Oxford University Press, 1955.

Wright, Gavin. *Old South, New South: Revolutions in the Southern Economy Since the Civil War.* New York: Basic Books, 1986.

Years, W. Buck, and John G. Barrett, eds. *North Carolina Civil War Documentary.* Chapel Hill: University of North Carolina Press, 2002.

Zuckerman, Michael. "The Power of Blackness: Thomas Jefferson and the Revolution in St. Domingue." In *Almost Chosen People: Oblique Biographies in the American Grain.* Berkeley: University of California Press, 1993, 175–218.

INDEX